D1339628

Mission Praise

II

Compiled by

Peter Horrobin and Greg Leavers

MUSIC EDITION

Marshall Morgan & Scott

Marshall Morgan and Scott
3 Beggarwood Lane, Basingstoke, Hants RG23 7LP, UK

Compilation copyright © 1987 Peter Horrobin and Greg Leavers

First published in 1987 by Marshall Morgan and Scott Publications Ltd
Part of the Marshall Pickering Holdings Group
A subsidiary of the Zondervan Corporation

Reprinted : Impression number
88 89 90   : 10 9 8 7 6 5 4 3 2

ISBN: 0 551 014164

Words edition pack of 50 copies ISBN: 0 551 014172

Music and text set by Barnes Music Engraving Ltd., East Sussex, England
Printed in Great Britain at the Bath Press, Avon

Foreword

Mission Praise 1 was originally published as Mission England Praise. Part of the objective of that volume was to meet the growing need of many churches for a supplementary hymn and song book. That objective was extensively fulfilled in thousands of church fellowships throughout the country and, more recently, overseas as well.

In many churches also, however, Mission Praise 1 has become the principle source of music for worship – in spite of its obvious limitations. Those limitations were, principally, the restricted number of items that could be included (only 282) and the almost total exclusion of the many important seasonal items for use at Christmas, Easter, Harvest, etc..

Mission Praise 2 has been specifically compiled to overcome these, and other, limitations. Mission Praise 1 & 2 together now form an all embracing hymn and song book for use throughout the year. They can be used as either a supplement to a traditional hymnbook or, with its large total selection of nearly 650 items, as a complete hymn and song book in its own right.

We have taken advantage of the opportunity also to include many new items which have now passed into widespread popular use during the intervening years. At the same time we have sought to maintain the balance that was achieved in Mission Praise 1 of music from the many different strands and traditions found in today's Christian music.

Once again the arrangement of the volume is largely alphabetical – but to assist users with tune selection there is now an extensive tune index covering both volumes.

We pray that, as with Mission Praise 1, this new volume will be extensively used as a means of uniting Christians of all denominations in praise and worship as they work together in the service of the Kingdom of God.

Peter Horrobin and Greg Leavers
June 1987

Acknowledgements

We would like to express our gratitude to: our many friends throughout the country who helped us with the compilation by sending us their suggestions for inclusion; Sue Cartwright for many hours of dedicated proof reading; Andy Silver and Phil Burt for their help with musical arrangements; and our families for patiently enduring the whole operation!

283 A new commandment

Author unknown
arr. Andy Silver

A new com-mand-ment I give un-to you, That you love one an-oth-er as I have loved you, That you love one an-oth-er as I have loved you. By this shall all men know that you are my dis-ci-ples, If

you have love one for an - oth - er._____ By

this shall all men know that you are my dis - ci - ples, If

you have love one for an - oth - er._____

A new commandment I give unto you,
That you love one another as I have loved you,
That you love one another as I have loved you.
By this shall all men know that you are my disciples,
If you have love one for another.
By this shall all men know that you are my disciples,
If you have love one for another.

284 A safe stronghold our God is still

EIN' FESTE BURG 8 7. 8 7. 6 6. 6 6 7

Present form of melody by
Martin Luther (1483–1546)

A safe strong - hold our God is still, A trus - ty shield and

wea - pon; He'll help us clear from all the ill That

has us now o'er - tak - en. The an - cient prince of hell Has

ris'n with pur - pose fell; Strong mail of craft and pow'r He

4

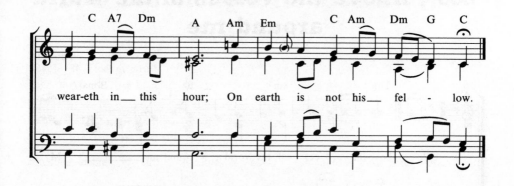

wear-eth in __ this hour; On earth is not his __ fel - low.

1 A safe stronghold our God is still,
   A trusty shield and weapon;
   He'll help us clear from all the ill
   That has us now o'ertaken.
   The ancient prince of hell
   Has ris'n with purpose fell;
   Strong mail of craft and pow'r
   He weareth in this hour;
   On earth is not his fellow.

2 With force of arms we nothing can,
   Full soon were we downridden;
   But for us fights the proper Man,
   Whom God Himself has bidden.
   Ask ye: Who is this same?
   Christ Jesus is His name,
   The Lord Sabaoth's Son;
   He, and no other one,
   Shall conquer in the battle.

3 And were this world all devils o'er,
   And watching to devour us,
   We lay it not to heart so sore;
   Not they can overpow'r us.
   And let the prince of ill
   Look grim as e'er he will,
   He harms us not a whit:
   For why? His doom is writ;
   A word shall quickly slay him.

4 God's word, for all their craft and force,
   One moment will not linger;
   But, spite of hell, shall have its course;
   'Tis written by His finger.
   And though they take our life,
   Goods, honour, children, wife,
   Yet is their profit small;
   These things shall vanish all;
   Th' city of God remaineth.

Martin Luther, 1483–1546
tr. Thomas Carlyle, 1795–1881

285 Above the voices of the world around me

Phil Burt

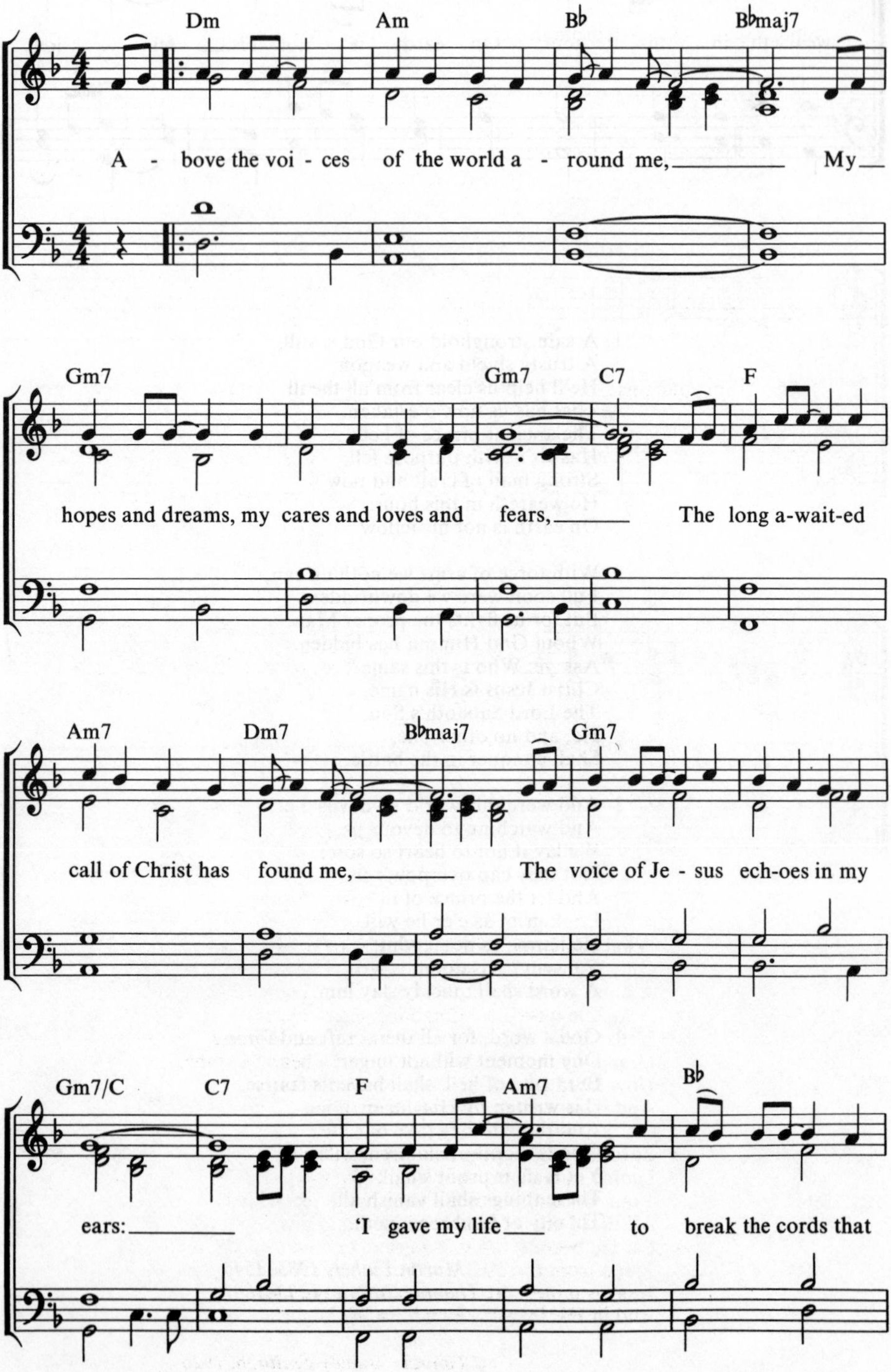

A - bove the voi - ces of the world a - round me,_____ My_____ hopes and dreams, my cares and loves and fears,_____ The long a-wait-ed call of Christ has found me,_____ The voice of Je - sus ech-oes in my ears:_____ 'I gave my life_____ to break the cords that

6

2 What can I offer Him who calls me to Him?
   Only the wastes of sin and self and shame;
   A mind confused, a heart that never knew Him,
   A tongue unskilled at naming Jesus' Name.
   Yet at Your call, and hungry for Your blessing,
   Drawn by that cross which moves a heart of stone,
   Now Lord I come, my tale of sin confessing,
   And in repentance turn to You alone.

3 Lord, I believe; help now my unbelieving;
   I come in faith because Your promise stands.
   Your word of pardon and of peace receiving,
   All that I am I place within Your hands.
   Let me become what You shall choose to make me,
   Freed from the guilt and burden of my sins.
   Jesus is mine, who never shall forsake me,
   And in His love my new-born life begins.

© *Timothy Dudley-Smith, b. 1926*

286 Ah Lord God

Lively

Kay Chance

Capo 2

Ah Lord God, Thou____ hast made the hea-vens and the earth By Thy great po-wer.____ Ah Lord God, Thou____ hast made the hea-vens and the earth By Thine out-stretched arm. No-thing is too dif-fi-cult for Thee,____ No-thing is too dif-fi-cult for

Thee._____ O ___ great and migh-ty God, Great in coun-sel and

migh - ty in deed,_____ No-thing, no-thing,

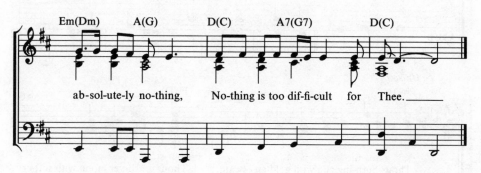

ab-sol-ute-ly no-thing, No-thing is too dif-fi-cult for Thee._____

1 Ah Lord God,
   Thou hast made the heavens and the earth
   By Thy great power.
   Ah Lord God,
   Thou hast made the heavens and the earth
   By Thine outstretched arm.

2 Nothing is too difficult for Thee,
   Nothing is too difficult for Thee.
   O great and mighty God,
   Great in counsel and mighty in deed,
   Nothing, nothing, absolutely nothing,
   Nothing is too difficult for Thee.

287 All creatures of our God and King

LASST UNS ERFREUEN L.M. with Hallelujahs
(Easter Hallelujah)

Geistliche Kirchengessang
Cologne (1623)

All crea-tures of our God and King, Lift up your voice and with us sing: Hal-le-lu-jah, Hal-le-lu-jah!

Thou burn-ing sun with gold-en beam, Thou sil-ver moon with soft-er gleam: O __ praise Him, O __ praise Him, Hal-le-

lu - jah, Hal - le - lu - jah, Hal - le - lu - jah!

1 All creatures of our God and King,
Lift up your voice and with us sing:
Hallelujah, Hallelujah!
Thou burning sun with golden beam,
Thou silver moon with softer gleam:

O praise Him, O praise Him,
Hallelujah, Hallelujah, Hallelujah!

2 Thou rushing wind that art so strong,
Ye clouds that sail in heav'n along,
O praise Him, Hallelujah!
Thou rising morn, in praise rejoice,
Ye lights of evening, find a voice:
O praise Him . . .

3 Thou flowing water, pure and clear,
Make music for thy Lord to hear,
Hallelujah, Hallelujah!
Thou fire so masterful and bright,
That givest man both warmth and light:
O praise Him . . .

4 And all ye men of tender heart,
Forgiving others, take your part,
O sing ye, Hallelujah!
Ye who long pain and sorrow bear,
Praise God and on Him cast your care:
O praise Him . . .

5 Let all things their Creator bless,
And worship Him in humbleness,
O praise Him Hallelujah!
Praise, praise the Father, praise the Son,
And praise the Spirit, Three in One:
O praise Him . . .

St. Francis of Assisi, 1182–1226
tr. William Henry Draper, 1855–1933

288   All earth was dark

1 All earth was dark until You spoke,
Then all was light and all was peace.
Yet still, oh God, so many wait,
To see the flame of love released.

Lights to the world, oh Light of man,
Kindle in us a mighty flame
Till ev'ry heart, consumed by love,
Shall rise to praise Your holy name.

2 In Christ You gave Your gift of life
To save us from the depth of night.
Oh come and set our spirits free,
And draw us to Your perfect light.
Lights to the world, . . .

3 Where there is fear, may we bring joy,
And healing to a world in pain.
Lord, build Your Kingdom through our lives,
Till Jesus walks this earth again.
Lights to the world, . . .

4 O burn in us that we may burn,
With love that triumphs in despair.
And touch our lives with such a fire,
That souls may search and find You there.
Lights to the world, . . .

13

289 All glory, laud, and honour

ST. THEODULPH 7 6. 7 6. D

Melody by Melchior Teschner (c.1615)
Harmony from J.S. Bach (1685–1750)

All glo-ry, laud and hon - our To Thee, Re-deem-er, King, To whom the lips of child - ren Made sweet ho-san-nas ring. Thou art the King of Is - rael, Thou Da - vid's roy - al Son, Who

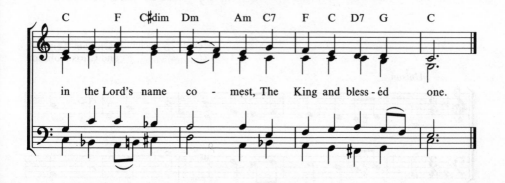

in the Lord's name co - mest, The King and bless - éd one.

1 All glory, laud and honour
To Thee, Redeemer, King,
To whom the lips of children
Made sweet hosannas ring.
Thou art the King of Israel,
Thou David's royal Son,
Who in the Lord's name comest,
The King and blesséd one.

2 The company of angels
Are praising Thee on high,
And mortal men and all things
Created make reply.
The people of the Hebrews
With psalms before Thee went;
Our praise and prayer and anthems
Before Thee we present.

3 To Thee before Thy passion
They sang their hymns of praise;
To Thee now high exalted
Our melody we raise.
Thou didst accept their praises;
Accept the prayers we bring,
Who in all good delightest,
Thou good and gracious King.

Theodulph of Orleans, c.750–821
Tr. J.M. Neale, 1818–1866

290　All heaven waits

Graham Kendrick
and Chris Rolinson

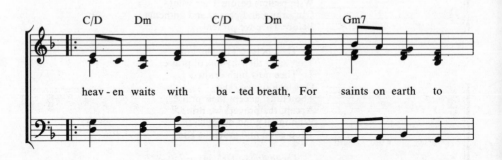

heav-en waits with ba-ted breath, For saints on earth to

pray.　Ma-jes-tic an-gels rea-dy stand With

swords of fi - ery blade. A - stound-ing power a -

waits a word, From God's re - splen - dent throne_____

_____ But God a - waits our prayer of faith That

cries 'Your will be done.'

A -

following verses overleaf

17

1 All heaven waits with bated breath,
   For saints on earth to pray.
   Majestic angels ready stand
   With swords of fiery blade.
   Astounding power awaits a word,
   From God's resplendent throne
   But God awaits our prayer of faith
   That cries 'Your will be done.'

2 Awake O church Arise and pray,
   Complaining words discard.
   The Spirit comes to fill your mouth
   With truth, His mighty sword.
   Go place your feet on Satan's ground
   And there proclaim Christ's name,
   In step with heaven's armies march
   To conquer and to reign!

3 Now in our hearts and on our lips
   The word of faith is near;   ⎤
   Let heaven's will on earth be done,   ⎬ ladies
   Let heaven flow from here.   ⎦
   Come blend your prayers with Jesus' own   ⎤
   Before the Father's throne;   ⎬ men
   And as the incense clouds ascend   ⎦
   God's holy fire rains down.

4 Soon comes the day when with a shout
   King Jesus shall appear,
   And with Him all the church
   From every age shall fill the air.
   The brightness of His coming shall
   Consume the lawless one;
   As with a word the breath of God
   Tears down his rebel throne.

5 One body here by heav'n inspired,
   We seek prophetic power.
   In Christ agreed one heart and voice
   To speak this day and hour.
   In every place where chaos rules
   And evil forces brood;
   Let Jesus voice speak like the roar
   Of a great multitude.

291 All around me, Lord

Words and music
Greg Leavers
arr. Phil Burt

A round in 3 parts

enter 2.

enter 3.

All around me, Lord, I see Your goodness,
All creation sings Your praises,
All the world cries, 'God is love!'

292 All my hope on God is founded

MICHAEL 8 7 8 7 3 3 7

Herbert Howells (1892–1983)

1 All my hope on God is founded,
  All my trust He shall renew;
  He, my guide through changing order,
  Only good and only true:
  God unknown,
  He alone,
  Calls my heart to be His own.

2 Pride of man and earthly glory,
  Sword and crown betray his trust;
  All that human toil can fashion,
  Tower and temple, fall to dust;
  But God's power
  Hour by hour
  Is my temple and my tower.

3 Day by day our mighty giver
  Grants to us His gifts of love;
  In His will our souls find pleasure,
  Leading to our home above:
  Love shall stand
  At His hand,
  Joy shall wait for His command.

4 Still from man to God eternal
  Sacrifice of praise be done;
  High above all praises praising
  For the gift of Christ His Son:
  Hear Christ's call
  One and all –
  We who follow shall not fall.

after J. Neander, 1650–1680
Robert Bridges, 1844–1930

293 All over the world

Roy Turner

1 All over the world the Spirit is moving,
  All over the world as the prophet said it would be;
  All over the world there's a mighty revelation
  Of the glory of the Lord, as the waters cover the sea.

2 All over His church God's Spirit is moving,
  All over His church as the prophet said it would be;
  All over His church there's a mighty revelation
  Of the Glory of the Lord, as the waters cover the sea.

3 Right here in this place the Spirit is moving,
  Right here in this place as the prophet said it would be;
  Right here in this place there's a mighty revelation
  Of the Glory of the Lord, as the waters cover the sea.

294 All praise to our redeeming Lord

LUCIUS. C.M.

Templi Carmina (1829)

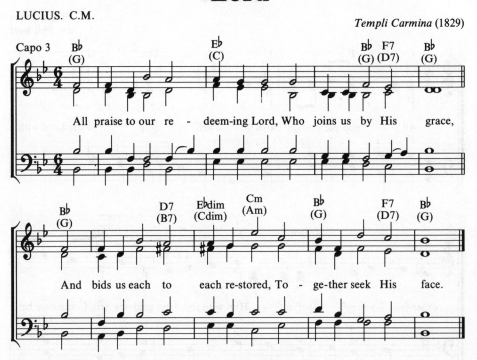

All praise to our re-deem-ing Lord, Who joins us by His grace,

And bids us each to each re-stored, To-ge-ther seek His face.

1 All praise to our redeeming Lord,
Who joins us by His grace,
And bids us each to each restored,
Together seek His face.

2 He bids us build each other up;
And, gathered into one,
To our high calling's glorious hope
We hand in hand go on.

3 The gift which He on one bestows,
We all delight to prove;
The grace through every vessel flows,
In purest streams of love.

4 Even now we think and speak the same,
And cordially agree;
Concentrated all, through Jesu's name,
In perfect harmony.

5 We all partake the joy of one,
The common peace we feel,
A peace to sensual minds unknown,
A joy unspeakable.

6 And if our fellowship below
In Jesus be so sweet,
What heights of rapture shall we know
When round His throne we meet.

Charles Wesley, 1707–88

295 All people that on earth do dwell

Roger Jones
arr. Phil Burt

All peo-ple that on earth do dwell Sing to the Lord with cheer-ful voice: Serve Him with joy, His prai-ses tell, Come now be - fore him and re - joice! Know that the Lord is God in - deed, He formed us all with - out our aid;___

We are the flock He loves to feed, The sheep who by His hand are made. - dore.

1 All people that on earth do dwell
   Sing to the Lord with cheerful voice:
   Serve Him with joy, His praises tell,
   Come now before Him and rejoice!
   Know that the Lord is God indeed,
   He formed us all without our aid;
   We are the flock He loves to feed,
   The sheep who by His hand are made.

2 O enter then His gates with praise,
   And in His courts His love proclaim;
   Give thanks and bless Him all your days:
   Let every tongue confess His name.
   The Lord our mighty God is good,
   His mercy is for ever sure;
   His truth at all times firmly stood,
   And shall from age to age endure.

3 All people that on earth do dwell
   Sing to the Lord with cheerful voice:
   Serve Him with joy, His praises tell,
   Come now before Him and rejoice!
   Praise God the Father, God the Son,
   And God the Spirit evermore;
   All praise to God the three-in-one,
   Let heaven rejoice and earth adore!

W. Kethe, d. 1594
© *in this version Jubilate Hymns*

296 All the way

ALL THE WAY 8. 7. 8. 7. D

Robert Lowry (1826–99)
arr. Phil Burt

All the way my Sav-iour leads me: What have I to ask be-side? Can I doubt His ten-der mer - cy, Who through life has been my Guide? Heav'n-ly peace, di - vin-est com - fort, Here by faith in Him to dwell! For I

know   what-e'er be - fall   me,   Je - sus do-eth all things   well.

1 All the way my Saviour leads me:
What have I to ask beside?
Can I doubt His tender mercy,
Who through life has been my Guide?
Heav'nly peace, divinest comfort,
Here by faith in Him to dwell!
For I know whate'er befall me,
Jesus doeth all things well.

2 All the way my Saviour leads me:
Cheers each winding path I tread;
Gives me grace for ev'ry trial,
Feeds me with the living bread.
Though my weary steps may falter,
And my soul a-thirst may be,
Gushing from the rock before me,
Lo! a spring of joy I see.

3 All the way my Saviour leads me:
O the fulness of His love!
Perfect rest to me is promised
In my Father's house above.
When my spirit, clothed immortal,
Wings its flight to realms of day,
This, my song through endless ages,
Jesus led me all the way.

Fanny J. Crosby, 1820-1915

297   All my life, Lord

Words and music
Andy and Becky Silver

For two groups of singers

All my life, Lord, _____ to You I want to give; _____

All my life, Lord, _____ to You I want to give; _____ This is my

_____This is my wor - ship, _____ please show me how to live. _____ Take ev-ery

wor - ship, _____ please show me how to live. _____ Take ev-ery part of me, _____

part of me, _____ make it Your own, Me on the cross, You on the throne.

make it Your own, Me on the cross, Lord, _____ You on the throne.

298(i) All things bright and beautiful

7.6.7.6. and chorus

W.H. Monk (1823–1889)

Chorus

All things bright and beau-ti-ful, All crea-tures great and small,

All things wise and won-der-ful, The Lord God made them all.

Verses

Each lit-tle flower that o-pens, Each lit-tle bird that sings, He

made their glow-ing co-lours, He made their ti-ny wings.

Following verses overleaf

29

298(ii) All things bright and beautiful

ROYAL OAK 7 6 7 6 and chorus

English traditional melody
seventeenth century
arr. M. Shaw (1875–1958)

All things bright and beau-ti-ful, All crea-tures great and small,

All things wise and won-der-ful, The Lord God made them all.

Each lit-tle flower that o-pens, Each lit-tle bird that sings, He

made their glow-ing col-ours, He made their ti-ny wings.

All things bright and beautiful,
All creatures great and small,
All things wise and wonderful,
The Lord God made them all.

1 Each little flower that opens,
  Each little bird that sings,
  He made their glowing colours,
  He made their tiny wings.
     All things bright . . .

2 The purple headed mountain,
  The river running by,
  The sunset, and the morning
  That brightens up the sky;
     All things bright . . .

3 The cold wind in the winter,
  The pleasant summer sun,
  The ripe fruits in the garden,
  He made them every one.
     All things bright . . .

4 He gave us eyes to see them,
  And lips that we might tell
  How great is God almighty,
  Who has made all things well.
     All things bright . . .

   Cecil F. Alexander, 1818–95

299 Almighty God

Austin Martin

Al-migh-ty God, _____ we bring You praise _____ For Your

Son, _____ the Word of God, _____ By whose power _____

_____ the world was made, _____ By whose blood _____ we are re - deemed.

Morn-ing star, _____ the Fa-ther's glo - ry, _____ We now

wor-ship____ and a-dore You.____ In our hearts____

_Your light has ris-en;____ Je-sus, Lord,____we wor-ship You.

Almighty God, we bring You praise
For Your Son, the Word of God,
By whose power the world was made,
By whose blood we are redeemed.
Morning star, the Father's glory,
We now worship and adore You.
In our hearts Your light has risen;
Jesus, Lord, we worship You.

300 All things praise Thee

TE LAUDANT OMNIA 7 7. 7 7. 7 7

J.F. Swift (1847–1931)

All things praise Thee, Lord most high, Heaven and earth and sea and sky,

All were for Thy glo-ry made, That Thy great-ness, thus dis-played,

Should all wor-ship bring to Thee; All things praise Thee: Lord, may we.

1 All things praise Thee, Lord most high,
Heaven and earth and sea and sky,
All were for Thy glory made,
That Thy greatness, thus displayed,
Should all worship bring to Thee;
All things praise Thee: Lord, may we.

2 All things praise Thee: night to night
Sings in silent hymns of light;
All things praise Thee: day to day
Chants Thy power in burning ray;
Time and space are praising Thee;
All things praise Thee, Lord, may we.

3 All things praise Thee, high and low,
Rain and dew, and seven-hued bow,
Crimson sunset, fleecy cloud,
Rippling stream, and tempest loud,
Summer, winter – all to Thee
Glory render: Lord, may we.

4 All things praise Thee, heaven's high shrine
Rings with melody divine;
Lowly bending at Thy feet,
Seraph and archangel meet;
This their highest bliss, to be
Ever praising: Lord, may we.

5 All things praise Thee, gracious Lord,
Great Creator, powerful Word,
Omnipresent Spirit, now
At Thy feet we humbly bow,
Lift our hearts in praise to Thee;
All things praise Thee, Lord, may we.

G.W. Conder, 1821–74

301 An army of ordinary people

With feeling

Dave Bilbrough

An ar-my of or-di-na-ry peo-ple,_____ A
king-dom where love is the key,_____ A ci-ty, a light to the
na-tions,_____ Heirs to the pro-mise are we._____ A
peo-ple__ whose life is in Je-sus,_____ A na-tion to-geth-er we

stand. On-ly through grace are we worth-y,_____ In-he-ri-tors of the

land._____ *A new day is dawn-ing,_____* *A new age to*

come, *When the child-ren of pro - mise_____*

Shall flow to-geth-er as one:_____ A truth long ne - glect-ed,_____

But the time has now come, When the child-ren of

pro-mise____ Shall flow to-geth-er as one._____

1 An army of ordinary people,
  A kingdom where love is the key,
  A city, a light to the nations,
  Heirs to the promise are we.
  A people whose life is in Jesus,
  A nation together we stand.
  Only through grace are we worthy,
  Inheritors of the land.

    A new day is dawning,
    A new age to come,
    When the children of promise
    Shall flow together as one:
    A truth long neglected,
    But the time has now come,
    When the children of promise
    Shall flow together as one.

2 A people without recognition,
  But with Him a destiny sealed,
  Called to a heavenly vision:
  His purpose shall be fulfilled.
  Come let us stand strong together,
  Abandon ourselves to the King.
  His love shall be ours for ever,
  This victory song we shall sing.
    A new day . . .

302 Angels from the realms of glory

IRIS 8.7.8.7 with chorus

French Carol Melody

An-gels from the realms of glo-ry, Wing your flight through all the earth;

Her-alds of cre - a - tion's sto-ry, Now pro-claim Mes - si - ah's birth!

Come _____ and ___

wor - ship, Christ, the new - born King: _____

Wor - ship Christ the new - born King.

1 Angels from the realms of glory,
  Wing your flight through all the earth;
  Heralds of creation's story,
  Now proclaim Messiah's birth!

    Come and worship,
    Christ, the new-born King:
    Come and worship,
    Worship Christ the new-born King.

2 Shepherds in the fields abiding,
  Watching by your flocks at night,
  God with man is now residing:
  See, there shines the infant light!
    Come and worship . . .

3 Wise men, leave your contemplations!
  Brighter visions shine afar;
  Seek in Him the hope of nations,
  You have seen His rising star:
    Come and worship . . .

4 Though an infant now we view Him,
  He will share His Father's throne,
  Gather all the nations to Him;
  Every knee shall then bow down:
    Come and worship . . .

J. Montgomery, 1771–1854
© *in this version Jubilee Hymns*

303 As the deer

As the deer pants for the wa-ter, So my soul longs af - ter You.

You a - lone are my heart's de - sire ___ And I long to wor - ship You.

You a - lone are my strength, my shield, To You a - lone may my spi - rit yield.

You a-lone are my heart's de - sire And I long to wor - ship You.

1 As the deer pants for the water,
  So my soul longs after You.
  You alone are my heart's desire
  And I long to worship You.

  You alone are my strength, my shield,
  To You alone may my spirit yield.
  You alone are my heart's desire
  And I long to worship You.

2 I want You more than gold or silver,
  Only You can satisfy.
  You alone are the real joy-giver
  And the apple of my eye.
    You alone are . . .

3 You're my Friend and You are my Brother,
  Even though You are a King.
  I love You more than any other,
  So much more than anything.
    You alone are . . .

304 Angel voices ever singing

ANGEL-VOICES 8 5.8 5. 8 4 3

Edwin George Monk (1819–1900)

An-gel voi-ces ev-er sing-ing Round thy throne of light,

An-gel harps for ev-er ring-ing, Rest not day nor night;

Thou-sands on-ly live to bless Thee, And con-fess Thee Lord of might.

1 Angel voices ever singing
Round thy throne of light,
Angel harps for ever ringing,
Rest not day nor night;
Thousands only live to bless Thee,
And confess Thee Lord of might.

2 Thou who art beyond the farthest
Mortal eye can scan,
Can it be that Thou regardest
Songs of sinful man?
Can we know that Thou art near us
And wilt hear us? Yes, we can.

3 Yes, we know that Thou rejoicest
O'er each work of Thine;
Thou didst ears and hands and voices
For Thy praise design;
Craftsman's art and music's measure
For Thy pleasure all combine.

4 In Thy house, great God, we offer
Of Thine own to Thee,
And for Thine acceptance proffer,
All unworthily,
Hearts and minds and hands and voices
In our choicest psalmody.

5 Honour, glory, might, and merit
Thine shall ever be,
Father, Son, and Holy Spirit,
Blessèd Trinity.
Of the best that Thou hast given
Earth and heaven render Thee.

Francis Pott 1832–1909

305 As with gladness

DIX 77.77.77

Adapted from a chorale by C. Kocher (1786–72)

As with glad-ness men of old Did the guid-ing star be-hold;

As with joy they hailed its light, Lead-ing on-ward, beam-ing bright,

So, most gra-cious God, may we Led by You for ev-er be.

1 As with gladness men of old
Did the guiding star behold;
As with joy they hailed its light,
Leading onward, beaming bright,
So, most gracious God, may we
Led by You for ever be.

2 As with joyful steps they sped,
Saviour, to Your lowly bed,
There to bend the knee before
You whom heaven and earth adore,
So may we with one accord,
Seek forgivness from our Lord.

3 As they offered gifts most rare
Gold and frankincense and myrrh
So may we cleansed from our sin
Lives of service now begin
As in love our treasures bring,
Christ, to You our heavenly King.

4 Holy Jesus, every day
Keep us in the narrow way;
And when earthly things are past,
Bring our ransomed souls at last
Where they need no star to guide,
Where no clouds Your glory hide.

5 In heavenly country bright
Need they no created light
You its light, its joy its crown,
You its sun which goes not down.
There for ever may we sing
Hallelujahs to our King.

W.C. Dix, 1837–98
Altered © 1986 Horrobin/Leavers

43

306 At even, ere the sun was set

ANGELUS L.M.

Scheffler's *Heilige Seelenlust* (1657)

At ev - en, ere the sun was set, The sick, O Lord, a - round Thee lay; O in what di - vers pains they met! O with what joy they went a - way!

1 At even, ere the sun was set,
   The sick, O Lord, around Thee lay;
   O in what divers pains they met!
   O with what joy they went away!

2 Once more 'tis eventide, and we
   Oppressed with various ills draw near:
   What if Thy form we cannot see?
   We know and feel that Thou art here.

3 O Saviour Christ, our woes dispel:
   For some are sick; and some are sad;
   And some have never loved Thee well;
   And some have lost the love they had.

4 And some have found the world is vain,
   Yet from the world they break not free;
   And some have friends who give them pain,
   Yet have not sought a Friend in Thee.

5 And none, O Lord, have perfect rest,
   For none are wholly free from sin;
   And they who fain would serve thee best
   Are concious most of wrong within.

6 O Saviour Christ, Thou too art Man;
   Thou hast been troubled, tempted, tried;
   Thy kind but searching glance can scan
   The very wounds that shame would hide.

7 Thy touch has still its ancient power;
   No word from Thee can fruitless fall;
   Hear, in this solemn evening hour,
   And in Thy mercy heal us all.

Henry Twells, 1823–1900

307   At Your feet O Lord

Janis Miller

Unhurried

At Your feet, O Lord, we wait for You,
Yearn-ing Lord, hun-gry Lord, for more of You.
Bow'd be-fore You, Lord, we de-sire on-ly You:
Fill us Lord, re-vive us Lord, with more of You.

308 At Your feet we fall

With steady strength

Dave Fellingham

Capo 2

At Your feet we fall,_____ migh-ty ris-en Lord,_____ As we come be-fore Your throne to wor-ship You._____ By Your Spi-rit's power_____ You now draw our hearts,_____ And we hear Your voice in tri-umph ring-ing clear._____

I am He that liv - eth, that liv-eth and was dead._____ Be-

hold, I am a - live for ev - er - more._____

1 At Your feet we fall, mighty risen Lord,
As we come before Your throne to worship You.
By Your Spirit's power You now draw our hearts,
And we hear Your voice in triumph ringing clear.

I am He that liveth, that liveth and was dead.
Behold, I am alive for evermore.

2 There we see You stand, mighty risen Lord,
Clothed in garments pure and holy, shining bright.
Eyes of flashing fire, feet like burnished bronze,
And the sound of many waters is Your voice.
I am He that liveth . . .

3 Like the shining sun in its noonday strength,
We now see the glory of Your wondrous face.
Once that face was marred, but now You're glorified,
And Your words like a two-edged sword have mighty power.
I am He that liveth . . .

309 Awake, awake, O Zion

David J. Hadden

Triumphantly

A - wake, a - wake, O Zi - on, Come

clothe your - self with strength._____ A -

Put on your gar - ments of splen -

dor, O Je - ru - sa - lem._____

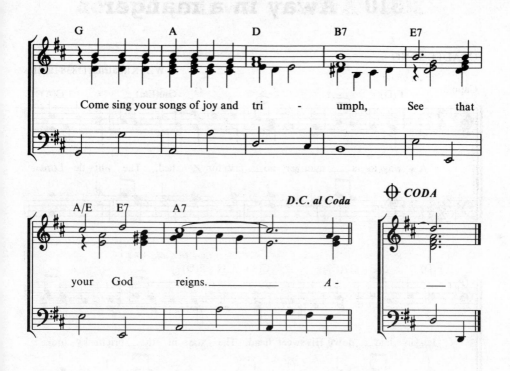

Awake, awake, O Zion,
Come clothe yourself with strength.
Awake, awake, O Zion,
Come clothe yourself with strength.

1 Put on your garments of splendour,
  O Jerusalem.
  Come sing your songs of joy and triumph,
  See that your God reigns.
      Awake, awake . . .

2 Burst into songs of joy together,
  O Jerusalem.
  The Lord has comforted His people,
  The redeemed Jerusalem.
      Awake, awake . . .

310 Away in a manger

CRADLE SONG

W.J. Kilpatrick (1838–1921)

A - way in a manger, no crib for a bed, The lit - tle Lord

Je - sus laid down His sweet head. The stars in the bright sky looked

down where He lay, The lit - tle Lord Je - sus a - sleep in the hay.

1 Away in a manger, no crib for a bed,
  The little Lord Jesus laid down His sweet head.
  The stars in the bright sky looked down where He lay,
  The little Lord Jesus asleep in the hay.

2 The cattle are lowing, the Baby awakes,
  But little Lord Jesus, no crying He makes.
  I love You Lord Jesus! Look down from the sky,
  And stay by my side until morning is nigh.

3 Be near me, Lord Jesus; I ask You to stay
  Close by me for ever and love me, I pray.
  Bless all the dear children in Your tender care,
  And fit us for heaven to live with You there.

311 Blest be the tie that binds

DENNIS S.M.

J.G. Nägeli (1768–1836)
arr. Phil Burt

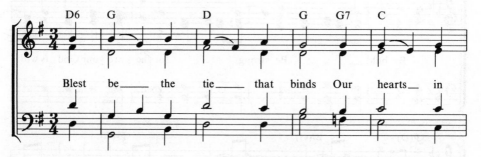

Blest be the tie that binds Our hearts in

Christ - ian love; The fel - low - ship of

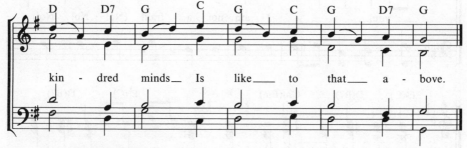

kin - dred minds Is like to that a - bove.

Arrangement Copyright © 1987 Phil Burt

1 Blest be the tie that binds
Our hearts in Christian love;
The fellowship of kindred minds
Is like to that above.

2 Before our Father's throne
We pour our ardent prayers;
Our fears, our hopes, our aims are one,
Our comforts and our cares.

3 We share our mutual woes,
Our mutual burdens bear,
And often for each other flows
The sympathizing tear.

4 When for awhile we part,
This thought will soothe our pain,
That we shall still be joined in heart,
And hope to meet again.

5 This glorious hope revives
Our courage by the way,
While each in expectation lives,
And longs to see the day.

6 From sorrow, toil, and pain,
And sin we shall be free;
And perfect love and friendship reign
Through all eternity.

John Fawcett, 1740–1817, altd.

51

312 Be bold

Anon
arr. Andy Silver

Rock feel

Capo 3 Bb(G) ... Eb(C)

Be bold, ___ Be strong, for the Lord your God is with ___

F(D) ... Bb(G) ... Eb(C)

___ you, Be bold, ___ Be strong, for the Lord your God is with ___

F(D) ... Eb(C) D(B7) Gm(Em)

___ you, ___ I am not a - fraid (No! No! No!)

Eb(C) D(B7) Gm(Em) ... Eb(C) D(B7)

I am not dis - mayed, For I'm walk-ing in faith and

Gm(Em) ... Eb(C) D(B7) Gm(Em)

vic - to - ry, Come on and walk in faith and vic - to - ry For the

Lord your God is with you.

Be bold, Be strong, for the Lord your God is with you,
Be bold, Be strong, for the Lord your God is with you,
I am not afraid (No! No! No!)
I am not dismayed,
For I'm walking in faith and victory,
Come on and walk in faith and victory
For the Lord your God is with you.

Copyright control

313 Blessed are the pure in heart

Betty Lou Mills

Bles-sed are the pure in heart, For they shall see God. Bles-sed are the pure in heart, For they shall see God.___ To see God,___ the Al-pha and O-me-ga, To see God,___ Cre-

Blessed are the pure in heart,
For they shall see God.
Blessed are the pure in heart,
For they shall see God.

1 To see God, the Alpha and Omega,
  To see God, Creator life sustainer,
  To see God, to think that this is possibility.
    Blessed are . . .

2 To see God, the everlasting Father.
  To see God, whose love endures for ever.
  To see God, how wonderful to think that this could be.
    Blessed are . . .

3 To see God, the God who talked with Moses.
  To see God, whose mercies are so endless.
  To see God, what better incentive for purity.
    Blessed are . . .

4 To see God, the One I've loved and longed for.
  To see God, the Father of my Saviour.
  To see God, a dream come true, at last His face I'll see.
    Blessed are . . .

314 Born by the Holy Spirit's breath

WHITSUN PSALM 8 8 8 8 (LM)

Noël Tredinnick (b. 1949)

This version Copyright © 1987 Noel Tredinnick

1 Born by the Holy Spirit's breath,
Loosed from the law of sin and death;
Now cleared in Christ from every claim
No judgement stands against our name.

2 In us the Spirit makes His home
That we in Him may overcome;
Christ's risen life, in all its powers,
Its all-prevailing strength, is ours.

3 Sons, then, and heirs of God most high,
We by His Spirit 'Father' cry;
That Spirit with our spirit shares
To frame and breathe our wordless prayers.

4 One is His love, His purpose one:
To form the likeness of His Son
In all who, called and justified,
Shall reign in glory at His side.

5 Nor death nor life, nor powers unseen,
Nor height nor depth can come between;
We know through peril, pain and sword,
The love of God in Christ our Lord.

From Romans 8
© Timothy Dudley-Smith, b. 1926

56

315 Born in the night

Geoffrey Ainger

1 Born in the night, Mary's child,
A long way from Your home;
Coming in need, Mary's child,
Born in a borrowed room.

2 Clear shining light, Mary's child,
Your face lights up our way;
Light of the world, Mary's child,
Dawn on our darkened day.

3 Truth of our life, Mary's child,
You tell us God is good;
Prove it is true, Mary's child,
Go to Your cross of wood.

4 Hope of the world Mary's child,
You're coming soon to reign;
King of the earth, Mary's child,
Walk in our streets again.

Geoffrey Ainger
© *1964 Stainer & Bell Ltd*

316 Break Thou the bread of life

LATHBURY 6 4.6 4 D

William F. Sherwin (1826–88)

Break Thou the bread of life, dear Lord to me,

As thou didst break the bread be - side the sea;

Be - yond the sa - cred page I seek Thee, Lord,

My Spi - rit longs for Thee, Thou liv - ing Word.

1 Break Thou the bread of life, dear Lord to me,
  As thou didst break the bread beside the sea;
  Beyond the sacred page I seek Thee, Lord,
  My Spirit longs for Thee, Thou living Word.

2 Thou art the bread of life, O Lord, to me,
  Thy holy Word the truth that saveth me;
  Give me to eat and live with Thee above,
  Teach me to love Thy truth, for Thou art love.

3 O send Thy Spirit, Lord, now unto me,
  That He may touch my eyes and make me see;
  Show me the truth concealed within Thy Word,
  And in Thy book revealed, I see Thee, Lord.

4 Bless Thou the bread of life to me, to me,
  As Thou didst bless the loaves by Galilee;
  Then shall all bondage cease, all fetters fall,
  And I shall find my peace, my all in all.

Mary A. Lathbury, 1841–1913
v.2 Alexander Groves, 1843–1909

317 Brightest and best

EPIPHANY HYMN 11.10.11.10

J.F. Thrupp (1827–67)

Bright-est and best of the sons of the morn-ing,

Dawn on our dark-ness and lend us thine aid;

Star of the east__ the ho-ri-zon a-dor-ing,

Guide where our in-fant Re-deem-er is laid.

1 Brightest and best of the sons of the morning,
Dawn on our darkness and lend us thine aid;
Star of the east the horizon adoring,
Guide where our infant Redeemer is laid.

2 Cold on His cradle the dew-drops are shining;
Low lies His head with the beasts of the stall:
Angels adore Him, in slumber reclining,
Maker and monarch, and Saviour of all.

3 Say, shall we yield Him, in costly devotion,
Odours of Edom, and offerings divine;
Gems of the mountain, and pearls of the ocean,
Myrrh from the forest, or gold from the mine?

4 Vainly we offer each ample oblation;
Vainly with gifts would His favour secure;
Richer by far is the heart's adoration;
Dearer to God are the prayers of the poor.

5 Brightest and best of the sons of the morning,
Dawn on our darkness and lend us thine aid;
Star of the east the horizon adorning,
Guide where our infant Redeemer is laid.

Reginald Heber, 1783–1826

318   Broken for me

Words and music by
Janet Lunt

Broken for me, broken for you, The Body of Jesus broken for you. He offered His body He poured out His Soul

Broken for me, broken for you,
The Body of Jesus broken for you.

1 He offered His body He poured out His Soul
   Jesus was broken that we might be whole:
      Broken for me . . .

2 Come to My table and with Me dine,
   Eat of My bread and drink of My wine:
      Broken for me . . .

3 This is My body given for you,
   Eat it rememb'ring I died for you:
      Broken for me . . .

4 This is my blood I shed for you,
   For your forgiveness, making you new:
      Broken for me . . .

319 Cause me to come

R. Edward Miller

Thoughtfully

Capo 2

1 Cause me to come to Thy river, O Lord, *(three times)*
Cause me to come, cause me to drink, cause me to live.

2 Cause me to drink from Thy river, O Lord, *(three times)*
Cause me to come, cause me to drink, cause me to live.

3 Cause me to live by Thy river, O Lord, *(three times)*
Cause me to come, cause me to drink, cause me to live.

320 Christ, whose glory fills the skies

RATISBON 7 7. 7 7. 7 7

Werner, *Choralbuch* (1815)

1 Christ, whose glory fills the skies,
  Christ, the true, the only light,
  Sun of righteousness, arise,
  Triumph o'er the shades of night;
  Dayspring from on high, be near;
  Daystar, in my heart appear.

2 Dark and cheerless is the morn
  Unaccompanied by Thee;
  Joyless is the day's return,
  Till Thy mercy's beams I see;
  Till they inward light impart,
  Glad my eyes, and warm my heart.

3 Visit then this soul of mine,
  Pierce the gloom of sin and grief;
  Fill me, radiancy divine,
  Scatter all my unbelief;
  More and more Thyself display,
  Shining to the perfect day.

Charles Wesley, 1707–88

321 Change my heart, O God

Eddie Espinosa

With feeling

Change my heart, O God,___ make it ev-er true,___

Change my heart, O God,___

to Coda ⊕

may I be like You. You are the

pot - ter, I am the clay,___

D.C. al Coda

CODA

Mould me and make _____ me, this is what I

pray.

You. _____

Change my heart, O God, make it ever true,
Change my heart, O God, may I be like You.

You are the potter, I am the clay,
Mould me and make me, this is what I pray.

Change my heart, O God, make it ever true,
Change my heart, O God, may I be like You.

322 Christ is risen! Hallelujah

MORGENLIED 8 7. 8 7. D and Chorus   Frederick Charles Maker (1844–1927)

Christ is ris - en! Hal - le - lu - jah! Ris - en our vic - tor-ious Head!

Sing His prais-es! Hal - le - lu - jah! Christ is ris - en from the dead.

Grate-ful-ly our hearts a - dore Him, As His light once more ap-pears,

Bow-ing down in joy be-fore Him, Ris - ing up from grief and tears.

Chorus

Christ is ris-en! Hal-le-lu-jah! Ris-en our vic-tor-ious Head!

Sing His prais-es! Hal-le-lu-jah! Christ is ris-en from the dead.

1 Christ is risen! Hallelujah!
  Risen our victorious Head!
  Sing His praises! Hallelujah!
  Christ is risen from the dead.
  Gratefully our hearts adore Him,
  As His light once more appears,
  Bowing down in joy before Him,
  Rising up from grief and tears.

  Christ is risen! Hallelujah!
  Risen our victorious Head!
  Sing His praises! Hallelujah!
  Christ is risen from the dead.

2 Christ is risen! All the sadness
  Of His earthly life is o'er,
  Through the open gates of gladness
  He returns to life once more;
  Death and hell before Him bending,
  He doth rise, the Victor now,
  Angels on His steps attending,
  Glory round His wounded brow.
    Christ is risen! . . .

3 Christ is risen! Henceforth never
  Death or hell shall us enthral,
  We are Christ's, in Him for ever
  We have triumphed over all;
  All the doubting and dejection
  Of our trembling hearts have ceased:
  'Tis His day of resurrection,
  Let us rise and keep the feast.
    Christ is risen! . . .

John Samuel Bewley Monsell, 1811–75

323 Christ is surely coming

LAND OF HOPE 11.11.11.11.11.

Edward Elgar (1857–1934)
arr. by Robin Sheldon (b. 1932)

Meet your Judge and Sav - iour, na-tions near and far!

1 Christ is surely coming, bringing His reward,
  Omega and Alpha, first and last and Lord:
  Root and stem of David, brilliant morning star,
  Meet your Judge and Saviour, nations near and far!
  Meet your Judge and Saviour, nations near and far!

2 See the holy city! There they enter in,
  Men by Christ made holy, washed from every sin:
  Thirsty ones, desiring all He loves to give,
  Come for living water, freely drink, and live!
  Come for living water, freely drink, and live!

3 Grace be with God's people! Praise His holy name!
  Father, Son, and Spirit, evermore the same.
  Hear the certain promise from the eternal home:
  'Surely I come quickly!' – Come, Lord Jesus, come!
  'Surely I come quickly!' – Come, Lord Jesus, come!

Christopher Idle, b. 1938

324 Christ the Lord is risen

EASTER HYMN 7 7. 7 7 with Hallelujahs

arr. W.A. Monk (1823–89)

Christ, the Lord, is risen to-day:— Hal - le - lu - jah!

Sons of men and an-gels say,— Hal - le - lu - jah!

Raise your joys and tri-umphs high; Hal - le - lu - jah!

Sing, ye heav'ns; thou earth, re - ply,— Hal - le - lu - jah!

1 Christ, the Lord, is risen today:
 Hallelujah!
Sons of men and angels say,
 Hallelujah!
Raise your joys and triumphs high;
 Hallelujah!
Sing, ye heav'ns; thou earth, reply,
 Hallelujah!

2 Love's redeeming work is done;
 Hallelujah!
Fought the fight, the battle won:
 Hallelujah!
Lo! our Sun's eclipse is o'er!
 Hallelujah!
Lo! He sets in blood no more!
 Hallelujah!

3 Vain the stone, the watch, the seal!
 Hallelujah!
Christ hath burst the gates of hell:
 Hallelujah!
Death in vain forbids Him rise;
 Hallelujah!
Christ hath opened paradise.
 Hallelujah!

4 Lives again our glorious King!
 Hallelujah!
Where, O death, is now thy sting?
 Hallelujah!
Once He died our souls to save;
 Hallelujah!
Where thy victory, O grave?
 Hallelujah!

5 Soar we now where Christ hath led,
 Hallelujah!
Following our exalted Head:
 Hallelujah!
Made like Him, like Him we rise,
 Hallelujah!
Ours the cross, the grave, the skies.
 Hallelujah!

6 Hail the Lord of earth and heaven,
 Hallelujah!
Praise to Thee by both be given;
 Hallelujah!
Thee we greet, in triumph sing
 Hallelujah!
Hail, our resurrected King.
 Hallelujah!

Charles Wesley, 1707–88

325 Christians awake!

YORKSHIRE 10. 10. 10. 10. 10. 10.

J. Wainwright (1723–68)

Christ - ians a - wake! sal - ute the hap - py morn,

Where - on the Sav - iour of man - kind was born;

Rise to a - dore the my - ste - ry of love

Which hosts of an - gels chant - ed from a - bove;

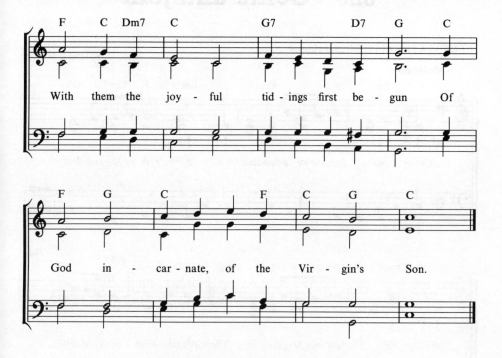

With them the joy-ful tid-ings first be-gun Of God in-car-nate, of the Vir-gin's Son.

1 Christians awake! salute the happy morn,
  Whereon the Saviour of mankind was born;
  Rise to adore the mystery of love
  Which hosts of angels chanted from above;
  With them the joyful tidings first begun
  Of God incarnate, of the Virgin's Son.

2 Then to the watchful shepherds it was told,
  Who heard the angelic herald's voice 'Behold,
  I bring good tidings of a Saviour's birth
  To you and all the nations upon earth:
  This day hath God fulfilled His promised word,
  This day is born a Saviour, Christ the Lord.'

3 He spake; and straightway the celestial choir,
  In hymns of joy unknown before conspire;
  High praise of God's redeeming love they sang,
  And heaven's whole orb with hallelujahs rang:
  God's highest glory was their anthem still,
  'On earth be peace, and unto men goodwill.'

4 O may we keep and ponder in our mind
  God's wondrous love in saving lost mankind;
  Trace we the Babe who hath retrieved our loss,
  From His poor manger to His bitter cross;
  Tread in His steps, assisted by His grace,
  Till man's first heavenly state again takes place.

5 Then may we hope, the angelic hosts among,
  To sing, redeemed, a glad triumphant song:
  He that was born upon this joyful day
  Around us all His glory shall display;
  Saved by His love, incessant we shall sing
  Eternal praise to heaven's almighty King.

John Byrom, 1692–1763, altd.

326 Come and join

CELEBRATIONS 11. 14. and chorus

Valerie Collison

Come and join the ce-le-bra-tion, It's a ve-ry spe-cial day;

Come and share our ju-bi-la-tion, There's a new King born to-day!

See the shep-herds Hur-ry down to Beth-le - hem;

Gaze in won - der At the Son of God who lay be-fore them.

327 Come and praise the living God

Come and praise the living God,
Come and worship, come and worship.
He has made you priest and king,
Come and worship the living God.

1 We come not to a mountain of fire and smoke,
  Not to gloom and darkness or trumpet sound;
  We come to the new Jerusalem,
  The holy city of God.
      Come and praise . . .

2 By His voice He shakes the earth,
  His judgements known throughout the world.
  But we have a city that for ever stands,
  The holy city of God.
      Come and praise . . .

328 Come let us bow down in worship

Andy Silver

He is our God, the peo-ple of__ His pas-ture, The flock
un-der His care.____ Come let__us bow down in
wor-ship,____ Let us kneel be-fore__the Lord.

Come let us bow down in worship,
Let us kneel before the Lord our Maker.
Come let us bow down in worship,
For He is our God and we are His people,
For He is our God, the people of His pasture,
The flock under His care.
Come let us bow down in worship,
Let us kneel before the Lord.

329 Come let us worship

I AM THE BREAD OF LIFE

S. Suzanne Toolan
arr. Christian Strover

Come let us wor-ship Christ, To the glo-ry of God the
Fa-ther, For He is wor-thy of all our love; He
died and rose for us! Praise Him as Lord and
Sav-iour. *And when the trum-pet shall sound, And Je-sus*

comes in great power, Then He will raise us to
be with Him For ev - er - more.

1 Come let us worship Christ,
   To the glory of God the Father,
   For He is worthy of all our love;
   He died and rose for us!
   Praise Him as Lord and Saviour.

   And when the trumpet shall sound,
   And Jesus comes in great power,
   Then He will raise us to be with Him
   For evermore.

2 'I am the bread of life;
   He who comes to Me shall not hunger:
   And all who trust in Me shall not thirst' –
   This is what Jesus said:
   Praise Him as Lord and Saviour.
     And when the trumpet . . .

3 'I am the door to life;
   He who enters by Me is saved,
   Abundant life He will then receive' –
   This is what Jesus said:
   Praise Him as Lord and Saviour.
     And when the trumpet . . .

4 'I am the light of the world;
   If you follow Me, darkness ceases,
   And in its place comes the light of life; –
   This is what Jesus said:
   Praise Him as Lord and Saviour,
     And when the trumpet . . .

5 Lord, we are one with You;
   We rejoice in Your new creation:
   Our hearts are fired by Your saving love –
   Take up our lives, O Lord,
   And use us for Your glory.
     And when the trumpet . . .

after S. Suzanne Toolan
© *Michael Baughan*
and GIA Publications Incorporated

Come on and celebrate

Very lively

Patricia Morgan

Come on and ce - le - brate His gift of love, we will ce - le - brate The Son of God who loved ___ us ___ And gave us life. ___ We'll shout Your praise, O King, You give us joy no-thing else can bring, ___

331 Come see the beauty of the Lord

Graham Kendrick

Thoughtfully, building throughout*

Come see the beau-ty of ___ the Lord,

Come see the beau-ty of ___ His face.

See the Lamb that once was slain,

See on His palms is carv'd your ___

name.

See how our pain has pierc'd His heart,

Come see the beauty of the Lord,
Come see the beauty of His face.
See the Lamb that once was slain,
See on His palms is carv'd your name.
See how our pain has pierc'd His heart,
And on His brow He bears our pride;
A crown of thorns.

But only love pours from His heart
As silently He takes the blame.
He has my name upon His lips,
My condemnation falls on Him.
This love is marvellous to me,
His sacrifice has set me free
And now I live.

Come see the beauty of the Lord,
Come see the beauty of His face.

*This song is sung as a call and response throughout,
the congregation copying the leader or the ladies following the men.

332 Come sing the praise of Jesus

American melody
arr. D.J. Langford

Come sing the praise of Je - sus, Sing His love with hearts a-flame. Sing His

won-d'rous birth of Ma - ry When to save the world He came. Tell the

life He lived for o - thers And His migh-ty deeds pro-claim, For Je-sus Christ is

King. Praise and glo - ry be to Je - sus.

88

Praise and glo-ry be to Je - sus. Praise and glo-ry be to
Je - sus, For Je - sus Christ is King.

1 Come sing the praise of Jesus,
 Sing His love with hearts aflame.
 Sing His wondrous birth of Mary
 When to save the world He came.
 Tell the life He lived for others
 And His mighty deeds proclaim,
 For Jesus Christ is King.

 Praise and glory be to Jesus.
 Praise and glory be to Jesus.
 Praise and glory be to Jesus,
 For Jesus Christ is King.

2 When foes arose and slew Him,
 He was victor in the fight;
 Over death and hell He triumphed
 In His resurrection-might;
 He has raised our fallen manhood
 And enthroned it in the height,
 For Jesus Christ is King.
  Praise and glory ...

3 There's joy for all who serve Him,
 More than human tongue can say;
 There is pardon for the sinner,
 And the night is turned to day;
 There is healing for our sorrows,
 There is music all the way,
 For Jesus Christ is King.
  Praise and glory ...

4 We witness to His beauty,
 And we spread His love abroad;
 And we cleave the host of darkness,
 With the Spirit's piercing sword;
 We will lead the souls in prison
 To the freedom of the Lord,
 For Jesus Christ is King.
  Praise and glory ...

5 To Jesus be the glory,
 The dominion, and the praise,
 He is Lord of all creation,
 He is guide of all our ways;
 And the world shall be His empire
 In the fulness of the days
 For Jesus Christ is King.
  Praise and glory ...

J.C. Winslow, 1882–1974
© *Mrs J. Tyrell*

333 Come, you thankful people, come

ST. GEORGE'S, WINDSOR 77.77.D

C.J. Elvey (1816–93)

Come, you thank-ful peo-ple, come, Raise the song of har-vest home!

Fruit and crops are gath-ered in Safe be-fore the storms be-gin:

God our ma-ker will pro-vide For our needs to be sup-plied:

Come, with all His peo-ple, come, Raise the song of har-vest home!

1 Come, you thankful people, come,
Raise the song of harvest home!
Fruit and crops are gathered in
Safe before the storms begin:
God our maker will provide
For our needs to be supplied:
Come, with all His people, come,
Raise the song of harvest home!

2 All the world is God's own field,
Harvests for His praise to yield;
Wheat and weeds together sown
Here for joy or sorrow grown:
First the blade and then the ear,
Then the full corn shall appear—
Lord of harvest, grant that we
Wholesome grain and pure may be.

3 For the Lord our God shall come
And shall bring His harvest home;
He Himself on that great day,
Worthless things shall take away,
Give His angels charge at last
In the fire the weeds to cast,
But the fruitful ears to store
In His care for evermore.

4 Even so, Lord, quickly come—
Bring Your final harvest home!
Gather all Your people in
Free from sorrow, free from sin,
There together purified,
Ever thankful at Your side—
Come, with all Your angels, come,
Bring that glorious harvest home!

H. Alford, 1810–71
© *in this version Jubilate Hymns*

334 Create in me

Dave Fellingham

Create in me a clean heart, O___ God, And renew a right spi-rit in me._____
Create in me a clean heart, O___ God, And renew a right spi-rit in me._____

Create in me a clean heart, O God,
And renew a right spirit in me.
Create in me a clean heart, O God,
And renew a right spirit in me.
Wash me, cleanse me, purify me,
Make my heart as white as snow.
Create in me a clean heart, O God,
And renew a right spirit in me.

335 Come, thou long expected Jesus

STUTTGART 87.87

Melody by
C.F. Witt (1660–1716)

Come, Thou long - ex - pec-ted Je-sus, Born to set Thy peo-ple free;

From our fears and sins re-lease us; Let us find our rest in Thee.

1 Come, Thou long-expected Jesus,
  Born to set Thy people free;
  From our fears and sins release us;
  Let us find our rest in Thee.

2 Israel's strength and consolation,
  Hope of all the earth Thou art;
  Dear desire of every nation,
  Joy of every longing heart.

3 Born thy people to deliver;
  Born a child, and yet a King;
  Born to reign in us for ever;
  Now Thy gracious kingdom bring.

4 By Thine own eternal Spirit
  Rule in all our hearts alone:
  By Thine all-sufficient merit
  Raise us to Thy glorious throne.

Charles Wesley, 1707–88

336 Ding dong! Merrily on high

Traditional French tune
arr. Charles Wood
adpt. B.V. Burnett

1 Ding dong! Merrily on high
In heav'n the bells are ringing:
Ding dong! Verily the sky
Is riv'n with angels singing.

Gloria, Hosanna in excelsis!
Gloria, Hosanna in excelsis!

2 E'en so here below, below,
Let steeple bells be swungen,
And i-o, i-o, i-o,
By priest and people sungen.
Gloria . . .

3 Pray you, dutifully prime
Your matin chime, ye ringers;
May you beautifully rime
Your eve-time song, ye singers.
Gloria . . .

G.R. Woodward, 1859–1934

95

337 Delight yourself in the Lord

Andy Silver

De - light your - self in the Lord,_____ And
He will give you the de - sires__ of your heart. Com - mit your
way to the Lord;_____ Trust in Him and He will make your
right-eous-ness shine,__ Shin-ing like the dawn and like the noon day sun.__

338 **Delight yourselves in the Lord**

The right-eous will dwell in the land for ev - er,____ To share His in - her - it-ance.____ De - light your - self in the Lord,_____ And He will give you the de - sires____ of your heart. Com - mit your way to the Lord,____ Com - mit your way to the Lord.

338   Delight yourselves in the Lord

David Bolton

De - light your-selves in the Lord,_____ De - light your-selves in the Lord,_____ For He de-lights in the prai - ses Of His own peo - ple,_____ For He de-lights in the prai - ses Of His own peo - ple.

Let your well spring up with-in And o-ver-flow to one an-o-ther, Let your well spring up with-in And o-ver-flow to the Lord.

Delight yourselves in the Lord,
Delight yourselves in the Lord,
For He delights in the praises
Of His own people,
For He delights in the praises
Of His own people.

Let your well spring up within
And overflow to one another,
Let your well spring up within
And overflow to the Lord.

339 Draw near to God

Draw near to God and He'll draw near to you,
Draw near to God and He'll draw near to you.
Lift up ho-ly hands to Him__ and sing of what He's done,
Op-en up your hearts to Him__ and praise__ Him for His
Son.__ He'll draw near to you.__

340   Eternal Father, strong to save

MELITA 88.88.88

John Bacchus Dykes (1823–76)

E - ter-nal Fa-ther, strong to save, Whose arm hath bound the rest-less wave,

Who bidd'st the migh-ty o-cean deep Its own ap - point-ed lim - its keep:

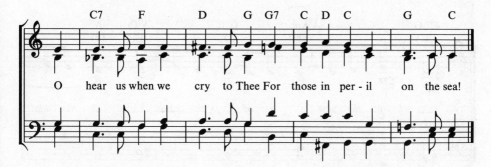

O hear us when we cry to Thee For those in per - il on the sea!

1 Eternal Father, strong to save,
Whose arm hath bound the restless wave,
Who bidd'st the mighty ocean deep
Its own appointed limits keep:
O hear us when we cry to Thee
For those in peril on the sea!

2 O Christ, whose voice the waters heard,
And hushed their raging at Thy word,
Who walkedst on the foaming deep,
And calm amid the storm didst sleep:
O hear us when we cry to Thee
For those in peril on the sea!

3 O Holy Spirit, who didst brood
Upon the waters dark and rude,
And bid their angry tumult cease,
And give, for wild confusion, peace:
O hear us when we cry to Thee
For those in peril on the sea!

4 O Trinity of love and power,
Our brethren shield in danger's hour;
From rock and tempest, fire and foe,
Protect them whersoe'er they go:
Thus evermore shall rise to Thee
Glad hymns of praise from land and sea.

William Whiting, 1825–78

341 El-Shaddai

(God Almighty)

John Thompson

We will praise___ and lift You high,___ El - Sha - ddai._

1–4.

1 Through your love

last time

El-Shaddai, El-Shaddai (God Almighty, God Almighty)
El-Elyon na Adonai (God in the highest, Oh Lord)
Age to age You're still the same by the power of the name.
El-Shaddai, El-Shaddai (God Almighty, God Almighty)
Erkamka na Adonai (We will love You, Oh Lord)
We will praise and lift You high, El-Shaddai.

1 Through Your love and through the ram
You saved the son of Abraham.
Through the power of Your hand,
Turned the sea into dry land.
To the outcast on her knees
You were the God who really sees
And by Your might You set Your children free.
    El-Shaddai, El-Shaddai . . .

2 Through the years You made it clear,
That the time of Christ was near.
Though the people couldn't see
What Messiah ought to be.
Though Your word contained the plan
They just could not understand.
Your most awesome work was done
Through the frailty of Your Son.
    El-Shaddai, El-Shaddai . . .

                                    Michael Card

103

342 Emmanuel

Music by Greg Leavers
and Phil Burt

104

Fine

Dm7　G7　C　C7

Lord of Lords　TOGETHER is　He.
Lord of Lords

F　Esus　E7　Am　Fmaj7

God Him-self＿will give a sign; A vir-gin shall bear a son Who shall be

C　Eb　Dm7　G　**D.C.**

called Em - ma - nu - el.＿＿＿＿＿＿

Emmanuel, (Emmanuel,)
God with us, (God with us,)
Wonderful (Wonderful)
Counsellor, (Counsellor,)
Prince of Peace – a Saviour is born
To redeem the world and His name is Jesus.
King of kings, (King of kings,)
Lord of Lords (Lord of Lords)
is He.

1　God Himself will give a sign;
　A virgin shall bear a son
　Who shall be called Emmanuel.
　　Emmanuel . . .

2　People who now walk in darkness
　Soon will see the light of Jesus,
　He is the light of the world.
　　Emmanuel . . .

3　Hear a voice cry in the desert,
　Clear a way for the Messiah,
　Make straight a highway for God.
　　Emmanuel . . .

4　Bringing good news; healing heartaches
　Preaching freedom; releasing captives,
　Giving a mantle of praise.
　　Emmanuel . . .

343　Eternal God

Dave Fellingham

Joyfully with strength

E - ter-nal God, we come to You,_____ We come be - fore Your throne._____ We en-ter by a new and liv-ing way,__ With con - fid - ence we come._____

We de - clare Your faith - ful - ness, Your pro - mi - ses are true;

We will now draw near to wor - ship You.

Ladies

O ho - ly God, full of

Men

O ho - ly God, we come to You,

344 Exalt the Lord our God

Rick Ridings

Steadily

Ex - alt the Lord our God,_____ Ex - alt the Lord our God,_____ And wor - ship at His foot - stool, Wor - ship at His foot - stool; Ho - ly is He, ho - ly is He._____

Exalt the Lord our God,
Exalt the Lord our God,
And worship at His footstool,
Worship at His footstool;
Holy is He, holy is He.

345 Father God

Graham Kendrick

1 Father God, we worship You,
  Make us part of all You do.
  As You move among us now
  We worship You.

2 Jesus King, we worship You,
  Help us listen now to You.
  As You move among us now
  We worship You.

3 Spirit pure, we worship You,
  With Your fire our zeal renew.
  As You move among us now
  We worship You.

346 Facing a task unfinished

AURELIA

Samuel Sebastian Wesley (1810–76)

Fac - ing a task un - fin - ished, That drives us to our
knees, A need that, un - dim - in - ished, Re -
bukes our sloth - ful ease, We who re - joice to
know Thee, Re - new be - fore Thy throne The

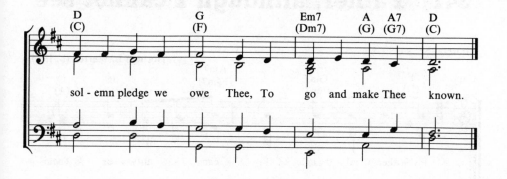

sol - emn pledge we owe Thee, To go and make Thee known.

1 Facing a task unfinished,
  That drives us to our knees,
  A need that, undiminished,
  Rebukes our slothful ease,
  We who rejoice to know Thee,
  Renew before Thy throne
  The solemn pledge we owe Thee,
  To go and make Thee known.

2 Where other lords beside Thee
  Hold their unhindered sway,
  Where forces that defied Thee
  Defy Thee still today;
  With none to heed their crying
  For life, and love, and light,
  Unnumbered souls are dying,
  And pass into the night.

3 We bear the torch that flaming
  Fell from the hands of those
  Who gave their lives proclaiming
  That Jesus died and rose.
  Ours is the same commission,
  The same glad message ours,
  Fired by the same ambition,
  To Thee we yield our powers.

4 O Father who sustained them,
  O Spirit who inspired,
  Saviour, whose love constrained them
  To toil with zeal untired,
  From cowardice defend us,
  From lethargy awake!
  Forth on Thine errands send us
  To labour for Thy sake.

Frank Houghton, 1894–1972
© *Overseas Missionary Fellowship*

347 Father, although I cannot see

MORDEN 868686

Norman L. Warren (b. 1934)

Fa - ther, al - though I can - not see The
fu - ture You have planned, And though the path is
some - times dark And hard to un - der - stand: Yet
give me faith, through joy and pain, To trace Your lov - ing

114

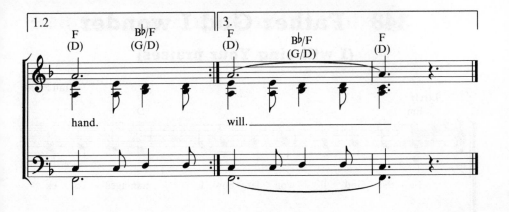

1 Father, although I cannot see
   The future You have planned,
   And though the path is sometimes dark
   And hard to understand:
   Yet give me faith, through joy and pain,
   To trace Your loving hand.

2 When I recall that in the past
   Your promises have stood
   Through each perplexing circumstance
   And every changing mood,
   I rest content that all things work
   Together for my good.

3 Whatever, then, the future brings
   Of good or seeming ill,
   I ask for strength to follow You
   And grace to trust You still;
   And I would look for no reward,
   Except to do Your will.

John Eddison, b. 1916

348 Father God I wonder

(I will sing Your praises)

Ian Smale

Father God I wonder how I man-aged To ex-ist with-out the know-ledge Of Your par-ent-hood And Your lov-ing care. But now I am Your son, I am a-dopt-ed in Your fam-i-ly And I can nev-er

349 Father make us one

Prayerfully

Rick Ridings

1. Fa - ther make us one,_____ Fa - ther make us____ one,_____ That the world may know Thou hast sent the Son,_____ Fa - ther make us one._____ 2. Be -

hold how plea-sant and how good it is_____ For
breth - ren to dwell in____ u - ni - ty,_____ For there the
Lord com - mands the bles - sing,_____
Life for ev - er - more._____

1 Father make us one,
  Father make us one,
  That the world may know Thou hast sent the Son,
  Father make us one.

2 Behold how pleasant and how good it is
  For brethren to dwell in unity,
  For there the Lord commands the blessing,
  Life for evermore.

350 Father God, the Lord creator

WALTHAM 8 7 8 7

H. Albert (1604–51)
Harmony by J.S. Bach (1685–1750)

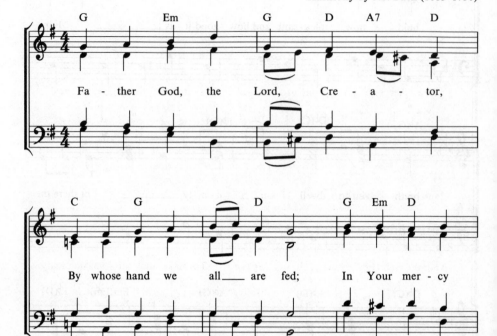

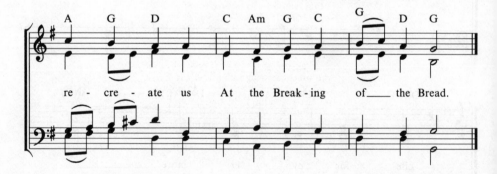

KYRIE (based on the 3-fold, 'Lord, have mercy'.)

1 Father God, the Lord, Creator,
By whose hand we all are fed;
In Your mercy recreate us
At the Breaking of the Bread.

2 Christ our Lord, be present with us,
Risen victorious from the dead!
In Your mercy may we know You
In the Breaking of the Bread.

3 Holy Spirit, God's empowering
By whose Life the Church is led;
In Your mercy, send us strengthened
From the Breaking of the Bread.

4 Father, Son and Holy Spirit
Hear our praises – sung and said.
From our hearts comes our Thanksgiving
For the Breaking of the Bread.

© *John Richards*

351 Father, sending Your anointed Son

ST. ANDREW 8. 7. 8. 7.

E.H. Thorne (1834–1916)

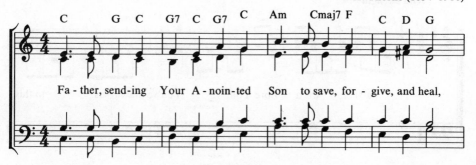

Fa - ther, send-ing Your A - noin-ted Son to save, for - give, and heal,

And, through Him, Your Ho - ly Spi - rit To make our sal - va - tion real;

1 Father, sending Your Anointed
Son to save, forgive, and heal,
And, through Him, Your Holy Spirit
To make our salvation real;

2 Look upon our ills and trouble
And on those who suffer much.
Send Your church the Spirit's unction
In Christ's Name to heal and touch.

3 Grant forgiveness to the faithful;
Bring to unity their prayer,
Use it for Your work unhindered
Through both sacrament and care.

*4 May the *one/ones* to be anointed
Outwardly with oil this hour,
Know Christ's fullest restoration
Through the Holy Spirit's power.

5 Heal Your church. Anoint and send us
Out into the world to tell
Of Your love and blessings to us;
How, in Christ, 'All will be well.'

John Richards

* Optional verse for when anointing takes place.

352 Father, we adore You

Carl Tuttle

With strength

Fa-ther, we a - dore You, You've drawn us to this place. We bow down be - fore You, Hum-bly on our face.

All the earth shall wor-ship At the throne of the

1 Father, we adore You,
  You've drawn us to this place.
  We bow down before You,
  Humbly on our face.

  All the earth shall worship
  At the throne of the King.
  Of His great and awesome power,
  We shall sing!

2 Jesus we love You,
  Because You first loved us,
  You reached out and healed us
  With Your mighty touch.
  All the earth . . .

3 Spirit we need You,
  To lift us from this mire,
  Consume and empower us
  With Your holy fire.
  All the earth . . .

  Holy is He; Blessèd is He;
  Worthy is He; Gracious is He;
  Faithful is He; Awesome is He;
  Saviour is He; Master is He;
  Mighty is He.
  Have mercy on me.

353 Fill your hearts with joy

REGENT SQUARE 8 7 8 7 8 7

H.T. Smart (1813–79)

Fill your hearts with joy and glad-ness, sing and praise your God and mine!

Great the Lord in love and wis-dom, Might and ma - jes - ty di-vine!

He who framed the star - ry hea-vens Knows and names them as they shine.

1 Fill your hearts with joy and gladness,
  Sing and praise your God and mine!
  Great the Lord in love and wisdom,
  Might and majesty divine!
  He who framed the starry heavens
  Knows and names them as they shine.

2 Praise the Lord, His people, praise Him!
  Wounded souls His comfort know;
  Those who fear Him find His mercies,
  Peace for pain and joy for woe;
  Humble hearts are high exalted,
  Human pride and power laid low.

3 Praise the Lord for times and seasons,
  Cloud and sunshine, wind and rain;
  Spring to melt the snows of winter
  Till the waters flow again;
  Grass upon the mountain pasture,
  Golden valleys thick with grain.

4 Fill your hearts with joy and gladness,
  Peace and plenty crown your days;
  Love His laws, declare His judgements,
  Walk in all His words and ways;
  He the Lord and we His children –
  Praise the Lord, all people, praise!

from Psalm 147
© *Timothy Dudley-Smith, b. 1926*

125

354 Father Your love is precious

(Your love overwhelms me)

Worshipfully

Everett Perry

Capo 3

Fa-ther __ Your love __ is pre-cious be-yond all loves,

1. Fa-ther Your love ov-er-whelms me. __

2. Fa-ther Your love ov-er-whelms me. __ So I

lift up __ my hands, An ex-pres-sion of my __ love, And I

give You___ my heart In joy-ful o - be - di-ence.

Fa - ther___ Your love___ is pre-cious be - yond all loves,

Fa - ther___ Your love ov - er-whelms me.___

Father Your love is precious beyond all loves,
Father Your love overwhelms me.
So I lift up my hands,
An expression of my love,
And I give You my heart
In joyful obedience.
Father Your love is precious beyond all loves,
Father Your love overwhelms me.

355 Fill the place Lord with Your glory

Words and music
Chris A. Bowater

With simplicity

Fill the place Lord with Your glo-ry At this gath-'ring of Your own; Reign in sove-reign grace and po-wer From your praise sur-roun-ded throne. Fill the place Lord with Your glo-ry At this gath-'ring of Your own;

We ex-alt You, we ____ a-dore You, _____ Thank-ful

hearts now join ____ as one. _____ You're the Christ, ____ the

King ____ of glo-ry, _____ Fa-ther's well ____ be-lov - ed

Son. _____ Fill the place Lord with Your glo-ry _____

___ At this gath - 'ring of Your own. _____

356 For the beauty of the earth

ENGLAND'S LANE 77.77.77

From an English melody
adpt. Geoffrey Shaw (1879–1943)

For the ___ beau - ty of the earth, For the
beau - ty ___ of the skies, For the ___ love which from our
birth O - ver and ___ a - round us lies, Fa - ther ___
un - to You we raise This our sac - ri - fice of praise.

1 For the beauty of the earth,
   For the beauty of the skies,
   For the love which from our birth
   Over and around us lies,
   Father unto You we raise
   This our sacrifice of praise.

2 For the beauty of each hour
   Of the day and of the night,
   Hill and vale and tree and flower,
   Sun and moon and stars of light,
   Father, unto You we raise
   This our sacrifice of praise.

3 For the joy of love from God,
   That we share on earth below.
   For our friends and family
   And the love that they can show,
   Father, unto You we raise
   This our sacrifice of praise.

4 For each perfect gift divine
   To our race so freely given,
   Thank You Lord that they are mine,
   Here on earth as gifts from heaven.
   Father, unto You we raise
   This our sacrifice of praise.

Folliott Pierpoint, 1835–1917
Altered © 1986 Horrobin/Leavers

357 For His name is exalted

For His name is ex-alt-ed, His glo-ry a-bove hea-ven and earth. Ho-ly is the Lord God Al-migh-ty, Who was and who is and who is to come. sit-teth on the throne and who lives for ev-er-more.

358   For this purpose

Graham Kendrick

One. Christ in us has

ov - er - come,_____ So with glad-ness we sing_____

_____ and wel - come His king - dom in._____

Rhythmic
Chorus

(MEN)

Ov - er sin He has con-quered, Hal - le -

(LADIES)

2 In the name of Jesus we stand,
By the power of His blood
We now claim this ground.
Satan has no authority here,
Powers of darkness must flee,
For Christ has the victory.
    Over sin . . .

135

359   For unto us a child is born

arr. Phil Burt

360 Forty days and forty nights

HEINLEIN 7 7. 7 7

M. Herbst (1654–81)

Forty days and forty nights
Thou wast fasting in the wild; Forty days and forty nights Tempted and yet undefiled.

1 Forty days and forty nights
Thou wast fasting in the wild;
Forty days and forty nights
Tempted and yet undefiled.

2 Sunbeams scorching all the day,
Chilly dew-drops nightly shed,
Prowling beasts about Thy way,
Stones Thy pillow, earth Thy bed.

3 Let us Thy endurance share
And from earthly greed abstain,
With Thee watching unto prayer
With Thee strong to suffer pain.

4 Then if evil on us press,
Flesh or spirit to assail,
Victor in the wilderness,
May we never faint or fail!

5 So shall peace divine be ours;
Holier gladness ours shall be;
Come to us angelic powers,
Such as ministered to Thee.

G.H. Smyttan, 1822–70, altd.

361 From heaven You came
(The Servant King)

Graham Kendrick

From heav'n You came, help-less babe, En-ter'd our world, Your glo-ry veil'd; Not to be served but to serve, And give Your life that we might live. *This is our* God,_____ *the Ser-vant King,*_____ *He calls us now to fol-low*

1 From heav'n You came, helpless babe,
   Enter'd our world, Your glory veil'd;
   Not to be served but to serve,
   And give Your life that we might live.

   This is our God, the Servant King,
   He calls us now to follow Him,
   To bring our lives as a daily offering
   Of worship to the Servant King.

2 There in the garden of tears,
   My heavy load He chose to bear;
   His heart with sorrow was torn,
   'Yet not my will but Yours,' He said.
   This is our God . . .

3 Come see His hands and His feet,
   The scars that speak of sacrifice,
   Hands that flung stars into space
   To cruel nails surrendered.
   This is our God . . .

4 So let us learn how to serve,
   And in our lives enthrone Him;
   Each other's needs to prefer,
   For it is Christ we're serving.
   This is our God . . .

362 Give me the faith

GIESSEN 88.88.88

from Gauntlett's
Comprehensive Tune Book (1851)

Give me____ the faith____ which can____ re - move, And
sink____ the moun - tain to____ a plain. Give me____ the
child - like, pray - ing love, Which longs____ to build____ Thy
house a - gain; Thy love,____ let it my heart____ o'er -

power, Let it____ my ran - somed soul____ de - vour.

1 Give me the faith which can remove,
  And sink the mountain to a plain.
  Give me the childlike, praying love,
  Which longs to build Thy house again;
  Thy love let it my heart o'erpower,
  Let it my ransomed soul devour.

2 I would the precious time redeem,
  And longer live for this alone—
  To spend and to be spent for them
  Who have not yet my Saviour known;
  Fully on these my mission prove,
  And only breathe to breathe Thy love.

3 My talents, gifts, and graces, Lord,
  Into Thy blessèd hands receive;
  And let me live to preach Thy word,
  And let me to Thy glory live;
  My every sacred moment spend
  In publishing the sinners' friend.

4 Enlarge, inflame, and fill my heart
  With boundless charity divine;
  So shall I all my strength exert,
  And love them with a zeal like Thine;
  And lead them to Thine open side,
  The sheep for whom their shepherd died.

Charles Wesley, 1707–88

363 Give to our God immortal praise

RIMINGTON L.M.

F. Duckworth (1862–1941)

1 Give to our God immortal praise;
Mercy and truth are all His ways:
Wonders of grace to God belong,
Repeat His mercies in your song.

2 Give to the Lord of lords renown;
The King of kings with glory crown:
His mercies ever shall endure,
When lords and kings are known no more.

3 He built the earth, He spread the sky,
And fixed the starry lights on high:
Wonders of grace to God belong,
Repeat His mercies in your song.

4 He fills the sun with morning light,
He bids the moon direct the night:
His mercies ever shall endure,
When suns and moons shall shine no more.

5 He sent His Son with power to save
From guilt and darkness and the grave:
Wonders of grace to God belong,
Repeat His mercies in your song.

Isaac Watts, 1674–1748, altd.

364 Glory be to God in Heaven

REGENT SQUARE 8 7. 8 7. 8 7

H. Smart (1813–79)

GLORIA (Based on the 'Gloria' of the Eucharistic Liturgy.)

1 Glory be to God in Heaven,
  And to all on earth, His Peace.
  Lord and Father, King in glory,
  Gifts of praise in us release
  So our worship and thanksgiving
  From our hearts will never cease.

2 Christ incarnate, sent by Father
  To redeem, renew, restore;
  Risen Lamb, in glory seated,
  Hear our prayers, Lord, we implore.
  Now to Father, Son and Spirit
  Be all glory evermore.

365 Glory to God in the highest

Words and music
Greg Leavers
arr. Phil Burt

Glo-ry to God in the high - est, Peace____ ____up-on earth. Je - sus Christ has come____ to earth, That's why we sing, Je - sus the King, Je - sus has come for you.____

Glory to God in the highest,
Peace upon earth.
Jesus Christ has come to earth,
That's why we sing,
Jesus the King,
Jesus has come for you.

1 The shepherds who were sitting there
   Were suddenly filled with fear,
   The dark night was filled with light
   Angels singing everywhere.
      Glory to God . . .

2 The next time we hear a song
   Of worship from a heavenly throng,
   Will be when Jesus comes again,
   Then with triumph we'll all sing,
      Glory to God . . .

© 1986 Greg Leavers

366 Glory to You, my God

TALLIS' CANON 8 8 8 8 (LM)

Shortened form of melody by
Thomas Tallis (1505–1585)

Glo - ry to You, my God, this night For all the bless-ings of the light;

Keep me, O keep me, King of kings, Be - neath Your own al - migh-ty wings.

1 Glory to You, my God, this night
  For all the blessings of the light;
  Keep me, O keep me, King of kings,
  Beneath Your own almighty wings.

2 Forgive me, Lord, through Your dear Son,
  The wrong that I this day have done,
  That peace with God and man may be,
  Before I sleep, restored to me.

3 Teach me to live, that I may dread
  The grave as little as my bed;
  Teach me to die, that so I may
  Rise glorious at the awesome day.

4 O may my soul on you repose
  And restful sleep my eyelids close;
  Sleep that shall me more vigorous make
  To serve my God when I awake.

5 If in the night I sleepless lie,
  My mind with peaceful thoughts supply;
  Let no dark dreams disturb my rest,
  No powers of evil me molest.

6 Praise God from whom all blessing flow
  In heaven above and earth below;
  One God, three persons, we adore,
  To Him be praise for evermore!

T. Ken, 1637–1710
© *in this version Jubilate Hymns*

367 God has spoken to His people

Israeli folk song
arr. Norman L. Warren

God has spo - ken to His peo - ple, al - le - lu - ia,
And His words are words of wis - dom, al - le - lu - ia!
O - pen your ears, O Christ-ian peo-ple, O - pen your ears and hear good news;
O - pen your hearts, O roy-al priest-hood, God has come to____ you.

Arrangement Copyright © Norman Warren

2 They who have ears to hear His message,
They who have ears, then let them hear;
They who would learn the way of wisdom,
Let them hear God's word.
God has spoken to His people, alleluia,
And His words are words of wisdom, alleluia!

3 Israel comes to greet the Saviour,
Judah is glad to see His day;
From east and west the peoples travel,
He will show the way.
God has spoken . . .

368 God holds the key

8 4. 8 8 4

George C. Stebbins (1846–1945)

Capo 1

God holds the key ___ of all un-known, And I am glad: ___

If oth-er hands should hold the key, Or if He trust-ed

it to me, I might be sad, ___ I might be sad. ___

1 God holds the key of all unknown,
And I am glad:
If other hands should hold the key,
Or if He trusted it to me,
I might be sad, I might be sad.

2 What if tomorrow's cares were here
Without its rest?
I'd rather He unlocked the day,
And, as the hours swing open, say,
'My will is best, My will is best."

3 The very dimness of my sight
Makes me secure;
For, groping in my misty way,
I feel His hand; I hear Him say,
'My help is sure, My help is sure.'

4 I cannot read His future plans;
But this I know:
I have the smiling of His face,
And all the refuge of His grace,
While here below, while here below.

5 Enough: this covers all my wants;
And so I rest!
For what I cannot, He can see,
And in His care I saved shall be,
For ever blest, for ever blest.

Joseph Parker, 1830–1902

369 God is building a house

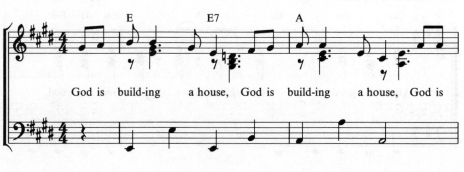

Anon
arr. Phil Burt

God is build-ing a house, God is build-ing a house, God is build-ing a house that will stand. He is build-ing by His plan With the

liv-ing stones of man, God is build-ing a house that will stand.

Arrangement Copyright © 1987 Phil Burt

1 God is building a house,
God is building a house,
God is building a house that will stand.
He is building by His plan
With the living stones of man,
God is building a house that will stand.

2 God is building a house,
God is building a house,
God is building a house that will stand.
With apostles, prophets, pastors,
With evangelists and teachers,
God is building a house that will stand.

3 Christ is head of this house,
Christ is head of this house,
Christ is head of this house that will stand.
He abideth in its praise,
Will perfect it in its ways,
Christ is head of this house that will stand.

4 We are part of this house,
We are part of this house,
We are part of this house that will stand.
We are called from every nation
To enjoy his full salvation,
We are part of this house that will stand.

370 God is Good

Graham Kendrick

Fast and rhythmic

God is good, we sing and shout it, God is good,
we ce-le-brate. God is good, no more we doubt it,
God is good, we know it's true.
And when I think of His love for me, My heart fills with praise and I

God is good, we sing and shout it,
God is good, we celebrate.
God is good, no more we doubt it,
God is good, we know it's true.

And when I think of His love for me,
My heart fills with praise and I feel like dancing.
For in His heart there is room for me
And I run with arms open'd wide.

God is good, we sing and shout it,
God is good, we celebrate.
God is good, no more we doubt it,
God is good, we know it's true. *Hey!*

371 God is love

ABBOT'S LEIGH 87.87.D

Cyril V. Taylor (b. 1907)

God is love: let heaven a-dore Him;
God is love: let earth re-joice; Let cre-
a-tion sing be-fore Him, And ex-alt Him
with one voice. He who laid the earth's foun-

1 God is love: let heaven adore Him;
   God is love: let earth rejoice;
   Let creation sing before Him,
   And exalt Him with one voice.
   He who laid the earth's foundation,
   He who spread the heavens above,
   He who breathes through all creation,
   He is love, eternal love.

2 God is love: and He enfoldeth
   All the world in one embrace;
   With unfailing grasp He holdeth
   Every child of every race.
   And when human hearts are breaking
   Under sorrow's iron rod,
   All the sorrow, all the aching,
   Wrings with pain the heart of God.

3 God is love: and though with blindness
   Sin afflicts the souls of men,
   God's eternal loving-kindness
   Holds and guides them even then.
   Sin and death and hell shall never
   O'er us final triumph gain;
   God is love, so love for ever
   O'er the universe must reign.

Timothy Rees, 1874–1939, altd.
© *A.R. Mowbray & Co. Ltd. Oxford*

God is our strength and refuge

DAMBUSTERS MARCH 7 7 7 5 7 7 11

E. Coates (1886–1958)
arranged John Barnard (b. 1948)

God is our strength and refuge, Our present help in trouble; And we therefore will not fear, Though the earth should change! Though mountains shake and tremble, Though swirling floods are raging, God the Lord of hosts is with us evermore!

God is our strength and refuge

God is our strength and refuge, Our present help in trouble; And we therefore will not fear, Though the earth should change! Though mountains shake and tremble, Though swirling floods are raging, God the Lord of hosts is with us evermore!

2 There is a flowing river,
   Within God's holy city;
   God is in the midst of her –
   She shall not be moved!
   God's help is swiftly given,
   Thrones vanish at His presence –
   God the Lord of hosts is with us evermore!

3 Come, see the works of our maker,
   Learn of His deeds all-powerful;
   Wars will cease across the world
   When He shatters the spear!
   Be still and know your creator,
   Uplift Him in the nations –
   God the Lord of hosts is with us evermore!

© *Richard Bewes, b. 1934*

373 God is working His purpose out

BENSON Irregular

M.D. Kingham (1866–1927)

God is work-ing His pur-pose out, As year suc-ceeds to year: God is work-ing His pur-pose out, And the time is draw-ing near: Near-er and near-er draws the time, The time that shall sure-ly be, When the

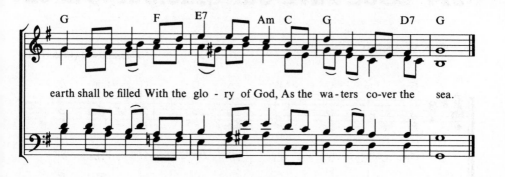

earth shall be filled With the glo - ry of God, As the wa - ters co-ver the sea.

1 God is working His purpose out,
   As year succeeds to year:
   God is working His purpose out,
   And the time is drawing near:
   Nearer and nearer draws the time,
   The time that shall surely be,
   When the earth shall be filled
   With the glory of God,
   As the waters cover the sea.

2 From the utmost east to utmost west
   Wherever man has trod,
   By the mouth of many messengers
   Rings out the voice of God:
   Listen to me you continents,
   You islands look to me,
   That the earth may be filled
   With the glory of God,
   As the waters cover the sea.

3 We shall march in the strength of God,
   With the banner of Christ unfurled,
   The the light of the glorious gospel of truth
   May shine throughout the world;
   We shall fight with sorrow and sin
   To set their captives free,
   That the earth may be filled
   With the glory of God,
   As the waters cover the sea.

4 All we can do is nothing worth
   Unless God blesses the deed;
   Vainly we hope for the harvest tide
   Till God gives life to the seed:
   Nearer and nearer draws the time,
   The time that shall surely be,
   When the earth shall be filled
   With the glory of God,
   As the waters cover the sea.

A. Ainger, 1841–1919
© *in this version Jubilate Hymns*

374 God save our gracious Queen

NATIONAL ANTHEM 6 6 4. 6 6 6. 4

Thesaurus Musicus (1745)

1 God save our gracious Queen,
   Long live our noble Queen,
   God save the Queen!
   Send her victorious,
   Happy and glorious,
   Long to reign over us;
   God save the Queen!

2 Thy choicest gifts in store
   On her be pleased to pour,
   Long may she reign;
   May she defend our laws,
   And ever give us cause
   To sing with heart and voice
   God save the Queen!

375 God moves in a mysterious way

LONDON NEW C.M.

Playford's Psalms (1671)
Adapted from NEWTOUN in *Scottish Psalter* (1635)

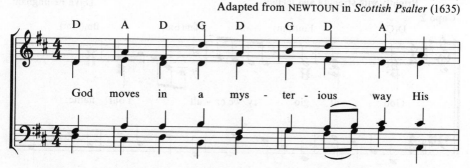

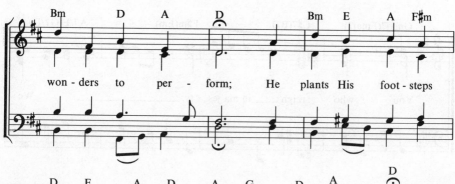

1 God moves in a mysterious way
His wonders to perform;
He plants His footsteps in the sea,
And rides upon the storm.

2 Deep in unfathomable mines
Of never-failing skill,
He treasures up His bright designs,
And works His sov'reign will.

3 Ye fearful saints, fresh courage take,
The clouds ye so much dread
Are big with mercy, and shall break
In blessings on your head.

4 Judge not the Lord by feeble sense,
But trust Him for His grace;
Behind a frowning providence
He hides a smiling face.

5 His purposes will ripen fast,
Unfolding every hour;
The bud may have a bitter taste,
But sweet will be the flower.

6 Blind unbelief is sure to err,
And scan His work in vain;
God is His own interpreter,
And He will make it plain.

William Cowper, 1731–1800

376 God of glory

Brightly with strength and feeling

Dave Fellingham

Capo 2

God of glo - ry, we ex - alt Your name,
You who reign in ma-jes - ty. We
lift our hearts to You And we will wor - ship, praise And
mag-ni-fy Your ho - ly name. In power res -

377 Gracious Spirit

CHARITY 7 7 7. 5

John Stainer (1840–1901)

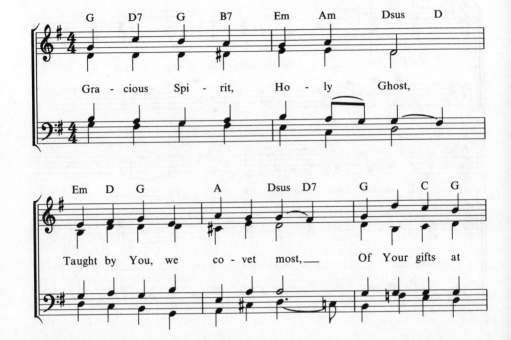

1 Gracious Spirit, Holy Ghost,
Taught by You, we covet most,
Of Your gifts at Pentecost,
Holy heavenly love.

2 Faith that mountains could remove,
Tongues of earth or heaven above,
Knowledge, all things, empty prove
Without heavenly love.

3 Though I as a martyr bleed,
Give my goods the poor to feed,
All is vain if love I need;
Therefore give me love.

4 Love is kind, and suffers long,
Love is meek, and thinks no wrong,
Love than death itself more strong:
Therefore give us love.

5 Prophecy will fade away
Melting in the light of day;
Love will ever with us stay:
Therefore give us love.

6 Faith, and hope, and love we see
Joining hand in hand, agree;
But the greatest of the three,
And the best, is love.

Christopher Wordsworth, 1807–85

162

378(i) God of grace and God of glory

WESTMINSTER ABBEY   87.87.87

The Psalmist (1842)
adapted from Henry Purcell (1659–95)

Capo 3

God of grace and God of glo-ry, On Thy peo-ple pour Thy power; Crown Thine an-cient Chur-ch's sto-ry; Bring her bud___to glor-ious flower. Grant us wis-dom, Grant us cour-age, For the fac-ing of this hour.

following verses overleaf

378(ii) God of grace and God of glory

RHUDDLAN 87.87.87.

Welsh traditional melody

God of grace and God of glo-ry, On Thy peo-ple pour Thy power; Crown Thine an-cient Chur-ch's sto-ry; Bring her bud to glor-ious flower. Grant us wis-dom, Grant us cour-age, For the fac-ing of this hour.

1 God of grace and God of glory,
  On Thy people pour Thy power;
  Crown Thine ancient Church's story;
  Bring her bud to glorious flower.
  Grant us wisdom,
  Grant us courage,
  For the facing of this hour.

2 Lo! the hosts of evil round us
  Scorn Thy Christ, assail His ways!
  Fears and doubts too long have bound us;
  Free our hearts to work and praise.
  Grant us wisdom,
  Grant us courage,
  For the living of these days.

3 Heal Thy children's warring madness;
  Bend our pride to Thy control;
  Shame our wanton, selfish gladness,
  Rich in things and poor in soul.
  Grant us wisdom,
  Grant us courage,
  Lest we miss Thy kingdom's goal.

4 Set our feet on lofty places;
  Gird our lives that they may be
  Armoured with all Christlike graces
  In the fight to set men free.
  Grant us wisdom,
  Grant us courage,
  That we fail not man nor Thee.

5 Save us from weak resignation
  To the evils we deplore;
  Let the search for Thy salvation
  Be our glory evermore.
  Grant us wisdom,
  Grant us courage,
  Serving Thee whom we adore.

© H.E. Fosdick, 1878–1969

379 Good Christian men, rejoice

IN DULCI JUBILO Irregular

German Carol Melody (14th century)

Good Christ - ian men, re - joice____ With heart and soul and voice!____ Give ye heed to what we say: News! News! Je - sus Christ is born to - day. Ox and ass be - fore Him bow, And

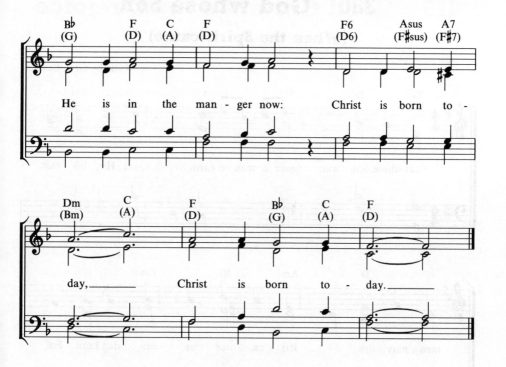

He is in the man-ger now: Christ is born to-day,_____ Christ is born to - day._____

1 Good Christian men, rejoice
  With heart and soul and voice!
  Give ye heed to what we say:
  News! News! Jesus Christ is born today.
  Ox and ass before Him bow,
  And He is in the manger now:
  Christ is born today,
  Christ is born today.

2 Good Christian men, rejoice
  With heart and soul and voice!
  Now ye hear of endless bliss:
  Joy! Joy! Jesus Christ was born for this.
  He hath oped the heav'nly door,
  And man is blest for evermore.
  Christ was born for this,
  Christ was born for this.

3 Good Christian men, rejoice
  With heart and soul and voice!
  Now ye need not fear the grave:
  Peace! Peace! Jesus Christ was born to save;
  Calls you one, and calls you all,
  To gain His everlasting hall.
  Christ was born to save,
  Christ was born to save.

John Mason Neale, 1818–66

380 God whose Son

(When the Spirit came)

Music by Greg Leavers

God whose Son was once a man on earth Gave His life that men may live. Ris - en, our as - cen - ded Lord Ful - filled His pro - mised word. When the Spi - rit came, the church was born, God's peo - ple shared in a bright new dawn. They

following verses overleaf

1 God whose Son was once a man on earth
Gave His life that men may live.
Risen, our ascended Lord
Fulfilled His promised word.

When the Spirit came, the church was born,
God's people shared in a bright new dawn.
They healed the sick,
They taught God's word,
They sought the lost,
They obeyed the Lord.
And it's all because the Spirit came
That the world will never be the same,
Because the Spirit came.

2 God whose power fell on the early church,
Sent to earth from heav'n above.
Spirit led, by Him ordained
They showed the world God's love.

When the Spirit came, the church was born,
God's people shared in a bright new dawn.
They healed the sick,
They taught God's word,
They sought the lost,
They obeyed the Lord.
And it's all because the Spirit came
That the world will never be the same,
Because the Spirit came.

3 Pour Your Spirit on the church today,
That Your life through me may flow.
Spirit filled, I'll serve Your Name
And live the truth I know.

When the Spirit comes, new life is born,
God's people share in a bright new dawn.
We'll heal the sick,
We'll teach God's word,
We'll seek the lost,
We'll obey the Lord.
And it's all because the Spirit came
That the world will never be the same,
Because the Spirit came.

© *1986 Peter Horrobin*

381 Hark, my Soul

ST. BEES 7 7. 7 7

John Bacchus Dykes (1823–76)

1 Hark, my soul! it is the Lord;
'Tis thy Saviour, hear His word;
Jesus speaks, and speaks to thee,
'Say, poor sinner, lov'st thou Me?'

2 'I delivered thee when bound,
And, when bleeding, healed thy wound;
Sought thee wand'ring, set thee right,
Turned thy darkness into light.'

3 'Mine is an unchanging love,
Higher than the heights above,
Deeper than the depths beneath,
Free and faithful, strong as death.'

4 'Thou shalt see My glory soon,
When the work of grace is done;
Partner of My throne shalt be;
Say, poor sinner, lov'st thou Me?'

5 Lord! it is my chief complaint
That my love is weak and faint;
Yet I love Thee, and adore:
O for grace to love Thee more!

William Cowper, 1731–1800

382 Hail the day

LLANFAIR 7 7 7 7 and Alleluias

R. Williams (1781–1821)

Hail the day that sees Him rise Al - le - lu - ia,

To His throne be - yond the skies, Al - le - lu - ia,

Christ, the Lamb for sin - ners given, Al - le - lu - ia,

En - ters now the high - est heaven: Al - le - lu - ia.

1 Hail the day that sees Him rise, *Alleluia,*
To His throne beyond the skies, *Alleluia,*
Christ, the Lamb for sinners given, *Alleluia,*
Enters now the highest heaven: *Alleluia.*

2 There for Him high triumph waits: *Alleluia,*
Lift your heads, eternal gates, *Alleluia,*
He has conquered death and sin, *Alleluia,*
Take the King of glory in: *Alleluia.*

3 See! the heaven its Lord receives, *Alleluia,*
Yet He loves the earth He leaves; *Alleluia,*
Though returning to His throne, *Alleluia,*
Still He calls mankind His own. *Alleluia.*

4 Still for us He intercedes, *Alleluia,*
His prevailing death He pleads, *Alleluia,*
Near Himself prepares our place, *Alleluia,*
He the first-fruits of our race. *Alleluia.*

5 Lord, though parted from our sight *Alleluia,*
Far beyond the starry height, *Alleluia,*
Lift our hearts that we may rise *Alleluia,*
One with You beyond the skies: *Alleluia.*

6 There with You we shall remain, *Alleluia,*
Share the glory of Your reign, *Alleluia,*
There Your face unclouded view, *Alleluia,*
Find our heaven of heavens in You: *Alleluia.*

C. Wesley, 1707–88
and T. Cotterill, 1779–1823

383 Hail, Thou once despised Jesus

LUX EOI 8 7 8 7 D

Arthur S. Sullivan (1842–1900)

Hail, thou once des - pi - sèd Je - sus, Hail, Thou Ga - li - le - an King!

Thou didst suf - fer to re - lease us, Thou didst free sal - va - tion bring.

Hail, Thou a - go - nis - ing Sav-iour, Bear-er of our sin and shame,

By Thy mer - its we find fa-vour; Life is giv - en through Thy Name.

1 Hail, thou once despisèd Jesus,
  Hail, Thou Galilean King!
  Thou didst suffer to release us,
  Thou didst free salvation bring.
  Hail, Thou agonising Saviour,
  Bearer of our sin and shame,
  By Thy merits we find favour;
  Life is given through Thy Name.

2 Paschal Lamb, by God appointed,
  All our sins on Thee were laid.
  By Almighty love anointed,
  Thou hast full atonement made.
  All Thy people are forgiven
  Through the virtue of Thy blood:
  Opened is the gate of heaven,
  Peace is made 'twixt man and God.

3 Jesus, hail! enthroned in glory,
  There for ever to abide;
  All the heavenly hosts adore Thee,
  Seated at Thy Father's side:
  There for sinners Thou art pleading,
  There Thou dost our place prepare,
  Ever for us interceding,
  Till in glory we appear.

4 Worship, honour, power, and blessing,
  Thou art worthy to receive:
  Loudest praises, without ceasing,
  Meet it is for us to give:
  Help, ye bright angelic spirits,
  Bring your sweetest, noblest lays;
  Help to sing our Saviour's merits,
  Help to chant Immanuel's praise.

John Bakewell, 1721–1819

384 Hark! the herald angels sing

Adapted by William Hayman Cummings (1831–1915)
from a chorus of Felix Mendelssohn-Bartholdy (1809–47)

Hark! The her-ald an-gels sing,— 'Glo-ry to the new-born King!

Peace on earth, and mer-cy mild,— God and sin-ners re-con-ciled.'

Joy-ful, all you na-tions, rise,— Join the tri-umph of the skies;—

With th'an-gel-ic host pro-claim: 'Christ is—born in Beth-le-hem!'

Hark! The her-ald an-gels sing, 'Glo-ry___ to the new-born King!'

1 Hark! The herald angels sing,
   'Glory to the new-born King!
   Peace on earth, and mercy mild,
   God and sinners reconciled.'
   Joyful, all you nations, rise,
   Join the triumph of the skies;
   With the angelic host proclaim:
   'Christ is born in Bethlehem!'
      Hark! The herald-angels sing,
      'Glory to the new-born King!'

2 Christ by highest heaven adored,
   Christ, the everlasting Lord,
   Late in time behold Him come,
   Offspring of a virgin's womb!
   Veiled in flesh the Godhead see!
   Hail, the incarnate Deity!
   Pleased as man with man to dwell,
   Jesus, our Immanuel.
      Hark! The herald-angels sing,
      'Glory to the new-born King!'

3 Hail, the heaven-born Prince of Peace!
   Hail, the Sun of Righteousness!
   Light and life to all He brings,
   Risen with healing in His wings.
   Mild He lays His glory by,
   Born that man no more may die;
   Born to raise the sons of earth,
   Born to give them second birth.
      Hark! The herald-angels sing,
      'Glory to the new-born King!'

Charles Wesley, 1707–88
George Whitfield, 1714–70
Martin Madan, 1726–90 and others

385 Hark, the glad sound

ST. SAVIOUR

Frederick George Baker (1840–1908)

Hark, the glad sound! The Sav - iour comes, The Sav - iour prom - ised long; Let ev - ery heart pre - pare a throne, And ev - ery voice a song.

1 Hark, the glad sound! The Saviour comes,
   The Saviour promised long;
   Let every heart prepare a throne,
   And every voice a song.

2 He comes, the prisoners to release
   In Satan's bondage held;
   The chains of sin before Him break,
   The iron fetters yield.

3 He comes to free the captive mind
   Where evil thoughts control;
   And for the darkness of the blind
   Gives light that makes them whole.

4 He comes the broken heart to bind,
   The wounded soul to cure;
   And with the treasures of His grace
   To enrich the humble poor.

5 Our glad hosannas, Prince of Peace,
   Your welcome shall proclaim;
   And heaven's eternal arches ring
   With Your belovéd name.

Philip Dodderidge, 1702–1751
Altered © 1986 Horrobin/Leavers

386 Have Thine own way, Lord

THINE OWN WAY, LORD! 5 4. 5 4. D

George C. Stebbins (1846–1945)

1 Have Thine own way, Lord,
   have Thine own way;
 Thou art the potter, I am the clay.
 Mould me and make me after thy will,
 While I am waiting yielded and still.

2 Have Thine own way, Lord,
   have Thine own way;
 Search me and try me, Master, today.
 Whiter than snow, Lord, wash me just now,
 As in Thy presence humbly I bow.

3 Have Thine own way, Lord,
   have Thine own way;
 Wounded and weary, help me, I pray.
 Power, all power, surely is Thine;
 Touch me and heal me, Saviour Divine.

4 Have Thine own way, Lord,
   have Thine own way;
 Hold o'er my being absolute sway.
 Fill with Thy Spirit till all shall see
 Christ only, always, living in me.

A.A. Pollard, 1862–1934

387 He gave His life

SELFLESS LOVE 8 6 8 6 D (DCM)

Andrew Maries (b. 1949)

He gave His life in self-less love For sin-ful man He came;

He had no stain of sin Him-self But bore our guilt and shame:

He took the cup of pain and death, His blood was free - ly shed;

We see His Bo - dy on the cross, We share the li - ving bread.

1 He gave His life in selfless love
  For sinful man He came;
  He had no stain of sin Himself
  But bore our guilt and shame:
  He took the cup of pain and death,
  His blood was freely shed;
  We see His Body on the cross,
  We share the living bread.

2 He did not come to call the good
  But sinners to repent;
  it was the lame, the deaf, the blind
  For whom His life was spent:
  To heal the sick, to find the lost –
  It was for such He came,
  And round His table all may come
  To praise His holy name.

3 They heard Him call His Father's name –
  Then 'Finished!' was His cry;
  Like them we have forsaken Him
  And left Him there to die:
  The sins that crucified Him then
  Are sins His blood was cured;
  The love that bound Him to a cross
  Our freedom has ensured.

4 His body broken once for us
  Is glorious now above;
  The cup of blessing we receive,
  A sharing of His love:
  As in His presence we partake,
  His dying we proclaim
  Until the hour of majesty
  When Jesus comes again.

388 He that is in us

Graham Kendrick
arr. Phil Burt

He that is in us is great-er than he that is in the world. He that is in us is great-er than he that is in the world. There-fore I will sing and I will re-joice For His Spi - rit

lives in me. _____ Christ the liv-ing One has o - ver -
come And we share in His vic - to - ry. _____ _____

He that is in us is greater
    than he that is in the world.
He that is in us is greater
    than he that is in the world.

1 Therefore I will sing and I will rejoice
   For His Spirit lives in me.
   Christ the living One has overcome
   And we share in His victory.
       He that is in us . . .

2 All the powers of death and hell and sin
   Lie crushed beneath His feet.
   Jesus owns the Name above all names
   Crowned with honour and majesty.
       He that is in us . . .

Repeat verse 2 slowly and majestically.

389 He who would valiant be

MONKS GATE 11 11. 12 11.

English traditional melody
adpt. Ralph Vaughan Williams (1872–1958)

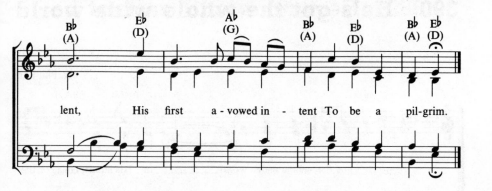

lent, His first a-vowed in - tent To be a pil-grim.

1 He who would valiant be
   'Gainst all disaster,
   Let him in constancy
   Follow the Master.
   There's no discouragement
   Shall make him once relent,
   His first avowed intent
   To be a pilgrim.

2 Who so beset him round
   With dismal stories,
   Do but themselves confound—
   His strength the more is.
   No foes shall stay his might,
   Though he with giants fight:
   He will make good his right
   To be a pilgrim.

3 Since, Lord, You do defend
   Us with Your Spirit,
   We know we at the end
   Shall life inherit.
   Then fancies flee away!
   I'll fear not what men say,
   I'll labour night and day
   To be a pilgrim.

P. Dearmer, 1867–1936
after J. Bunyan, 1628–1688

390 He's got the whole wide world

arr. Phil Burt

He's got the whole wide world_____ in His hands, He's got the

whole wide world_____ in His hands, He's got the

whole wide world_____ in His hands, He's got the

whole world in His hands. He's got the hands.

186

1 He's got the whole wide world in His hands,
He's got the whole wide world in His hands,
He's got the whole wide world in His hands,
He's got the whole world in His hands.

2 He's got ev'rybody here, in His hands,
He's got ev'rybody here, in His hands,
He's got ev'rybody here, in His hands,
He's got the whole world in His hands.

3 He's got the tiny little baby, in His hands,
He's got the tiny little baby, in His hands,
He's got the tiny little baby, in His hands,
He's got the whole world in His hands.

4 He's got you and me brother, in His hands,
He's got you and me brother, in His hands,
He's got you and me brother, in His hands,
He's got the whole world in His hands.

391 Healing God, Almighty Father

HYFRYDOL 8.7.8.7.D

R.H. Prichard (1811–87)

Heal - ing God,___ Al - migh - ty Fa - ther,
Ac - tive through - out his - to - ry; Ev - er
sav - ing, guid - ing, work - ing For Your
child - ren to___ be free. Shep - herd, King,___ in -

spir - ing pro - phets To fore - see___ Your
suf - f'ring role – Lord,___ we raise___ our prayers and
voi - ces Make us one___ and make us whole.

(Alternative tune, ABBOTTS LEIGH, No. 371)

1 Healing God, Almighty Father,
   Active throughout history;
   Ever saving, guiding, working
   For Your children to be free.
   Shepherd, King, inspiring prophets
   To foresee Your suffering role –
   Lord, we raise our prayers and voices
   Make us one and make us whole.

2 Healing Christ, God's Word incarnate,
   Reconciling man to man.
   God's atonement, dying for us
   In His great redemptive plan.
   'Jesus', Saviour, Healer, Victor
   Drawing out for us death's sting,
   Lord, we bow our hearts in worship,
   And united praises bring.

3 Healing Spirit, Christ-annointing
   Raising to new Life in Him;
   Help the poor; release to captives;
   Cure of body; health within.
   Life-renewing and empowering
   Christ-like service to the lost.
   Lord, we pray 'Renew Your wonders
   As of a New Pentecost!'

4 Healing Church, called-out and chosen
   To enlarge God's Kingdom here.
   Lord-obeying; Spirit-strengthened
   To bring God's salvation near.
   For creation's reconciling
   Gifts of love in us release.
   Father, Son and Holy Spirit
   'Make us instruments of peace.'

189

392 Hear my cry O God

Andy Silver

Slow

Hear my cry, O God, Lis-ten to my
prayer; From the ends of the earth Will I call to you.
Hear my cry, O God, When my heart is ov - er-
whelmed; Lead me to the rock That is high-er than I.

Teach me to trust in You,_____ To pour out my heart to You;

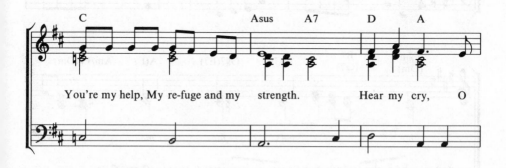

You're my help, My re-fuge and my strength. Hear my cry, O

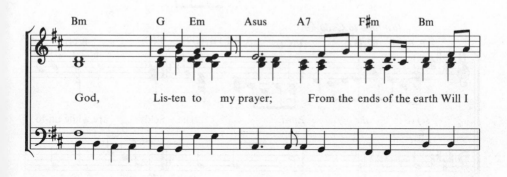

God, Lis-ten to my prayer; From the ends of the earth Will I

call to you.___ Hear my cry, O God.

393 Here I am

Chris A. Bowater

Here I am, wholly available.
As for me, I will serve the Lord.

1 The fields are white unto harvest
  But O, the lab'rers are so few,
  So Lord I give myself to help the reaping,
  To gather precious souls unto You.
      Here I am . . .

2 The time is right in the nation
  For works of power and authority;
  God's looking for a people who are willing
  To be counted in His glorious victory.
      Here I am . . .

3 As salt are we ready to savour,
  In darkness are we ready to be light,
  God's seeking out a very special people
  To manifest His truth and His might.
      Here I am . . .

394 Here, O my Lord

TOULON (Old 124th) 10 10. 10 10

Louis Bourgeois (1510–61)

Here, O my Lord, I see Thee face to face;

Here would I touch and han-dle things un-seen,

Here grasp with firm-er hand th'e-ter-nal grace,

And all my wea-ri-ness up-on Thee lean.

1 Here, O my Lord, I see Thee face to face;
   Here would I touch and handle things unseen,
   Here grasp with firmer hand th'eternal grace,
   And all my weariness upon Thee lean.

2 Here would I feed upon the bread of God,
   Here drink with Thee the royal wine of heav'n;
   Here would I lay aside each earthly load,
   Here taste afresh the calms of sin forgiv'n.

3 Too soon we rise, the symbols disappear;
   The feast, though not the love, as past and gone;
   The bread and wine remove, but Thou art here,
   Nearer than ever, still my Shield and Sun.

4 I have no help but Thine; nor do I need
   Another arm save Thine to lean upon;
   It is enough, my Lord, enough indeed;
   My strength is in Thy might, Thy might alone.

5 Mine is the sin, but Thine the righteousness;
   Mine is the guilt, but Thine the cleansing blood;
   Here is my robe, my refuge, and my peace—
   Thy blood, Thy righteousness, O Lord my God.

6 Feast after feast thus comes and passes by,
   Yet, passing, points to the glad feast above,
   Giving sweet foretaste of the festal joy,
   The Lamb's great bridal feast of bliss and love.

Horatius Bonar, 1808–89

395 He gave me beauty

(Beauty for ashes)

Robert Whitney Manzano

He gave me beau-ty for ash-es, __ The oil of joy for mourn-ing, __ The gar-ment of praise For the spi-rit of heav-i-ness. That we might be trees of right-eous-ness, The plant-ing of the Lord, That He might be glo-ri-fied. __

396 Hévénu shalom

(Peace unto you)

Traditional melody

Brightly

Hé-vé-nu sha - lom a - lé-chem, Hé-vé-nu sha - lom a -

lé-chem, Hé-vé-nu sha - lom a - lé-chem, Hé-vé-nu

Repeat for verses   *last time*

sha - lom sha - lom sha-lom a - lé-chem. Hé - vé - nu sha-lom a - lé-chem.

Arrangement Copyright © A & C. Black (Publishers) Ltd. From *Alleluya.*
Used by permission

> *Hévénu shalom aléchem,*
> *Hévénu shalom aléchem,*
> *Hévénu shalom aléchem,*
> *Hévénu shalom, shalom, shalom aléchem.*

1 Because He died and is risen,
  Because He died and is risen,
  Because He died and is risen,
  We now have peace with God
      through Jesus Christ our Lord.
    Hévénu shalom . . .

2 His peace destroys walls between us,
  His peace destroys walls between us,
  His peace destroys walls between us,
  For only He can reconcile
      us both to God.
    Hévénu shalom . . .

3 My peace I give you, said Jesus,
  My peace I give you, said Jesus,
  My peace I give you, said Jesus,
  Don't let your heart be troubled,
      do not be afraid.
    Hévénu shalom . . .

4 The peace beyond understanding,
  The peace beyond understanding,
  The peace beyond understanding,
  Will guard the hearts and minds
      of those who pray to Him.
    Hévénu shalom . . .

Chorus Traditional Israeli song
Verses © Michael Baughen

197

397 Hold me Lord

398 How I love You

(You are the One)

Keith Green

Brightly

How I love You, You are the One, You are the One, —

4th time **to Coda** ⊕

How I love You, You are the One for me.

1 I was so lost   But You showed the way,   'Cause You are the Way.
2 I was lied to   But You told the truth,   'Cause You are the Truth.
3 I was dy-ing   But You gave me life,   'Cause You are the Life.

I was so lost   But You showed the way to   me!
I was lied to   But You showed the truth to   me!
I was dy-ing   And You gave Your life for   me!

CODA

You are the One, God's ri-sen Son, You are the One, for____ me.

4 Hal - le - lu - jah! You are the One, You are the One.__
How I love You, You are the One, You are the One.__

Hal - le - lu - jah! You are the One for me!
How I love You, You are the One for me.

How I love You,
You are the One,
You are the One,
How I love You,
You are the One for me.

1 I was so lost
But You showed the way,
'Cause You are the Way.
I was so lost
But You showed the way to me!
How I love You . . .

2 I was lied to
But You told the truth,
'Cause You are the Truth.
I was lied to
But You showed the truth to me!
How I love You . . .

3 I was dying
But You gave me life,
'Cause You are the Life.
I was dying
And You gave Your life for me!
How I love You,
You are the One,
You are the One,
How I love You,
You are the One,
God's risen Son.
You are the One for me!

4 Hallelujah!
You are the One,
You are the One.
Hallelujah!
You are the One for me!
How I love You . . .

201

399 How lovely is Thy dwelling place

Traditional Scottish folk melody
arr. Jonathan Asprey

With gentle lyricism

Capo 3

1. and 4. How— love - ly is———— thy———— dwell-ing place,—
2. Ev - en the spar - row——— finds a home—
3. And I'd ra - ther be——— a——— door-keep - er—

—O———Lord of hosts,— to— me.———— My—
— Where——— he can set-tle— down.——— And the
— And——— on - ly stay— a— day,——— Than—

soul is long-ing and faint - ing The courts of the
swal - low, she can build a nest Where she may
live the life of a sin - ner And have to

Lord to see. My heart and flesh, they are
lay her young With - in the courts of the
stay a - way. For the Lord is shi - ning

sing - ing For joy to the liv - ing God.
Lord of hosts, My King, my Lord, and my God.
as the sun, And the Lord, He's like a shield;

How love - ly is____ Thy____dwell-ing place,____ O_
And hap-py are those who are____dwell-ing where____ The_
And no good thing____does____ He with-hold____ From_

____Lord of hosts,____ to___ me.____
____song of praise____ is___ sung.____
____those who walk____ His_ way.____

final ending

1 How lovely is thy dwelling place,
   O Lord of hosts, to me.
   My soul is longing and fainting
   The courts of the Lord to see.
   My heart and flesh, they are singing
   For joy to the living God.
   How lovely is Thy dwelling place,
   O Lord of hosts, to me.

2 Even the sparrow finds a home
   Where he can settle down.
   And the swallow, she can build a nest
   Where she may lay her young
   Within the courts of the Lord of hosts,
   My King, my Lord, and my God.
   And happy are those who are dwelling where
   The song of praise is sung.

3 And I'd rather be a door-keeper
   And only stay a day,
   Than live the life of a sinner
   And have to stay away.
   For the Lord is shining as the sun,
   And the Lord, He's like a shield;
   And no good thing does He withhold
   From those who walk His way.

4 How lovely is thy dwelling place,
   O Lord of hosts, to me.
   My soul is longing and fainting
   The courts of the Lord to see.
   My heart and flesh, they are singing
   For joy to the living God.
   How lovely is thy dwelling place,
   O Lord of hosts, to me.

400 How precious, O Lord

401 How great is our God

Author unknown
arr. Phil Burt

With life

How great is our God,_____ How great is His name,_____

_____How great is His love_____ For-ev-er the same._____

_____He rolled back the wa - ters_____ Of the migh-ty Red Sea,_____

_____And He said, I'll ne-ver leave you,_____Put your trust in me._____

How great is our God,   He rolled back the waters
How great is His name,   Of the mighty Red Sea,
How great is His love   And He said, I'll never leave you,
Forever the same.   Put your trust in me.

402 How shall they hear

OMBERSLEY L.M.

W.H. Gladstone (1840–91)

1 'How shall they hear,' who have not heard
News of a Lord who loved and came;
Nor known His reconciling word,
Nor learned to trust the Saviour's name?

2 'To all the world,' to every place,
Neighbours and friends and far-off lands,
Preach the good news of saving grace;
Go while the great commission stands.

3 'Whom shall I send?' Who hears the call,
Constant in prayer, through toil and pain,
Telling of one who died for all,
To bring a lost world home again?

4 'Lord, here am I:' Your fire impart
To this poor cold self-centred soul;
Touch but my lips, my hands, my heart,
And make a world for Christ my goal.

5 Spirit of love, within us move:
Spirit of truth, in power come down!
So shall they hear and find and prove
Christ is their life, their joy, their crown.

403 Hushed was the evening hymn

SAMUEL 66.66.88

Arthur S. Sullivan (1842–1900)

Hushed was the eve - ning hymn, The tem - ple courts were dark;___ The lamp was burn - ing dim Be - fore the sa - cred ark, When sud - den - ly a voice di - vine Rang through the sil - ence of the shrine.

1 Hushed was the evening hymn,
   The temple courts were dark;
   The lamp was burning dim
   Before the sacred ark,
   When suddenly a voice divine
   Rang through the silence of the shrine.

2 The old man, meek and mild,
   The priest of Israel, slept;
   His watch the temple child,
   The little Samuel, kept:
   And what from Eli's sense was sealed
   The Lord to Hannah's son revealed.

3 O give me Samuel's ear,
   The open ear, O Lord,
   Alive and quick to hear
   Each whisper of Your word—
   Like him to answer at Your call,
   And to obey You first of all.

4 O give me Samuel's heart,
   A lowly heart, that waits
   To serve and play the part
   You show us at Your gates
   By day and night, a heart that still
   Moves at the breathing of Your will.

5 O give me Samuel's mind,
   A sweet, unmurmuring faith,
   Obedient and resigned
   To You in life and death,
   That I may read with childlike eyes
   Truths that are hidden from the wise.

J.D. Burns, 1823–64
Altered © 1986 Horrobin/Leavers

404   I am a new creation

Dave Bilbrough

With drive

Capo 3

I am a new cre-a - tion, No more in con-dem - na - tion, Here in the grace of God I stand.

My heart is ov - er-flow-ing, My love just keeps on grow-ing, Here in the grace of God I stand. And I will praise

405   I am not mine own

Words and music
Chris A. Bowater

Very simply

Capo 3

I am not mine own, I've been bought with a price.

Pre - cious blood of Christ, I am not mine own.

1 I am not mine own,
   I've been bought with a price.
   Precious blood of Christ,
   I am not mine own.

2 I belong to You,
   I've been bought with a price.
   Precious blood of Christ,
   I belong to You.

3 How could I ever say
   'I will choose another way',
   Knowing the price that's paid;
   Precious blood of Christ.

406 I am not skilled

EWHURST 8 8 8. 7

Cecil John Allen (1886–1973)

1 I am not skilled to understand
   What God has willed, what God has planned;
   I only know at His right hand
   Stands One Who is my Saviour!

2 I take Him at His word indeed:
   'Christ died for sinners,' this I read;
   And in my heart I find a need
   Of Him to be my Saviour!

3 That He should leave His place on high,
   And come for sinful man to die,
   You count it strange? so once did I,
   Before I knew my Saviour!

4 And O that He fulfilled may see
   The glory of His life in me.
   And with His work contented be,
   As I with my dear Saviour!

5 Yea, living, dying, let me bring
   My life, to Him an offering
   That He Who lives to be my King
   Once died to be my Saviour.

Dora Greenwell, 1821–82 altd.
altered © 1987 Horrobin/Leavers

215

407 I confess

Words and music by
Chris A. Bowater

I con-fess that Je-sus Christ is Lord,____
__ I con-fess that Je-sus Christ is Lord.____
__ He's om-ni-po-tent, mag-ni-fi-cent, All glor-ious, vic-
to-ri-ous;__ I con-fess that Je-sus Christ is Lord.____

I confess that Jesus Christ is Lord,
I confess that Jesus Christ is Lord.
He's omnipotent, magnificent,
All glorious, victorious;
I confess that Jesus Christ is Lord.

216

408   I delight greatly in the Lord

Chris A. Bowater

With swing

Capo 5

I de-light great-ly in the Lord, My soul re-joic-es in my God.____ I de-light great-ly in the Lord, My soul re-joic-es in my God. For He has clothed me with gar-ments of sal-va - tion And ar-rayed me in a robe of right-eous-ness; He has clothed me with gar-ments of sal-va - tion And ar-rayed me in a robe of right-eous-ness.

409 I do not know what lies ahead

(I know who holds the future)

Words and music
Alfred B. Smith and Eugene Clarke

I do not know what lies a-head, The way I can-not see; Yet one stands near to be my guide, He'll show the way to me:

I know who holds the fu-ture, And He'll guide me with His hand, With God things don't just hap-pen, Ev-'ry-thing by Him is planned; So

as I face to-mor-row With its prob-lems large and small, I'll
trust the God of mir-a-cles, Give to Him my all.

1 I do not know what lies ahead,
The way I cannot see;
Yet one stands near to be my guide,
He'll show the way to me:

I know who holds the future,
And He'll guide me with His hand,
With God things don't just happen,
Ev'rything by Him is planned;
So as I face tomorrow
With its problems large and small,
I'll trust the God of miracles,
Give to Him my all.

2 I do not know how many days
Of life are mine to spend;
But one who knows and cares for me
Will keep me to the end:
I know who holds . . .

3 I do not know the course ahead,
What joys and griefs are there;
But one is near who fully knows,
I'll trust His loving care:
I know who holds . . .

410 I get so excited, Lord
(I'm forgiven)

Mick Ray

Bm(Am)   E(D)   D(C) A(G)

gi - ven, I'm for - gi - ven, I'm for - gi - ven._____

Bm(Am)   E(D)   E7(D7)

_____I'm for - gi - ven, I'm for - gi - ven, I'm for -

1.
D(C) A(G)

gi - ven._____

2.
D(C) A(G)

gi - ven._____

1 I get so excited, Lord, ev'ry time I realize
   I'm forgiven, I'm forgiven.
   Jesus Lord, You've done it all,
   You've paid the price.
   I'm forgiven, I'm forgiven.

   Hallelujah, Lord,
   My heart just fills with praise,
   My feet start dancing, my hands rise up,
   And my lips they bless Your name.
   I'm forgiven, I'm forgiven, I'm forgiven.
   I'm forgiven, I'm forgiven, I'm forgiven.

2 Living in Your presence, Lord, is life itself.
   I'm forgiven, I'm forgiven.
   With the past behind, grace for today
   And a hope to come.
   I'm forgiven, I'm forgiven.
   Hallelujah . . .

222

411 I just want to praise You

Arthur Tannous

412 I give You all the honour

(I worship You)

Carl Tuttle

Majestically

I give You all the hon-our And praise that's due Your name, For You are the King of Glo-ry, The Cre-a-tor of all things. And I wor-ship You, I give my life to You, I fall down on my

1 I give You all the honour
   And praise that's due Your name,
   For You are the King of Glory,
   The Creator of all things.

   And I worship You,
   I give my life to You,
   I fall down on my knees.
   Yes, I worship You,
   I give my life to You,
   I fall down on my knees.

2 As Your Spirit moves upon me now
   You meet my deepest need,
   And I lift my hands up to Your throne,
   Your mercy, I've received.
   And I worship . . .

3 You have broken chains that bound me,
   You've set this captive free,
   I will lift my voice to praise Your name
   For all eternity.
   And I worship . . .

413 I hear the sound

Dave Moody
arr. Roland Fudge

I hear the sound of the ar-my of the Lord, __
I hear the sound of the ar-my of the Lord. __ It's the
sound of praise, It's the sound of __ war, __ The
ar-my of the Lord, __ The ar-my of the Lord, __ The

ar - my of the Lord____   is march-ing on.____

I hear the sound of the army of the Lord,
I hear the sound of the army of the Lord.
It's the sound of praise,
It's the sound of war,
The army of the Lord,
The army of the Lord,
The army of the Lord is marching on.

414 I lift my hands

(Most of all)

I lift my hands, I raise my voice, I give my heart to You my Lord And I re-joice. There are man-y, man-y rea-sons why I do the things I do, O but

most of all, I praise You, Most of all I
praise You, Je-sus, most of all I praise You be-cause You're

1.2.
You.
2. I lift my___ You.

3.

1 I lift my hands,
  I raise my voice,
  I give my heart to You my Lord
  And I rejoice.
  There are many, many reasons why I do the things I do,
  O but most of all, I praise You,
  Most of all I praise You,
  Jesus, most of all I praise You because You're You.

2 I lift my hands,
  I raise my voice,
  I give my life to You my Lord
  And I rejoice.
  There are many, many reasons why I do the things I do,
  O but most of all, I love You,
  Most of all I love You,
  Jesus, most of all I love You because You're You.

3 I lift my hands,
  I raise my voice,
  I give my love to You my Lord
  And I rejoice.
  There are many, many reasons why I love You like I do,
  O but most of all, I love You,
  Most of all I love You,
  Jesus, most of all I love You because You're You.

415   I live

Rich Cook

Majestically

I live, I live be-cause He is ri-sen, I live, I live with power ov-er sin. I live, I live be-cause He is ri-sen, I live, I live to wor-ship Him. Thank You

I live, I live because He is risen,
I live, I live with power over sin.
I live, I live because He is risen,
I live, I live to worship Him.
Thank You Jesus, thank You Jesus,
Because You're alive,
Because You're alive,
Because You're alive I live.

416 I lift my eyes

Michael Baughen
and Elisabeth Crocker

1 I lift my eyes
  To the quiet hills
  In the press of a busy day;
  As green hills stand
  In a dusty land
  So God is my strength and stay.

2 I lift my eyes
  To the quiet hills
  To a calm that is mine to share;
  Secure and still
  In the Father's will
  And kept by the Father's care.

3 I lift up my eyes
  To the quiet hills
  With a prayer as I turn to sleep;
  By day, by night,
  Through the dark and light
  My Shepherd will guard His sheep.

4 I lift up my eyes
  To the quiet hills
  And my heart to the Father's throne;
  In all my ways
  To the end of days
  The Lord will preserve His own.

© *Timothy Dudley-Smith, b. 1926*

417 I receive You

John Lai

418 I receive Your love

Paul Armstrong

1 I receive Your love,
I receive Your love,
In my heart I receive Your love, O Lord.
I receive Your love
By Your Spirit within me,
I receive, I receive Your love.

2 I confess Your love,
I confess Your love,
In my heart I confess Your love, O Lord.
I confess Your love
By Your Spirit within me,
I confess, I confess Your love.

419 I sing the almighty power of God

JACKSON C.M.

Thomas Jackson (1715–81)

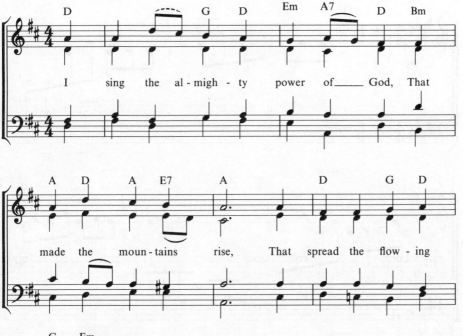

1 I sing the almighty power of God,
That made the mountains rise,
That spread the flowing seas abroad,
And built the lofty skies.

2 I sing the wisdom that ordained
The sun to rule the day;
The moon shines full at His command,
And all the stars obey.

3 I sing the goodness of the Lord,
That filled the earth with food;
He formed the creatures with His word,
And then pronounced them good.

4 Creatures, as numerous as they be,
Are subject to His care;
There's not a place where we can flee
But God is present there.

5 Lord, how Thy wonders are displayed
Where'er I turn mine eye,
If I survey the ground I tread,
Or gaze upon the sky.

6 God's hand is my perpetual guard,
He guides me with His eye;
Why should I then forget the Lord,
Whose love is ever nigh?

Isaac Watts, 1674–1748

420 I sing a new song

Carl Tuttle and John Wimber

1. I sing a new song to the Lord, my God. I lift_____ my voice to Je - sus, the King. And I wor - ship You, I wor - ship

You, I wor - ship You,_____ I
wor - ship You._____ 2. I
bow down_____my face at the foot - stool of the
Lamb, I lay down_____ my
life at the al - ter of_ God. And I

237

421 I stand amazed in the presence

Words and music by
Charles H. Gabriel (1858–1932)

I stand a-mazed in the pre-sence Of Je-sus the Na-za-rene, And
won-der how He could love me, A sin-ner, con-demned, un-clean.

How mar-vel-lous! How won-der-ful!
O, how mar-vel-lous! O, how won-der-ful! *And my song shall ev-er be;*

How mar-vel-lous! How won-der-ful!
O, how mar-vel-lous! O, how won-der-ful! *Is my Sav-iour's love for me!*

1 I stand amazed in the presence
Of Jesus the Nazarene,
And wonder how He could love me,
A sinner, condemned, unclean.

How marvellous! How wonderful!
And my song shall ever be;
How marvellous! How wonderful!
Is my Saviour's love for me!

2 For me it was in the garden
He prayed – 'Not My will, but Thine':
He had tears for His own griefs,
But sweat drops of blood for mine.
How marvellous! . . .

3 In pity angels beheld Him,
And came from the world of light
To comfort Him in the sorrows
He bore for my soul that night.
How marvellous! . . .

4 He took my sins and my sorrows,
He made them His very own;
He bore the burden to Calvary,
And suffered, and died alone.
How marvellous! . . .

5 When with the ransomed in glory
His face I at last shall see,
'Twill be my joy through the ages
To sing of His love for me.
How marvellous! . . .

422 I stand before the presence

Mavis Ford

Thoughtfully

Capo 5

I stand be-fore the pre-sence Of the Lord God of hosts, A

child of my Fath-er And an heir of His grace,_____For

Je - sus paid the debt for me, The veil was torn in two, And the

Ho - ly of Ho - lies Has be - come my dwel-ling place.

423 I want to learn to appreciate You

John Kennett

With pace and swing

Capo 3

I want to learn to ap - pre - ci - ate You Lord in ev - 'ry way, —

— I want to learn to walk with You — Lord,

day by day, With You al - ways

there to guide me, Hand in hand, There be - side — me,

Walk-ing in the Spi - rit day by day. _____

Often sung colloquially *I wanna learn to . . .* etc.

424 I will rejoice, I will rejoice

With pace

Dave Fellingham

Capo 3

I will re-joice, I will re-joice,

I will re-joice in the Lord with my whole heart.

I will re-joice, I will re-joice,

I will re-joice in the Lord.

425　I will sing about Your love

Phil Potter

I will sing a-bout Your love,

I will mag-ni-fy Your name.

I will be glad and re-joice in You,

I will praise You a-gain,

I will sing about Your love,
I will magnify Your name.
I will be glad and rejoice in You,
I will praise You again,
Praise the Lord, lift your voices high.
Praise the Lord,
Tell them He's alive.
Praise the Lord, praise the Lord.

426   I will wait upon the Lord

Andy Silver

Slowly and prayerfully

I will wait u - pon the Lord, My hope is all in Him. He on - ly is my rock and strength, My re - fuge is in God. I will trust Him at all times, Pour out my heart to Him.

246

427 I'll praise my Maker

MONMOUTH 8 8. 8. D

Gabriel Davis (c.1768–1924)

I'll praise my Ma - ker while I've breath;

And when my voice is lost in death, Praise

shall em - ploy my no - bler pow'rs: My

days of praise shall ne'er be past, While

life,___ and thought,___ and be - ing last,___ Or

im - mor - ta - li - ty en - dures.

1 I'll praise my Maker while I've breath;
   And when my voice is lost in death,
   Praise shall employ my nobler pow'rs:
   My days of praise shall ne'er be past,
   While life, and thought, and being last,
   Or immortality endures.

2 Happy the man whose hopes rely
   On Israel's God! He made the sky,
   And earth, and sea, with all their train:
   His truth for ever stands secure;
   He saves th'oppressed, He feeds the poor,
   And none shall find His promise vain.

3 The Lord gives eyesight to the blind;
   The Lord supports the fainting mind;
   He sends the lab'ring conscience peace;
   He helps the stranger in distress,
   The widow, and the fatherless,
   And grants the pris'ner sweet release.

4 I'll praise Him while He lends me breath;
   And when my voice is lost in death,
   Praise shall employ my nobler pow'rs:
   My days of praise shall ne'er be past,
   While life, and thought, and being last,
   Or immortality endures.

Isaac Watts, 1674–1748

428 I will rejoice in You

Anon.
arr. Phil Burt

I will re - joice_____ in You and be glad,_____

I will ex - tol____ Your love more than wine,_____

Draw me af - ter You and let us run to - geth - er,

I will re - joice_____ in You and be glad.____

429 I'm confident of this very thing

Composer unknown

In a marching style

LADIES: I'm con-fi-dent of this ve-ry thing___

MEN: I'm con-fi-dent of this ve-ry thing_____ That

That he_____ who has be-gun_____ a good work_____

he_____ who has be - gun a good work in___

in___ you

you ALL: He will per - form it un - til the day___ of

Je - sus Christ, He will per - form it un - til the day___ of

Je - sus Christ, He will per - form it un - til the day___ of Je - sus Christ.___

430 I'm redeemed

Tony Humphries

With pace and swing

I'm re-deemed, Yes I am, By the blood of the Lamb, Je-sus Christ has done it all for me.

I am His, He is mine, I'm part of the roy-al vine, All my sins were washed a-way at Cal-va-ry.

Fine

Once I was lost, I had no-where to go, My
life was just a lone-ly round of sin. Till
Je-sus said to me, By My blood shed on the tree I've
paid the price, Brought you back, You're mine, Oh what a friend!

I'm redeemed, Yes I am,
By the blood of the Lamb,
Jesus Christ has done it all for me.
I am His, He is mine,
I'm part of the royal vine,
All my sins were washed away at Calvary.

Once I was lost, I had nowhere to go,
My life was just a lonely round of sin.
Till Jesus said to me,
By My blood shed on the tree
I've paid the price,
Brought you back,
You're mine,
Oh what a friend!

431 I'm special

Words and music
Graham Kendrick

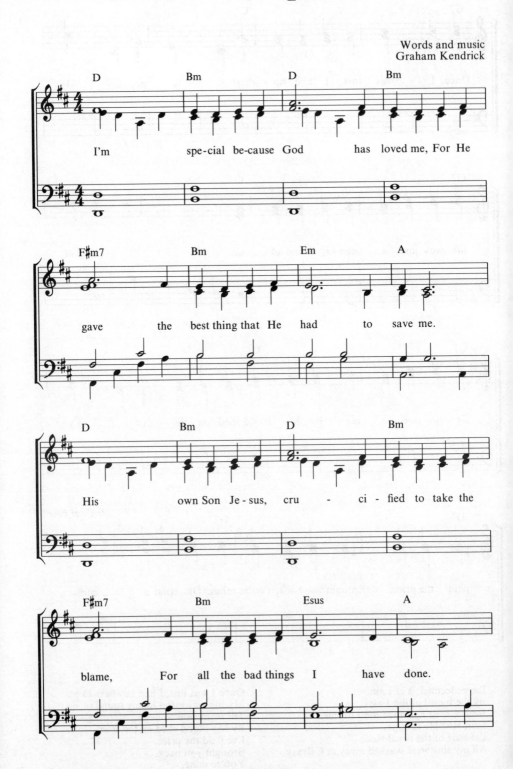

I'm spe-cial be-cause God has loved me, For He gave the best thing that He had to save me.

His own Son Je-sus, cru - ci - fied to take the blame, For all the bad things I have done.

Thank You Jesus, thank You Lord, For lov-ing me so much. I know I don't de-serve a-ny-thing, Help me feel your love right now To know deep in my heart that I'm Your spe-cial friend.

I'm special because God has loved me,
For He gave the best thing that He had to save me.
His own Son Jesus, crucified to take the blame,
For all the bad things I have done.

Thank You Jesus, thank You Lord,
For loving me so much.
I know I don't deserve anything,
Help me feel Your love right now
To know deep in my heart that I'm Your special friend.

432 I am trusting

Words and music
Andy and Becky Silver

433　In Him we live and move

Randy Spier
arr. Phil Burt

With energy

In Him we live and move and have our being,____ In Him we live and move and have our being.____

last time **to Coda** ⊕

Make a joy - ful noise, sing un-to____ the Lord,

Tell Him of___ your love, dance be-fore Him.

Make a joy-ful noise, sing un-to___ the Lord,

Tell Him of___ your love, Hal - le - lu -

CODA

jah! In Him we being.___

434 In moments like these

David Graham
arr. G. Baker

Flowing

In mo-ments like these,___ I sing out a song,___ I sing out a love song to Je - sus, In mo-ments like these,___ I lift up my hands,___I lift up my hands to the Lord, Sing-ing I love You Lord, Sing-ing I love You

Lord, Sing-ing I love You Lord,___

I love You. Sing-ing You.___

In moments like these, I sing out a song,
I sing out a love song to Jesus,
In moments like these, I lift up my hands,
I lift up my hands to the Lord,
Singing I love You Lord,
Singing I love You Lord,
Singing I love You Lord,
I love You.

435 In Christ there is no East or West

ST. STEPHEN C.M.

William Jones (1726–1800)

In Christ there is no___ East or West, In___

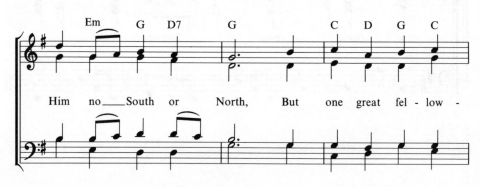

Him no___South or North, But one great fel - low -

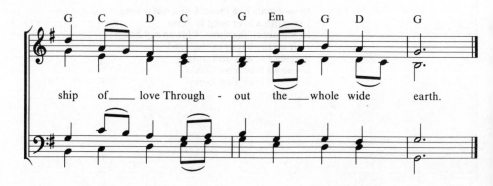

ship of___ love Through - out the___whole wide earth.

1 In Christ there is no East or West,
In Him no South or North,
But one great fellowship of love
Throughout the whole wide earth.

2 In Him shall true hearts everywhere
Their high communion find:
His service is the golden cord
Close-binding all mankind.

3 Join hands then, brothers of the faith,
Whate'er your race may be!
Who serves my Father as a son
Is surely kin to me.

4 In Christ now meet both East and West,
In Him meet South and North,
All Christly souls are one in Him,
Throughout the whole wide earth.

John Oxenham, 1852–1941

262

436 In my need Jesus found me

Words and music
Gordon Brattle

In my need Je-sus found me, Put His strong arm a-round me, Brought me safe home, In-to the shel-ter of the fold._____ Gra-cious Shep-herd that sought me, Pre-cious life-blood that bought me; Out of the night, In-to the light and near to God.____

437 In the bleak mid-winter

CRANHAM 6 5. 6 5. D

Gustav Holst (1874–1934)

1. In the bleak mid - win - ter / Fros - ty wind made moan,
2. Our God, heav'n can - not hold Him, / Nor ___ earth sus - tain;
3. An - gels and arch - an - gels / May have gath - ered there,
4. What ___ can I give Him, / Poor ___ as I am?

Earth stood hard as / ir - on, / Wa - ter like a stone;
Heav'n and earth shall / flee a - way / When He comes to reign;
Cher - u - bim and / se - ra-phim / Thronged ___ the air;
If I were a / shep - herd, / I would bring a lamb;

Snow had fall - en, snow on snow, / Snow ___ on ___ snow,
In the bleak mid - win - ter / A sta - ble-place suf - ficed
But His mo - ther on - ly, / In her maid - en bliss,
If I were a wise ___ man, / I would do my part; Yet

264

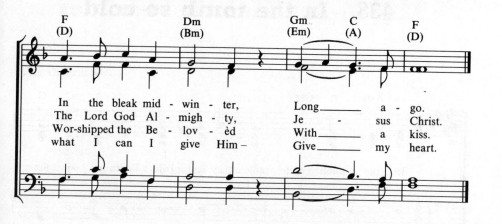

In the bleak mid - win - ter,   Long_____ a - go.
The Lord God Al - migh - ty,   Je - sus Christ.
Wor-shipped the Be - lov - èd   With_____ a kiss.
what I can I give Him –   Give_____ my heart.

1 In the bleak mid-winter
Frosty wind made moan,
Earth stood hard as iron,
Water like a stone;
Snow had fallen, snow on snow,
Snow on snow,
In the bleak mid-winter,
Long ago.

2 Our God, heaven cannot hold Him,
Nor earth sustain;
Heaven and earth shall flee away
When He comes to reign;
In the bleak mid-winter
A stable-place sufficed
The Lord God Almighty,
Jesus Christ.

3 Angels and archangels
May have gathered there,
Cherubim and seraphim
Thronged the air;
But His mother only,
In her maiden bliss,
Worshipped the Belovèd
With a kiss.

4 What can I give Him,
Poor as I am?
If I were a shepherd,
I would bring a lamb;
If I were a wise man,
I would do my part;
Yet what I can I give Him –
Give my heart.

Christina Georgina Rossetti, 1830–94

438 In the tomb so cold

Graham Kendrick

In the tomb so cold they laid Him, Death its vic-tim claimed. Powers of hell they could not hold Him, Back to life He came! Christ is ris-en, (Christ is ris-en) Death has been con-quered, (Death has been con-quered)

Christ is ris - en, (Christ is ris - en) He shall reign for

last time

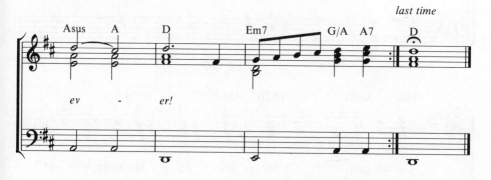

ev - er!

1 In the tomb so cold they laid Him,
  Death its victim claimed.
  Powers of hell they could not hold Him,
  Back to life He came!

  Christ is risen, (Christ is risen),
  Death has been conquered, (Death has been conquered),
  Christ is risen, (Christ is risen),
  He shall reign for ever!

2 Hell had spent its fury on Him,
  Left Him crucified.
  Yet by blood He boldly conquered
  Sin and death defied.
    Christ is risen . . .

3 Now the fear of death is broken,
  Love has won the crown.
  Prisoners of the darkness listen,
  Walls are tumbling down.
    Christ is risen . . .

4 Raised from death to heav'n ascending
  Love's exalted King.
  Let His song of joy unending
  Through the nations ring!
    Christ is risen . . .

439 Infant holy

INFANT HOLY   447.447.44447

Polish Carol
arr. A.E. Rusbridge (1917–1969)

In-fant ho - ly, In-fant low - ly, For His bed a
cat - tle stall; Ox - en low - ing, Lit - tle know - ing
Christ the babe is Lord of all. Swift are wing - ing
An - gels sing - ing, No-wells ring - ing, Ti - dings bring - ing,

Christel the babe is Lord of all, Christ the babe is Lord of all.

1 Infant holy,
   Infant lowly,
   For His bed a cattle stall;
   Oxen lowing,
   Little knowing
   Christ the babe is Lord of all.
   Swift are winging
   Angels singing,
   Nowells ringing,
   Tidings bringing,
   Christ the babe is Lord of all,
   Christ the babe is Lord of all.

2 Flocks were sleeping,
   Shepherds keeping
   Vigil till the morning new.
   Saw the glory,
   Heard the story,
   Tidings of a gospel true.
   Thus rejoicing,
   Free from sorrow,
   Praises voicing,
   Greet the morrow,
   Christ the babe was born for you!
   Christ the babe was born for you!

tr. E.M.G Reed
Kingsway Carol Book

440 Is this the Church of our God?

Words and music
Anne Horrobin and Stephen Poxon
arr. Phil Burt

1 Is this the church___ of our God?___
2 If we're de - pen - dant on Him,___

Is this the church___ of the Word?___
If we be - lieve___ God's own Word,___

Is this the church___ of His Son Je - sus Christ?
If we're re - deemed by the blood of His Son,

Is this the church of His Spi - rit?___
If we are filled___ with His Spi - rit.___

1.

2. 3 Then

this is the church__ of our God,_____ Then
(4) this is the church__ of our God,_____ Yes,

this is the church__ of His Word,_____ Then
this is the church__ of His Word,_____ Yes,

this is the church__ of His Son Je - sus Christ, Then
this is the church__ of His Son Je - sus Christ, Yes,

this is the church of our Lord._____ 4 Yes
this is the church of our Lord.__

441   Isn't He?

John Wimber
arr. Christopher Norton

With simplicity and adoration

men — Is - n't He, — beau - ti - ful? —
ladies — is - n't He _____ beau - ti - ful, —

Beau - ti - ful, — is - n't He? —
beau - ti - ful, _____ is - n't He? —

together

Prince of Peace, _____ Son of God, _____

Is - n't He? _____ Is - n't He, —
is - n't He _____

2 Yes You are beautiful,   Wonderful, yes You are!
   Beautiful, yes you are!   Counsellor,
   Prince of Peace,   Almighty God,
   Son of God,   Yes You are, yes You are,
   Yes You are!   Yes You are, yes You are,
   Yes You are wonderful,   Yes You are!

442 It came upon the midnight clear

NOEL 8 6 8 6 D (DCM)

English traditional melody
arr. Arthur S. Sullivan (1842–1900)

It__ came up-on the__ mid night clear, That glo-rious song of

old, From_ an-gels bend-ing near the earth To__

touch their harps of gold: 'Peace on the earth, good-

will to men From heaven's all-gra-cious king!' The

world in sol-emn still-ness lay To__ hear the an-gels sing.

1 It came upon the midnight clear,
  That glorious song of old,
  From angels bending near the earth
  To touch their harps of gold:
  'Peace on the earth, goodwill to men
  From heaven's all-gracious king!'
  The world in solemn stillness lay
  To hear the angels sing.

2 With sorrow brought by sin and strife
  The world has suffered long,
  And, since the angels sang, have passed
  Two thousand years of wrong:
  For man at war with man hears not
  The love-song which they bring:
  O hush the noise, you men of strife,
  And hear the angels sing!

3 And those whose journey now is hard,
  Whose hope is burning low,
  Who tread the rocky path of life
  With painful steps and slow:
  O listen to the news of love
  Which makes the heavens ring!
  O rest beside the weary road
  And hear the angels sing!

4 And still the days are hastening on—
  By prophets seen of old—
  Towards the fulness of the time
  When comes the age foretold:
  Then earth and heaven renewed shall see
  The Prince of Peace, their king;
  And all the world repeat the song
  Which now the angels sing.

E.H. Sears, 1810–76
© *in this version Jubilate Hymns*

443 It may be at morn

O LORD JESUS HOW LONG   12.12.12.7. and Refrain   James McGranahan
(1840–1907)

It may be at morn, when the day is a - wak - ing When
sun - light through dark - ness and sha - dow is break - ing, That
Je - sus will come in the ful - ness of glo - ry, To re - ceive from the
world__ 'His own'. O Lord Je - sus, how long? How

long ere we shout the glad song? Christ re - turn - eth, Hal - le -

lu - jah! Hal - le - lu - jah! A - men, Hal - le - lu - jah! A - men.

1 It may be at morn, when the day is awaking
When sunlight through darkness and shadow is breaking,
That Jesus will come in the fulness of glory,
To receive from the world 'His own'.

O Lord Jesus, how long?
How long ere we shout the glad song?
Christ returneth, Hallelujah! Hallelujah! Amen,
Hallelujah! Amen.

2 It may be at mid-day it may be at twilight,
It may be, perchance, that the blackness of midnight
Will burst into light in the blaze of His glory,
When Jesus receives 'His own'.
O Lord Jesus . . .

3 While hosts cry Hosanna, from heaven descending,
With glorified saints and the angels attending,
With grace on His brow, like a halo of glory,
Will Jesus receive 'His own'.
O Lord Jesus . . .

4 Oh, joy! Oh, delight! Should we go without dying;
No sickness, no sadness, no dread and no crying;
Caught up through the clouds with our Lord into glory,
When Jesus receives 'His own'.
O Lord Jesus . . .

H.L. Turner

444 I want to walk

Swiss folk tune
(*Es Buurebuebli*)
arr. Phil Burt

I want to walk___ with Je - sus
Christ, All the days I live of this life on
earth, To give to Him___ com - plete con -
trol Of bo - dy and___ of soul:___
Fol-low Him, *fol-low Him,* *yield your life* *to*

Him, He has con - quered death, He is King of kings. Ac - cept the joy which He gives to those Who yield their lives to Him.

1 I want to walk with Jesus Christ,
All the days I live of this life on earth,
To give to Him complete control
Of body and of soul:

Follow Him, follow Him, yield your life to Him,
He has conquered death, He is King of kings.
Accept the joy which He gives to those
Who yield their lives to Him.

2 I want to learn to speak to Him,
To pray to Him, confess my sin,
To open my life and let Him in,
For joy will then be mine:
  Follow Him, follow Him . . .

3 I want to learn to speak of Him,
My life must show that He lives in me,
My deeds, my thoughts, my words must speak
All of His love for me:
  Follow Him, follow Him . . .

4 I want to learn to read His Word,
For this is how I know the way,
To live my life as pleases Him,
In holiness and joy:
  Follow Him, follow Him . . .

5 O Holy Spirit of the Lord,
Enter now into this heart of mine,
Take full control of my selfish will
And make me wholly Thine:
  Follow Him, follow Him . . .

© 1964 C. Simmonds

279

445 It is no longer I that liveth

Sally Ellis

Joyfully

It is no long-er I that liv-eth___ But Christ that liveth in
me, It is no lon-ger I that liv-eth___ But
Christ that liv-eth in me. He lives, He
lives, Je-sus is a-live in me. It is
no long-er I that liv-eth___ But Christ that liveth in me.

446 Jesus at Your Name

(You are the Christ)

Words and music by
Chris A. Bowater

Je - sus at Your Name__ we bow the knee.

Je-sus at Your Name we bow the knee. Je-sus at Your Name we

bow the knee, And ac - know-ledge You as Lord.

You are the Christ__ You are the Lord.

Through Your Spi-rit in our lives__ We know who You are;__

447 Jesus Christ is risen today

LLANFAIR 7 7. 7 7 and Hallelujahs

Melody by
Robert Williams (1781–1821)

Je - sus Christ is risen to - day, *Hal - le -*
lu - jah! Our tri - umph - ant ho - ly___ day,
Hal - le - lu - jah! Who did once, up -
on___ the___cross, *Hal - le - lu - jah!*

Suf-fer to re-deem our loss. *Hal - le - lu - jah!*

1 Jesus Christ is risen today, *Hallelujah!*
Our triumphant holy day, *Hallelujah!*
Who did once, upon the cross, *Hallelujah!*
Suffer to redeem our loss. *Hallelujah!*

2 Hymns of praise then let us sing, *Hallelujah!*
Unto Christ, our heavenly King, *Hallelujah!*
Who endured the cross and grave, *Hallelujah!*
Sinners to redeem and save. *Hallelujah!*

3 But the pains which He endured, *Hallelujah!*
Our salvation have procured, *Hallelujah!*
Now in heaven above He's King, *Hallelujah!*
Where the angels ever sing: *Hallelujah!*

Lyra Davidica, 1708

448 Jesus has sat down

Triumphantly

Jonathan Wallis

Capo 5

Je - sus has sat down at God's right hand, He is reign-ing now on Dav-id's throne. God has placed all things be-neath His feet, His en - e-mies will be His footstool. *For the gov-ern-ment is now up - on His shoul-der, For the gov-ern-ment is*

now up - on His shoul-der,_____And of the in-crease of His

gov - ern - ment and peace There will be no end, There will

be no end, There will be no end._____

1 Jesus has sat down at God's right hand,
  He is reigning now on David's throne.
  God has placed all things beneath His feet,
  His enemies will be His footstool.

  For the government is now upon His shoulder,
  For the government is now upon His shoulder,
  And of the increase of His government and peace
  There will be no end,
  There will be no end,
  There will be no end.

2 God has exalted Him on high,
  Given Him a name above all names.
  Every knee will bow and tongue confess
  That Jesus Christ is Lord.
  For the government ...

3 Jesus is now living in His church,
  Men who have been purchased by His blood.
  They will serve their God, a royal priesthood,
  And they will reign on earth.
  For the government ...

4 Sounds the trumpet, good news to the poor,
  Captives will go free, the blind will see,
  The kingdom of this world will soon become
  The kingdom of out God.
  For the government ...

449 Jesus is King

Je - sus is King and I will ex-tol Him,
Give Him the glo - ry and hon - our His name.
He reigns on high, en - throned in the hea - vens,
Word of the Fa - ther, ex - alt - ed for us.

1 Jesus is King and I will extol Him,
   Give Him the glory and honour His name.
   He reigns on high, enthroned in the heavens,
   Word of the Father, exalted for us.

2 We have a hope that is steadfast and certain,
   Gone through the curtain and touching the throne.
   We have a Priest who is there interceding,
   Pouring His grace on our lives day by day.

3 We come to Him, our Priest and Apostle,
   Clothed in His glory and bearing His name,
   Laying our lives with gladness before Him;
   Filled with His Spirit we worship the King.

4 O holy One, our hearts do adore You;
   Thrilled with Your goodness we give You our praise.
   Angels in light with worship surround Him,
   Jesus, our Saviour, for ever the same.

450 Jesus is Lord of all

Marilyn Baker

Majestically

Je - sus is Lord of all,___ Sa - tan is un-der His feet,___ Je - sus is reign-ing on high___ And all pow'r is giv - en to Him In heaven and earth. Him.

2 We are joined to Him,
Satan is under our feet,
We are seated on high
And all authority is given
To us through Him.

3 One day we'll be like Him,
Perfect in every way,
Chosen to be His bride,
Ruling and reigning with Him
For evermore.

451 Jesus, I worship You

Worshipfully

Chris A. Bowater

Je-sus, I wor-ship You, Wor-ship, hon-our and a-dore Your

love - ly name. Je - sus, I wor - ship You,

Lord of lords and King of kings, I wor - ship

You, From a thank - ful heart I sing;

I wor - ship You. You.

452 Jesus is the Lord

Dennis Merry

With steady pace

Je - sus is the Lord, Je - sus the Lord reigns,

We will take the king-doms of this world in His name.

Ev - 'ry tribe and na - tion, ev - 'ry si - tu - a - tion,

Must de-clare that Je - sus is the Lord. For the

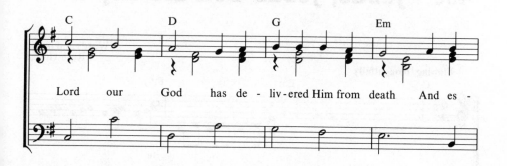

Lord our God has de - liv-ered Him from death And es -

tab - lished Je - sus as Lord,_____ He has

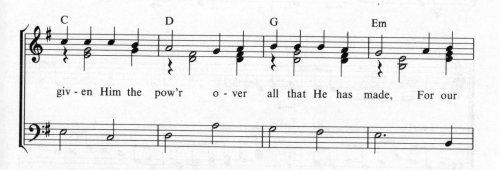

giv - en Him the pow'r o - ver all that He has made, For our

God has__ made Him Christ the Lord._____

453 Jesus, Jesus You are my Lord

Words and music
Ruth Hooke

Keep   us   in_____Your love._____

1 Jesus, Jesus,
  You are my Lord and my heart's desire.
  Jesus, Jesus,
  Keep us in Your love.

2 Jesus, Jesus,
  You are my King and my Sovereign Master.
  Jesus, Jesus,
  I will serve Your Lord.

454 Jesus lives

ST. ALBINUS 7 8. 7 8. 4   Henry John Gauntlett (1805–76)

1   Jesus lives! thy terrors now
Can, O death, no more appal us;
Jesus lives! by this we know
Thou, O grave, canst not enthral us.
    Hallelujah!

2   Jesus lives! henceforth is death
But the gate of life immortal;
This shall calm our trembling breath
When we pass its gloomy portal.
    Hallelujah!

3   Jesus lives! for us He died;
Then, alone to Jesus living,
Pure in heart may we abide,
Glory to our Saviour giving.
    Hallelujah!

4   Jesus lives! our hearts know well
Naught from us His love shall sever;
Life, nor death, nor powers of hell
Tear us from His keeping ever.
    Hallelujah!

5   Jesus lives! to Him the throne
Over all the world is given;
May we go where He is gone,
Rest and reign with Him in heaven.
    Hallelujah!

Christian Fürchtegott Gellert, 1715–69
tr. Frances Elizabeth Cox, 1812–97, and others

455 Jesus, Jesus, Jesus

Chris A. Bowater

Worshipfully
Capo 3

Je - sus, Je - sus, Je - sus, Your love has mel - ted my heart.

Je - sus, Je - sus, Je - sus, Your love has mel - ted my heart.

456 Jesus, Prince and Saviour

ST. GERTRUDE 6 5 6 5 Triple

Arthur S. Sullivan (1842–1900)

Je - sus, Prince and Sav - iour, Lord of life who died:

Christ, the friend of sin - ners, Sin - ners cru - ci - fied.

For a lost world's ran - som All Him - self He gave,

Lay at last death's vic - tim___ Life - less in the grave.

Lord of life triumphant, Risen now to reign!
King of endless ages, Jesus lives again!

1 Jesus, Prince and Saviour,
  Lord of life who died:
  Christ, the friend of sinners,
  Sinners crucified.
  For a lost world's ransom
  All Himself He gave,
  Lay at last death's victim
  Lifeless in the grave.

    Lord of life triumphant,
    Risen now to reign!
    King of endless ages,
    Jesus lives again!

2 In His power and Godhead
  Every victory won,
  Pain and passion ended,
  All His purpose done:
  Christ the Lord is risen!
  Sighs and sorrows past,
  Death's dark night is over,
  Morning comes at last!
    Lord of life . . .

3 Resurrection morning!
  Sinners' bondage freed.
  Christ the Lord is risen—
  He is risen indeed!
  Jesus, Prince and Saviour,
  Lord of life who died,
  Christ the King of glory
  Now is glorified!
    Lord of life . . .

© *Timothy Dudley-Smith, b. 1926*

457 Jesus put this song into our hearts

Graham Kendrick

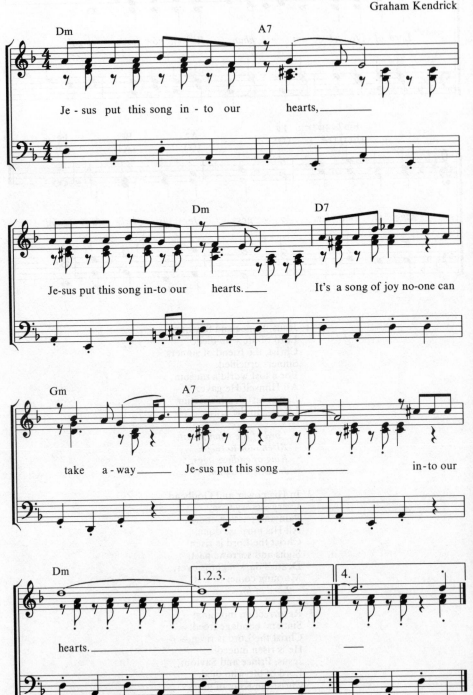

1 Jesus put this song into our hearts,
  Jesus put this song into our hearts.
  It's a song of joy no-one can take away
  Jesus put this song into our hearts.

2 Jesus taught us how to live in harmony,
  Jesus taught us how to live in harmony,
  Different faces, different races, He made us one,
  Jesus taught us how to live in harmony.

3 Jesus taught us how to be a family,
  Jesus taught us how to be a family,
  Loving one another with the love that He gives,
  Jesus taught us how to be a family.

4 Jesus turned our sorrow into dancing,
  Jesus turned our sorrow into dancing,
  Changed our tears of sadness into rivers of joy,
  Jesus turned our sorrow into a dance.

458 Jesus the Lord

YISU NE KAHA

Urdu melody harmonised by
Francis B. Westbrook (1903–75)

Je - sus the Lord said: 'I am the bread, The bread of ___ life ___ for man -

kind am I, The bread of ___ life ___ for man - kind am I, The

bread of ___ life ___ for man - kind am I.' Je - sus the Lord said:

'I am the bread, The bread of ___ life ___ for man - kind am I.'

1 Jesus the Lord said: 'I am the bread,
The bread of life for mankind am I,
The bread of life for mankind am I,
The bread of life for mankind am I.'
Jesus the Lord said: 'I am the bread,
The bread of life for mankind am I.'

2 Jesus the Lord said: 'I am the way,
The true and living way am I,
The true and living way am I,
The true and living way am I.'
Jesus the Lord said: 'I am the way,
The true and living way am I.'

3 Jesus the Lord said: 'I am the light,
The one true light of the world am I,
The one true light of the world am I,
The one true light of the world am I.'
Jesus the Lord said: 'I am the light,
The one true light of the world am I.'

4 Jesus the Lord said: 'I am the shepherd,
The one good shepherd of the sheep am I,
The one good shepherd of the sheep am I,
The one good shepherd of the sheep am I.'
Jesus the Lord said: 'I am the shepherd,
The one good shepherd of the sheep am I.'

5 Jesus the Lord said: 'I am the life,
The resurrection and the life am I,
The resurrection and the life am I,
The resurrection and the life am I.'
Jesus the Lord said: 'I am the life,
The resurrection and the life am I.'

Translated from Urdu
by D. Monahan, 1906–1957
© The Methodist Church,
Division of Education and Youth

459 Jesus, You are changing me

Words and music by
Marilyn Baker

Je - sus,_____ You are chang-ing me._____

__ By Your Spi - rit You're mak-ing me like You._____

__ Je - sus,_____ You're trans - for-ming me,_____

__ That Your love - li-ness may be seen in all I

460 Jesus, You are the radiance

Dave Fellingham

461 Join all the glorious names

ST. GODRIC 6 6. 6 6. 8 8   John Bacchus Dykes (1823–76)

Join all the glo-rious names Of wis-dom, love, and pow'r, That ev – er mor – tals knew, That an – gels ev – er bore: All are too mean to speak His worth, Too mean to set my Sav – iour forth.

1 Join all the glorious names
Of wisdom, love, and power,
That ever mortals knew,
That angels ever bore:
All are too mean to speak His worth,
Too mean to set my Saviour forth.

2 Great Prophet of my God,
My tongue would bless Thy Name:
By Thee the joyful news
Of our salvation came:
The joyful news of sins forgiven,
Of hell subdued and peace with heaven.

3 Jesus, my great High Priest,
Offered His blood, and died;
My guilty conscience seeks
No sacrifice beside:
His powerful blood did once atone,
And now it pleads before the throne.

4 My Saviour and my Lord,
My Conqueror and my King,
Thy sceptre and Thy sword,
Thy reigning grace I sing:
Thine is the power; behold, I sit
In willing bonds beneath Thy feet.

5 Now let my soul arise,
And tread the tempter down:
My Captain leads me forth
To conquest and a crown:
March on, nor fear to win the day,
Though death and hell obstruct the way.

6 Should all the hosts of death,
And powers of hell unknown,
Put their most dreadful forms
Of rage and malice on,
I shall be safe; for Christ displays
Superior power and guardian grace.

Isaac Watts, 1674–1748

462 King of glory, King of peace

GWALCHMAI 74.74.D

J.D. Jones (1827–70)

King of glo-ry,— King of peace, I will love Thee;

And, that love may— ne-ver cease, I will move Thee.

Thou hast gran-ted my re - quest, Thou hast heard— me;

Thou didst note my— work-ing breast, Thou hast spared me.

1 King of glory, King of peace,
I will love Thee;
And, that love may never cease,
I will move Thee.
Thou hast granted my request,
Thou hast heard me;
Thou didst note my working breast,
Thou hast spared me.

2 Wherefore with my utmost art
I will sing Thee,
And the cream of all my heart
I will bring Thee.
Though my sins against me cried,
Thou didst clear me;
And alone, when they replied,
Thou didst hear me.

3 Seven whole days, not one in seven,
I will praise Thee;
In my heart, though not in heaven,
I can raise Thee.
Small it is, in this poor sort
To enrol Thee:
E'en eternity's too short
To extol Thee.

George Herbert, 1593–1633

463 King of kings and Lord of lords

Round

Hebrew folk melody
Sophie Conty and Naomi Batya

Brightly with increasing pace

Capo 3

King of kings and Lord of___lords, Glo-ry, Hal - le - lu - jah!

Je - sus, Prince of Peace, Glo-ry, Hal - le - lu - jah!

King of kings and Lord of lords,
Glory, Hallelujah!
King of kings and Lord of lords,
Glory, Hallelujah!
Jesus, Prince of Peace,
Glory, Hallelujah!
Jesus, Prince of Peace,
Glory, Hallelujah!

464 Lead kindly light

SANDON 10.4.10.4.10.10

C.H. Purday (1799–1885)

Lead kind-ly Light, a - mid th'en-circ-ling gloom, Lead
The night is dark, and I am far from home; Lead

Thou me on; Keep Thou my feet; I do not ask to
Thou me on.

see The dis - tant scene; one step e - nough for me.

1 Lead kindly Light, amid th'encircling gloom,
   Lead Thou me on;
   The night is dark, and I am far from home;
   Lead Thou me on.
   Keep Thou my feet; I do not ask to see
   The distant scene; one step enough for me.

2 I was not ever thus, nor prayed that Thou
   Shouldst lead me on;
   I loved to choose and see my path; but now
   Lead Thou me on.
   I loved the garish day, and, spite of fears,
   Pride ruled my will: remember not past years.

3 So long Thy power has blest me, sure it still
   Will lead me on
   O'er moor and fen, o'er crag and torrent, till
   The night is gone;
   And with the morn those angel faces smile
   Which I have loved long since, and lost awhile.

J.H. Newman, 1801–90

311

465 Lead us, heavenly Father

MANNHEIM 8 7. 8 7. 8 7

Altered from Chorale by
F. Filitz (1804–76)

Lead us, heav'n-ly Fa-ther, lead us O'er the world's tem-pest-uous sea; Guard us, guide us, keep us, feed us, For we have no help but Thee; Yet pos-sess-ing ev-'ry bless-ing If our God our Fa-ther be.

2 Saviour, breathe forgiveness o'er us;
All our weakness Thou dost know:
Thou didst tread this earth before us,
Thou didst feel its keenest woe;
Lone and dreary, faint and weary,
Through the desert Thou didst go.

3 Spirit of our God, descending,
Fill our hearts with heav'nly joy,
Love with ev'ry passion blending,
Pleasure that can never cloy:
Thus provided, pardoned, guided,
Nothing can our peace destroy.

James Edmeston, 1791–1867

466 Let saints on earth

DUNDEE 8 6 8 6

Scottish Psalter Edinburgh (1615)

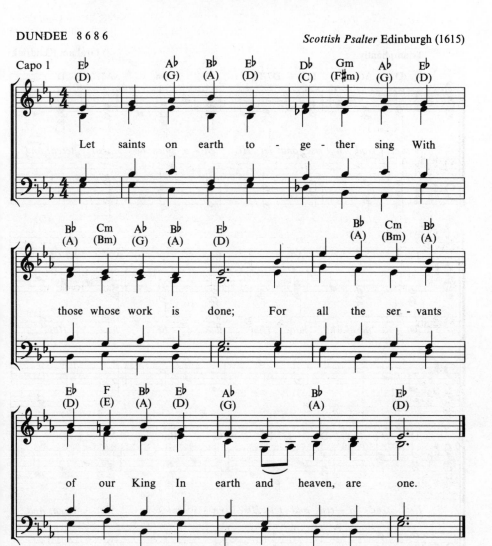

1 Let saints on earth together sing
With those whose work is done;
For all the servants of our King
In earth and heaven, are one.

2 One family, we live in Him,
One church above, beneath,
Though now divided by the stream,
The narrow stream of death.

3 One army of the living God,
To His command we bow;
Part of His host have crossed the flood
And part are crossing now.

4 But all unite in Christ their head,
And love to sing His praise:
Lord of the living and the dead,
Direct our earthly ways!

5 So shall we join our friends above
Who have obtained the prize;
And on the eagle wings of love
To joys celestial rise.

C. Wesley, 1707–88
© *in this version Jubilate Hymns*

467 Let God arise

Triumphantly

Graham Kendrick

Let God a-rise, and let His en-e-mies be scat-tered; And

let those who hate Him flee be-fore Him.

Let God a-rise, and let His en-e-mies be scat-tered; And

let those who hate Him flee a-way.

315

468 Let our praise to You be as incense

Brent Chambers

Worshipfully

Capo 1

Let our praise to You be as in - cense, Let our praise to You be as pil - lars of Your throne.

Let our praise to You be as in - cense, As we come be - fore You and wor - ship You a - lone.

As we see You in Your splen-dour, As we gaze up-on Your ma-jes-ty; As we join the hosts of an - gels, And pro - claim to - geth - er Your ho-li-ness. Let our Ho - ly, ho-ly, ho - ly, ho - ly is the Lord!

Repeat last line ad lib. increasing then decreasing in intensity

317

469 Let us acknowledge the Lord

HOSEA 6. 3.

Andy Silver

Let us ac - know - ledge the Lord,

Let us press on to ac - know - ledge Him, Let us ac -

know - ledge the Lord. Let us ac -

know - ledge Him As sure - ly as the

Let us acknowledge the Lord,
Let us press on to acknowledge Him,
Let us acknowledge the Lord.
Let us acknowledge Him
As surely as the sun rises,
He will appear, He will come to us
Like the winter rains,
Like the spring rains
That water the earth.

470 Let us break bread together

Calhoun melody
arr. Norman Warren

VERSION 1 (TRADITIONAL)

1 Let us break bread together on our knees,
  Let us break bread together on our knees:

  When I fall on my knees,
  With my face to the rising sun,
  O Lord, have mercy on me!

2 Let us drink wine together on our knees,
  Let us drink wine together on our knees:
  When I fall . . .

3 Let us praise God together on our knees,
  Let us praise God together on our knees:
  When I fall . . .

VERSION 2

1 Let us praise God together, let us praise;
  Let us praise God together all our days:
  He is faithful in all His ways,
  He is worthy of all our praise,
  His name be exalted on high!

2 Let us seek God together, let us pray;
  Let us seek His forgiveness as we pray:
  He will cleanse us from all sin,
  He will help us the fight to win,
  His name be exalted on high!

3 Let us serve God together, Him obey;
  Let our lives show His goodness through each day:
  Christ the Lord is the world's true light—
  Let us serve Him with all our might,
  His name be exalted on high!

J.E. Seddon, 1915–83
© *Mavis Seddon / Jubilate Hymns*

471 Let us with a gladsome mind

John Antes (1740–1811)
Melody from *Hymn Tunes of the United Brethren* (1824)
arr. John Bernard Wilkes (1785–1869)

MONKLAND 7 7.7 7

1 Let us with a gladsome mind
   Praise the Lord, for He is kind;

   For His mercies shall endure,
   Ever faithful, ever sure.

2 He, with all-commanding might,
   Filled the new-made world with light:
   For His mercies . . .

3 All things living He doth feed,
   His full hand supplies their need:
   For His mercies . . .

4 He His chosen race did bless
   In the wasteland wilderness:
   For His mercies . . .

5 He hath with a piteous eye
   Looked upon our misery:
   For His mercies . . .

6 Let us, then, with gladsome mind,
   Praise the Lord, For He is kind!
   For His mercies . . .

John Milton, 1608–74

322

472 Lift Jesus higher

Author unknown
arr. Phil Burt

Cheerfully

Lift Je-sus high - er, lift Je-sus high - er, Lift Him
up for the world to see._____ He said if I be lift - ed
up from the earth I will draw all men un-to me._____

Lift Jesus higher, lift Jesus higher,
Lift Him up for the world to see.
He said if I be lifted up from the earth
I will draw all men unto me.

Copyright control

323

473 Lift up your heads

Steven L. Fry

be pure and ho - ly, Giv - ing glo - ry

to the King of kings. kings.

Lift up your heads to the coming King.
Bow before Him and adore Him,
Sing to His majesty,
Let your praises be pure and holy,
Giving glory to the King of kings.

474 Living under the shadow of His wing

David J.Hadden
and Bob Silvester

Living under the shadow of His wing

We find security.

Standing in His presence we will bring

Our worship, worship,

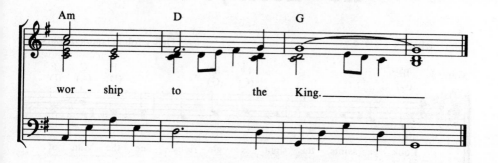

wor - ship to the King.

1 Living under the shadow of His wing
We find security.
Standing in His presence we will bring
Our worship, worship, worship to the King.

2 Bowed in adoration at His feet
We dwell in harmony.
Voices joined together that repeat,
Worthy, worthy, worthy is the Lamb.

3 Heart to heart embracing in His love
Reveals His purity.
Soaring in my spirit like a dove.
Holy, holy, holy is the Lord.

475 Look ye saints

TRIUMPH 8 7. 8 7. 8 7

Henry John Gauntlett (1805–76)

Look, ye saints, the sight is glorious! See the Man of Sorrows now, From the fight returned victorious, Ev'ry knee to Him shall bow: Crown Him! Crown Him! Crown Him! Crown Him! Crowns become the Victor's brow.

328

1 Look, ye saints, the sight is glorious!
  See the Man of Sorrows now,
  From the fight returned victorious,
  Every knee to Him shall bow:
  Crown Him! Crown Him!
  Crown Him! Crown Him!
  Crowns become the Victor's brow.

2 Crown the Saviour! angels, crown Him!
  Rich the trophies Jesus brings;
  In the seat of power enthrone Him,
  While the vault of heaven rings:
  Crown Him! Crown Him!
  Crown Him! Crown Him!
  Crown the Saviour King of kings!

3 Sinners in derision crowned Him,
  Mocking thus the Saviour's claim;
  Saints and angels crowd around Him,
  Own His title, praise His name:
  Crown Him! Crown Him!
  Crown Him! Crown Him!
  Spread abroad the Victor's fame.

4 Hark, those bursts of acclamation!
  Hark, those loud triumphant chords!
  Jesus takes the highest station:
  O what joy the sight affords!
  Crown Him! Crown Him!
  Crown Him! Crown Him!
  King of kings, and Lord of lords!

Thomas Kelly, 1769–1854

476 Lord, enthroned in heavenly splendour

ST. HELEN 8 7 8 7 8 7

G.C. Martin (1844–1916)

Lord en-throned in heaven-ly splen-dour, Glor-ious first born from the dead,

You a - lone our strong de - fend - er, Lift-ing up Your peo - ple's head:

Al - le - lu - ia, al - le - lu - ia, Je - sus, true and liv - ing bread!

2 Prince of life, for us now living,
By Your body souls are healed;
Prince of peace, Your pardon giving,
By Your blood our peace is sealed:
Alleluia, alleluia,
Word of God in flesh revealed.

3 Paschal Lamb! Your offering finished,
Once for all, when You were slain;
In its fulness undiminished
Shall for evermore remain:
Alleluia, alleluia,
Cleansing souls from every stain.

4 Great High Priest of our profession,
Through the veil You entered in,
By Your mighty intercession
Grace and mercy there to win:
Alleluia, alleluia,
Only sacrifice for sin.

5 Life-imparting heavenly manna,
Stricken rock, with streaming side;
Heaven and earth, with loud hosanna,
Worship You, the Lamb who died:
Alleluia, alleluia,
Risen, ascended, glorified!

G. Bourne, 1840–1925

330

477 Lord, I was blind

BODMIN 8 8 8 8 (LM)

A. Scott-Gatty (1847–1918)

1 Lord, I was blind; I could not see
In Your marred visage any grace:
But now the beauty of Your face
In radiant vision dawns on me.

2 Lord, I was deaf; I could not hear
The thrilling music of Your voice:
But now I hear You and rejoice,
And all Your spoken words are dear.

3 Lord, I was dumb; I could not speak
The grace and glory of Your name:
But now as touched with living flame
My lips will speak for Jesus' sake.

4 Lord, I was dead; I could not move
My lifeless soul from sin's dark grave:
But now the power of life You gave
Has raised me up to know Your love.

5 Lord, You have made the blind to see,
The deaf to hear, the dumb to speak,
The dead to live – and now I break
The chains of my captivity!

W.T. Matson (1833–1899)
© *in this version Jubilate Hymns*

331

478 Lord, it is eventide

CHRIST'S OWN PEACE Irregular

Words and music
H. Ernest Nichol (1862–1926)

Lord, it is ev-en-tide: the light of day is wan-ing; Far o'er the gold-en land earth's voi-ces faint and fall; Low-ly we pray to You for strength and love sus-tain-ing, Low-ly we ask of You Your

following verses overleaf

1 Lord, it is eventide: the light of day is waning;
  Far o'er the golden land earth's voices faint and fall;
  Lowly we pray to You for strength and love sustaining,
  Lowly we ask of You Your peace upon us all.
  O grant unto our souls –

    Light that grows not pale with day's decrease.
    Love that never can fail till life shall cease;
    Joy no trial can mar, Hope that shines afar.
    Faith serene as a star, and Christ's own peace.

2 Lord, it is eventide: we turn to You for healing,
  Like those of Galilee who came at close of day;
  Speak to our waiting souls, their hidden needs revealing;
  Touch us with hands divine that take our sin away.
  O grant unto our souls –
    Light that grows . . .

3 Saviour, You know of every trial and temptation,
  Know of the wilfulness and waywardness of youth,
  Help us to hold to You, our strength and our salvation,
  Help us to find in You the one eternal Truth.
  O grant unto our souls –
    Light that grows . . .

4 Lord, it is eventide: our hearts await Your giving,
  Wait for that peace divine that none can take away,
  Peace that shall lift our souls to loftier heights of living,
  Till we abide with You in everlasting day.
  O grant unto our souls –
    Light that grows . . .

479 Lord of creation

CHEDWORTH 10 11 11 11

John Barnard (b. 1948)

Lord of cre-a-tion, to You be all praise! Most
migh-ty Your work-ing, most won-drous Your ways! Your glo-ry and might are beyond us to tell, And yet in the heart of the hum-ble You dwell.

2 Lord of all power, I give to You my will,
In joyful obedience Your tasks to fulfil;
Your bondage is freedom, Your service is song,
And, held in Your keeping, my weakness is strong.

3 Lord of all wisdom, I give You my mind;
Rich truth that surpasses man's knowledge to find,
What eye has not seen and what ear has not heard
Is taught by Your Spirit and shines from Your word.

4 Lord of all bounty, I give You my heart;
I praise and adore You for all You impart –
Your love to inspire me, Your counsel to guide,
Your presence to cheer me, whatever betide.

5 Lord of all being, I give You my all;
For if I disown You I stumble and fall,
But, sworn in glad service Your word to obey,
I walk in Your freedom to the end of the way.

J.C. Winslow, 1882–1974
© Mrs. J. Tyrrell

335

480 Lord Jesus Christ

Words and Music by
P. Appleford

Capo 2

Lord Je-sus Christ, You have come to us,
You are one with us, Ma - ry's Son.
Clean-sing our souls from all their sin, Pour-ing Your love And
good - ness in, Je - sus, our love For You we sing,

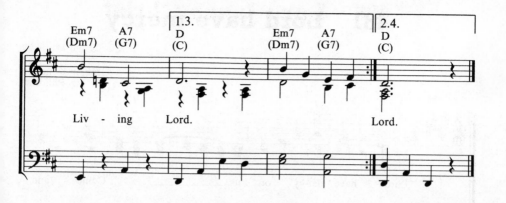

Liv - ing Lord.   Lord.

1 Lord Jesus Christ,
   You have come to us,
   You are one with us,
   Mary's Son.
   Cleansing our souls
   from all their sin,
   Pouring Your love
   And goodness in,
   Jesus, our love
   For You we sing,
   Living Lord.

2 Lord Jesus Christ,
   Now and every day,
   Teach us how to pray,
   Son of God.
   You have commanded
   Us to do
   This in remembrance,
   Lord, of You:
   Into our lives
   Your power breaks through,
   Living Lord.

3 Lord Jesus Christ,
   You have come to us,
   Born as one of us,
   Mary's Son.
   Led out to die
   On Calvary,
   Risen from death
   To set us free,
   Living Lord Jesus,
   Help us see
   You are Lord.

4 Lord Jesus Christ,
   I would come to You,
   Live my life for You,
   Son of God.
   All Your commands
   I know are true,
   Your many gifts
   Will make me new,
   Into my life
   Your power breaks through,
   Living Lord.

481 Lord have mercy

Graham Kendrick
arr. Phil Burt

Lord have mer-cy on us,_____ Come and

heal our land,_____ Cleanse with Your fire,

Heal with Your touch, Hum-bly we bow and call up-on_You

now, O_ Lord,_____ have mer-cy_____ on_

482 Lord have mercy

Lord have mercy on us,
Come and heal our land,
Cleanse with Your fire,
Heal with Your touch,
Humbly we bow and call upon You now,
O Lord, have mercy on us.
O Lord, have mercy on us.

482   Lord have mercy

Gerald Markland
arr. Roland Fudge

Lord have mer - cy, Lord have mer - cy, Lord have mer - cy on__ Your peo-ple.__ peo-ple.__

1 Give me the heart of stone with -
2 You'll find Me near the bro - ken -

in you,— And I'll give
heart-ed,— Those crushed in

you a heart of flesh. Clean wa - ter
spi - rit I will save. So turn to

mp

I will use to cleanse all your wounds. My Spi - rit
Me— for My par - don is great, My word will

D.C. ⊕ *CODA*

I give to you.————
heal all your wounds.————

peo-ple.————————

341

483 Lord make me a mountain

Words and music
Paul Field

Lord make me a moun - tain stand-ing tall for You,___ Strong and free and ho - ly, in ev-ery-thing I do.___ Lord, make me a ri - ver of wa-ter pure and sweet, Lord, make me the

ser - vant   of ev-ery-one   I   meet.   meet.

1 Lord make me a mountain standing tall for You,
  Strong and free and holy, in everything I do.
  Lord, make me a river of water pure and sweet,
  Lord, make me the servant of everyone I meet.

2 Lord make me a candle with Your light,
  Steadfastly unflickering, standing for the right,
  Lord make me a fire burning strong for You,
  Lord, make me be humble in everything I do.

3 Lord make me a mountain, strong and tall for You,
  Lord make me a fountain of water clear and new,
  Lord make me a shepherd that I may feed Your sheep,
  Lord make me the servant of everyone I meet.

484 Lord of our life

CLOISTERS 11 11 11. 5

Joseph Barnby (1838–96)

Lord of our life, and God of our sal - va - tion,
Star of our night, and Hope of ev - 'ry
na - tion, Hear and re - ceive Thy church - 's sup - pli -
ca - tion, Lord God Al - migh - ty!

1 Lord of our life, and God of our salvation,
Star of our night, and Hope of every nation,
Hear and receive Thy church's supplication,
Lord God Almighty!

2 Lord, Thou canst help when earthly armour faileth,
Lord, Thou canst save when sin itself assaileth,
Lord, o'er Thy church nor death nor hell prevaileth;
Grant us Thy peace, Lord.

3 Peace in our hearts our evil thoughts assuaging,
Peace in Thy church when disputes are engaging,
Peace when the world its busy war is waging,
Calm Thy foes' raging.

4 Grant us Thy help till backward they are driven,
Grant them Thy truth, that they may be forgiven,
Grant peace on earth, and after we have striven,
Peace in Thy heaven.

Philip Pusey, 1799–1855
based on Matthaus Apelles von Löwenstern, 1594–1648

485 Lord of the Church

LONDONDERRY AIR Irregular

Irish traditional melody
arr. Roland Fudge

Lord of the church, we pray for our re-new-ing:___Christ o-ver all, our un-di-vi-ded aim;___Fire of the Spi-rit, burn for our en-du-ing,___Wind of the Spi-rit, fan the liv-ing flame!___We turn to Christ a-mid our fear and fail-ing,___The will that lacks the cour-age to be

free,_____ The wea-ry la - bours, all but un - a - vail - ing,____ To bring us near-er what a church___should be.____

1 Lord of the church, we pray for our renewing:
   Christ over all, our undivided aim;
   Fire of the Spirit, burn for our enduing,
   Wind of the Spirit, fan the living flame!
   We turn to Christ amid our fear and failing,
   The will that lacks the courage to be free,
   The weary labours, all but unavailing,
   To bring us nearer what a church should be.

2 Lord of the church, we seek a Father's blessing,
   A true repentance and a faith restored,
   A swift obedience and a new possessing,
   Filled with the Holy Spirit of the Lord!
   We turn to Christ from all our restless striving,
   Unnumbered voices with a single prayer –
   The living water for our souls' reviving,
   In Christ to live, and love and serve and care.

3 Lord of the church, we long for our uniting,
   True to one calling, by one vision stirred;
   One cross proclaiming and one creed reciting,
   One in the truth of Jesus and His word!
   So lead us on, till toil and trouble ended,
   One church triumphant one new song shall sing,
   To praise His glory, risen and ascended,
   Christ over all, the everlasting King!

© *Timothy Dudley-Smith, b. 1926*

486 Lord, Thy word abideth

Melody abridged by
William Henry Monk (1823–89) from *Ave Hierarchia*,
Michael Weisse (1480–1534)

RAVENSHAW 6 6. 6 6

1 Lord, Thy Word abideth,
And our footsteps guideth;
Who its truth believeth
Light and joy receiveth.

2 Who can tell the pleasure,
Who recount the treasure,
By Thy Word imparted
To the simple-hearted?

3 When the storms are o'er us,
And dark clouds before us,
Then its light directeth,
And our way protecteth.

4 When our foes are near us,
Then Thy Word doth cheer us,
Word of consolation,
Message of salvation.

5 Word of mercy, giving
Succour to the living;
Word of life, supplying
Comfort to the dying.

6 O that we discerning
Its most holy learning,
Lord, may love and fear Thee,
Evermore be near Thee!

Henry Williams Baker, 1821–77

487　Lord, You are more precious

Lord, You are more pre-cious than sil - ver,
Lord, You are more cost - ly than gold.
Lord, You are more beau - ti - ful__ than dia-monds, And
no-thing I de-sire com-pares with You.

488 Loved with everlasting love

EVERLASTING LOVE 7 7. 7 7. D

James Mountain (1843–1933)

Loved with ev-er-last-ing love, Led by grace that love to know, Spi-rit, breath-ing from a-bove, You have taught me it is so. O this full and per-fect peace! O this pres-ence so di-vine! In a

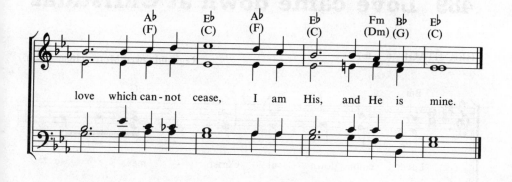

love which can‑not cease, I am His, and He is mine.

1 Loved with everlasting love,
  Led by grace that love to know,
  Spirit, breathing from above,
  You have taught me it is so.
  O this full and perfect peace!
  O this presence so divine!
  In a love which cannot cease,
  I am His, and He is mine.

2 Heaven above is softer blue,
  Earth around is sweeter green;
  Something lives in every hue
  Christless eyes have never seen:
  Birds with gladder songs o'er‑flow,
  Flowers with deeper beauties shine,
  Since I know, as now I know,
  I am His, and He is mine.

3 His for ever, only His;
  Who the Lord and me shall part?
  Ah, with what a rest of bliss
  Christ can fill the loving heart!
  Heaven and earth may fade and flee;
  First‑born light in gloom decline;
  But while God and I shall be,
  I am His, and He is mine.

George Wade Robinson, 1838–77

489 Love came down at Christmas

HERMITAGE 6 7. 6 7

Reginald Owen Morris (1886–1948)

Love came down at Christ - mas,

Love all love - ly, Love Di - vine; Love was born__ at

Christ - mas, Star and an - gels gave__ the sign.

1 Love came down at Christmas,
   Love all lovely, Love Divine;
   Love was born at Christmas,
   Star and angels gave the sign.

2 Worship we the God-head,
   Love Incarnate, Love Divine;
   Worship we our Jesus:
   But where-with for sacred sign?

3 Love shall be our token,
   Love be yours and love be mine,
   Love to God and all men,
   Love for plea and gift and sign.

Christina Georgina Rossetti, 1830–94

490 May the Lord bless you

Gently

Susie Hare

Capo 5

May the Lord bless you and keep you,

Make His face to shine up-on you And be gra-cious un - to you.

May the Lord lift up the light Of His

coun - te-nance up - on you And give you peace.

491 Make way, make way

Graham Kendrick

Make way, make way, for Christ the King In splen - dour ar -

rives. Fling wide the gates and wel - come Him In -

to your lives. *Make way! (Make way!) Make way! (Make way!) For the*

King of kings. (For the King of kings.) Make way! (Make way!) Make

way! (Make way!) And__ let His king - dom in.

1 Make way, make way, for Christ the King
In splendour arrives.
Fling wide the gates and welcome Him
Into your lives.

Make way! Make way!
For the King of kings.
Make way! Make way!
And let His kingdom in.

2 He comes the broken hearts to heal,
The prisoners to free;
The deaf shall hear, the lame shall dance,
The blind shall see.
Make way! . . .

3 And those who mourn with heavy hearts,
Who weep and sigh,
With laughter, joy and royal crown
He'll beautify.
Make way! . . .

4 We call You now to worship Him
As Lord of all.
To have no gods before Him,
Their thrones must fall.
Make way! . . .

492 May the fragrance

Graham Kendrick

356

1 May the fragrance of Jesus fill this place, *(men)*
  May the fragrance of Jesus fill this place, *(ladies)*
  May the fragrance of Jesus fill this place, *(men)*
  Lovely fragrance of Jesus *(ladies)*
  Rising from the sacrifice
  Of lives laid down in adoration. ⎤ *(all)*

2 May the glory of Jesus fill His church, *(men)*
  May the glory of Jesus fill His church, *(ladies)*
  May the glory of Jesus fill His church, *(men)*
  Radiant glory of Jesus *(ladies)*
  Shining from our faces
  As we gaze in adoration. ⎤ *(all)*

3 May the beauty of Jesus fill my life, *(men)*
  May the beauty of Jesus fill my life, *(ladies)*
  May the beauty of Jesus fill my life, *(men)*
  Perfect beauty of Jesus *(ladies)*
  Fill my thoughts, my words, my deeds,
  My all I give in adoration. ⎤ *(all – twice)*

493 Meekness and majesty

Graham Kendrick

Meek-ness and ma-jes-ty, Man-hood and De-i-ty,

In per-fect har-mo-ny, The man who is God.

Lord of e-ter-ni-ty Dwells in hu-man-i-ty, Kneels in hu-

mil-i-ty___ And___ wash-es our feet. *Oh, what a*

my-ste-ry, *Meek-ness and ma-jes-ty,*___ *Bow down and*

wor - ship,_____ For this is your God,_____

This is your God._____

God._____

This is your God._____

2 Father's pure radiance,
   Perfect in innocence,
   Yet learns obedience
   To death on a cross.
   Suffering to give us life,
   Conquering through sacrifice;
   And as they crucify
   Prays Father forgive.
     Oh, what a . . .

3 Wisdom unsearchable,
   God the invisible;
   Love indestructable
   In frailty appears.
   Lord of infinity
   Stooping so tenderly
   Lifts our humanity
   To the heights of His throne.
     Oh, what a . . .

494 My heart overflows

Carolyn Govier

With warmth

My heart ov-er-flows with a good-ly__ theme, I will add-ress my ver-ses to the King;__ My heart ov-er-flows with__ praise to my God, I'll give Him the love of my heart.____

last time **to Coda** ⊕

__For He is Lord of all the earth, He's ri-sen a-bove, He's

seat-ed at God's right hand,_____ And from Him and

through Him and to Him are all things, That His glo-ry might fill__ the

D.C. CODA

land._____ heart._____

My heart overflows with a goodly theme,
I will address my verses to the King;
My heart overflows with praise to my God,
I'll give Him the love of my heart.

1 For He is Lord of all the earth, He's risen above,
  He's seated at God's right hand,
  And from Him and through Him and to Him are all things,
  That His glory might fill the land.
    My heart overflows . . .

2 For He has chosen Mount Zion as His resting place,
  He says, 'Here will I dwell,
  I will abundantly bless and satisfy,
  And her saints will shout for joy.
    My heart overflows . . .

3 'Lift up your eyes round about and see,
  Your heart shall thrill and rejoice,
  For the abundance of the nations is coming to you,
  I am glorifying My house.'
    My heart overflows . . .

361

495   My life is Yours

Words and music
Ruth Hooke

Capo 1

My life is Yours, ___ O Lord,

My life is Yours, O Lord, ___ So

do as You will, Do what is pleas-ing to You ___

___ For my ___ life ___ be-longs to You. ___

496 My Lord, He is the fairest of the fair

Joan Parsons

With swing

My Lord, He is the fair-est of the fair, He is the li-ly of the val - ley, The bright and mor-ning star, His love is writ-ten deep with-in my heart, He is the ne-ver end-ing foun - tain Of ev-er-last-ing

My Lord, He is the fairest of the fair,
He is the lily of the valley,
The bright and morning star,
His love is written deep within my heart,
He is the never ending fountain
Of everlasting life.
And He lives, He lives,
He lives, He lives in me.

497 My peace

Keith Routledge

Gently

My— peace——— I give———un-to you,———

It's a peace——that the world——can-not give,———

It's a peace——that the world——can-not un - der -

stand. Peace to know, peace to

live._____ My peace I give_____ un-to you._____

1 My peace I give unto you,
  It's a peace that the world cannot give,
  It's a peace that the world cannot understand.
  Peace to know, peace to live.
  My peace I give unto you.

2 My joy I give unto you,
  It's a joy that the world cannot give,
  It's a joy that the world cannot understand.
  Joy to know, joy to live.
  My joy I give unto you.

3 My love I give unto you,
  It's a love that the world cannot give,
  It's a love that the world cannot understand.
  Love to know, love to live.
  My love I give unto you.

498 My God, how wonderful

WESTMINSTER C.M.

James Turle (1802–82)

My God, how won-der-ful You are, Your
ma-jes-ty how bright! How beau-ti-ful Your
mer-cy seat, In depths of burn-ing light!

1 My God, how wonderful You are,
   Your majesty how bright!
   How beautiful Your mercy seat,
   In depths of burning light!

2 In awe I glimpse eternity,
   O everlasting Lord,
   By angels worshipped day and night,
   Incessantly adored!

3 O how I love You, Living God,
   Who my heart's longing hears,
   And worship You with certain hope
   And penitential tears!

4 Yes I may love You, O my Lord,
   Almighty King of Kings,
   For You have stooped to live in me,
   With joy my heart now sings.

5 How wonderful, how beautiful,
   Your loving face must be,
   Your endless wisdom, boundless power,
   And awesome purity!

Frederick William Faber, 1814–63
Altered © 1987 Horrobin/Leavers

499 Name of all majesty

MAJESTAS 6 6 5 5 6 6 6 4

Michael Baughen (b. 1930)
arr. Noël Tredinnick (b. 1949)

1 Name of all majesty,
Fathomless mystery,
King of the ages
By angels adored;
Power and authority,
Splendour and dignity,
Bow to His mastery –
Jesus is Lord!

2 Child of our destiny,
God from eternity,
Love of the Father
On sinners outpoured;
See now what God has done
Sending His only Son,
Christ the belovèd One –
Jesus is Lord!

3 Saviour of Calvary,
Costliest victory,
Darkness defeated
And Eden restored –
Born as a man to die,
Nailed to a cross on high,
Cold in the grave to lie –
Jesus is Lord!

4 Source of all sovereignty,
Light, immortality,
Life everlasting
And heaven assured;
So with the ransomed, we
Praise Him eternally,
Christ in His majesty –
Jesus is Lord!

500   No weapon formed

Tom Dowell

Fast march

No wea-pon formed, or ar-my or king,— Shall be
ab-le to stand— A-gainst the Lord and His A-noint-ed.
All prin-ci-pa-li-ties and pow-ers————— Shall
crum-ble be-fore the Lord; And men's hearts shall

No weapon formed, or army or king,
Shall be able to stand
Against the Lord and His Anointed.
All principalities and powers
Shall crumble before the Lord;
And men's hearts shall be released,
And they shall come unto the Lord.
No weapon form'd, or army or king,
Shall be able to stand
Against the Lord and His Anointed.

501 Now I have found the ground

ANCHOR 88.88.88

Alfred Beer

Now I have found the ground where - in Sure
my soul's an - chor may re - main -
The wounds of Je - sus, for my sin Be -
fore the world's foun - da - tion slain;

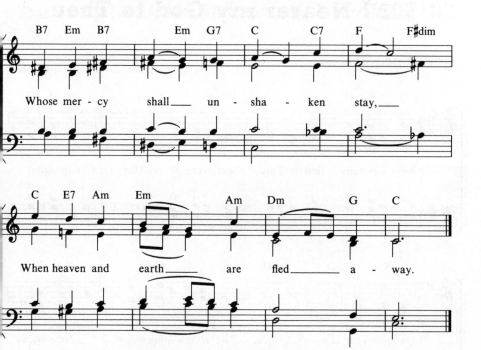

Whose mer - cy shall___ un - sha - ken stay,___

When heaven and earth___ are fled___ a - way.

1 Now I have found the ground wherein
  Sure my soul's anchor may remain –
  The wounds of Jesus, for my sin
  Before the world's foundation slain;
  Whose mercy shall unshaken stay,
  When heaven and earth are fled away.

2 Father, Your everlasting grace
  Our human thought surpassing far,
  Your heart still melts with tenderness,
  Your arms of love still open are
  Returning sinners will receive,
  Eternal life as they believe.

3 Your love, eternal hope, no less,
  My sins consumed at Calvary!
  Covered is my unrighteousness,
  Nor spot of guilt remains on me,
  While Jesu's blood through earth and skies
  Mercy, free, boundless mercy! cries.

4 Though waves and storms go o'er my head,
  Though strength, and health, and friends be gone,
  Though joys be withered all and dead,
  Though every comfort be withdrawn,
  On this my steadfast soul relies—
  Father, Your mercy never dies!

5 Fixed on this ground will I remain,
  Though my heart fail and flesh decay;
  This anchor shall my soul sustain,
  When earth's foundations melt away:
  Mercy's full power I then shall prove,
  Loved with an everlasting love.

Johann Andreas Rothe, 1688–1758
tr. John Wesley, 1703–91
Altered © 1987 Horrobin/Leavers

502 Nearer my God to Thee

PROPIOR DEO 64.64.664

Arthur S. Sullivan (1842–1900)

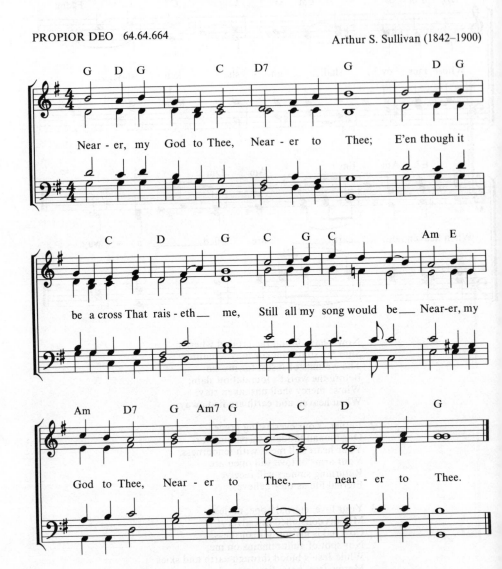

Near - er, my God to Thee, Near - er to Thee; E'en though it
be a cross That rais - eth___ me, Still all my song would be___ Near-er, my
God to Thee, Near - er to Thee,___ near - er to Thee.

2 Though, like the wanderer,
  The sun gone down,
  Darkness be over me,
  My rest a stone,
  Yet in my dreams I'd be
  Nearer, my God to Thee,
  Nearer to Thee, nearer to Thee.

3 There let the way appear,
  Steps up to heaven;
  All that Thou sendest me,
  In mercy given;
  Angels to beckon me
  Nearer, my God to Thee,
  Nearer to Thee, nearer to Thee.

4 Then, with my waking thoughts
  Bright with Thy praise,
  Out of my stony griefs
  Bethel I'll raise;
  So by my woes to be
  Nearer, my God to Thee,
  Nearer to Thee, nearer to Thee.

5 Or, if on joyful wing
  Cleaving the sky,
  Sun, moon, and stars forgot,
  Upwards I fly,
  Still all my song shall be,
  Nearer, my God to Thee,
  Nearer to Thee, nearer to Thee.

Sarah Flower Adams, 1805–48

374

503 O God our help

ST. ANNE C.M.

William Croft (1678–1727)

O God, our help in a - ges past, Our

hope for years to come, Our shel - ter from the

stor - my blast, And our e - ter - nal home.

1 O God, our help in ages past,
Our hope for years to come,
Our shelter from the stormy blast,
And our eternal home.

2 Under the shadow of Your throne
Your saints have dwelt secure;
Sufficient is Your arm alone,
And our defence is sure.

3 Before the hills in order stood,
Or earth received her frame,
From everlasting You are God,
To endless years the same.

4 A thousand ages in Your sight
Are like an evening gone,
Short as the watch that ends the night
Before the rising sun.

5 Time, like an ever-rolling stream,
Bears all its sons away;
They fly forgotten, as a dream
Dies with the dawning day.

6 O God, our help in ages past,
Our hope for years to come,
Be our defence while life shall last,
And our eternal home.

Isaac Watts, 1674–1748

504 O come, all you faithful

ADESTE FIDELES Irreg.

Eighteenth century melody,
probably by J.F. Wade (1711–86)
Harmonised mainly by W.H. Monk (1823–89)

O come, all you faith-ful, Joy-ful and tri-um-phant, O

come now, O come— now to Beth-le-hem;

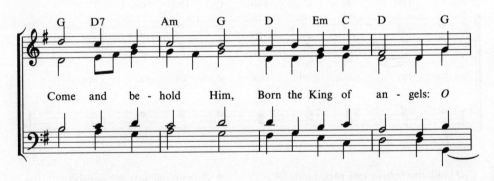

Come and be-hold Him, Born the King of an-gels: O

come, let us a-dore Him, O come, let us a-dore Him, O

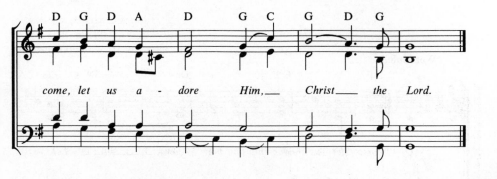

come, let us a-dore Him,— Christ— the Lord.

1 O come, all you faithful,
   Joyful and triumphant,
   O come now, O come now to Bethlehem;
   Come and behold Him,
   Born the King of angels:

   O come, let us adore Him,
   O come, let us adore Him,
   O come, let us adore Him,
   Christ the Lord.

2 True God of true God,
   Light of light eternal,
   He, who abhors not the virgin's womb;
   Son of the Father,
   Begotten not created:
   O come, let us adore Him . . .

3 Sing like the angels,
   Sing in exultation,
   Sing with the citizens of heaven above,
   'Glory to God,
   Glory in the highest':
   O come, let us adore Him . . .

ON CHRISTMAS DAY SING WORDS IN ITALICS
4 Yes, Lord, we greet You,
   Born that *(this)* happy morning,
   Jesus, to you be glory given;
   Word of the Father,
   Then *(Now)* in flesh appearing:
   O come, let us adore Him . . .

Latin, 18th century
tr. Frederick Oakley, 1802–80
Altered © 1986 Horrobin/Leavers

505 O come let us worship

Iain Anderson

O come let us wor-ship and bow down,_____ Let us
kneel be - fore the Lord our King._____ Let us whis - per His
name, won - der-ful name, Je - sus our Lord and
King._____ O Je - sus our Lord and King._____

For He is Lord of all the earth,_____ His

glo - ry out - shines the sun._____ See Him clothed in His

robes of right-eous - ness, God's be - lov - ed

D.C. al Coda

Son._____

✟ *CODA*

Je-sus our Lord and King._____

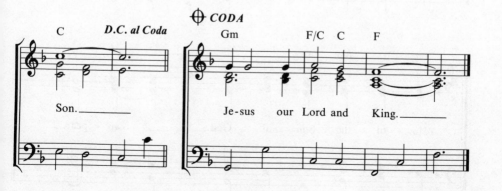

506 O come, O come, Emmanuel

VENI IMMANUEL 8 8. 8 8. 8 8

Hymnal Noted (1854)

In free rhythm. Unison

O come, O come, Em - man - u - el,
And ran - som cap - tive Is - ra - el,
That mourns in lone - ly ex - ile here
Un - til the Son of God ap - pear.

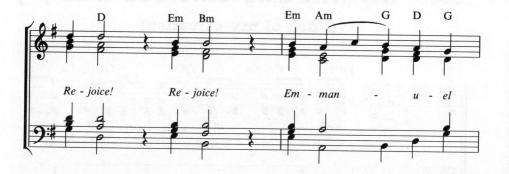

Re - joice!   Re - joice!   Em - man - u - el

Shall   come   to   thee,   O   Is - ra - el.

1 O come, O come, Emmanuel,
   And ransom captive Israel,
   That mourns in lonely exile here
   Until the Son of God appear.

   Rejoice! Rejoice! Emmanuel
   Shall come to thee, O Israel.

2 O come, O come, Thou Lord of might,
   Who to Thy tribes, on Sinai's height,
   In ancient times didst give the law
   In cloud, and majesty, and awe.
   Rejoice! Rejoice! . . .

3 O come, Thou Rod of Jesse, free
   Thine own from Satan's tyranny;
   From depths of hell Thy people save,
   And give them victory o'er the grave.
   Rejoice! Rejoice! . . .

4 O come, Thou Day-spring, come and cheer
   Our spirits by Thine advent here;
   Disperse the gloomy clouds of night,
   And death's dark shadows put to flight.
   Rejoice! Rejoice! . . .

5 O come, Thou Key of David, come,
   And open wide our heavenly home;
   Make safe the way that leads on high,
   And close the path to misery.
   Rejoice! Rejoice! . . .

From Antiphons in 'Latin Breviary', 12th century
tr. John Mason Neale, 1818–66

507 O I will sing unto You with joy

(Rock of my salvation)

Joyfully

Shona Sauni

O, I will sing un-to You with joy,___ O___ Lord, For You're the rock of my sal-va-tion, Come be-fore You with thanks-giv-ing___ And ex-tol___ You with a___ song. ___ For You're the great-est___ King___ a-bove all___ else,___ You hold the depths of the earth in Your hand. _

508 O let the Son of God enfold you

(Spirit song)

John Wimber

Worshipfully

Capo 2

1. O let the Son of God en-fold you With His Spi-rit and His
(2.) sing this song with glad-ness As your hearts are filled with

love, Let Him fill your heart and sat-is-fy your
joy, Lift your hands in sweet sur-ren-der to His

soul. O let Him have the things that
name. O give Him all your tears and

hold you, And His Spi-rit like a dove Will de-
sad-ness, Give Him all your years of pain, And you'll

509(i)   O little town of Bethlehem

CHRISTMAS CAROL C.M.D.

Walford Davies (1869–1941)

all __ the __ years Are met _____ in you to - night.

1 O little town of Bethlehem,
   How still we see you lie!
   Above your deep and dreamless sleep
   The silent stars go by:
   Yet in your dark streets shining
   Is everlasting Light;
   The hopes and fears of all the years
   Are met in you tonight.

2 For Christ is born of Mary;
   And, gathered all above
   While mortals sleep, the angels keep
   Their watch of wondering love.
   O morning stars, together
   Proclaim the holy birth,
   And praises sing to God the King,
   And peace to men on earth.

3 How silently, how silently,
   The wondrous gift is given!
   So God imparts to human hearts
   The blessings of His heaven.
   No ear may hear His coming;
   But in this world of sin,
   Where meek souls will receive Him, still
   The dear Christ enters in.

4 O holy child of Bethlehem,
   Descend to us, we pray;
   Cast out our sin, and enter in;
   Be born in us today.
   We hear the Christmas angels
   The great glad tidings tell;
   O come to us, abide with us,
   Our Lord Immanuel.

Phillips Brooks, 1835–93

509(ii)   O little town of Bethlehem

English traditional melody
arr. Ralph Vaughan Williams (1872–1958)

FOREST GREEN 8 6 8 6 D (DCM)

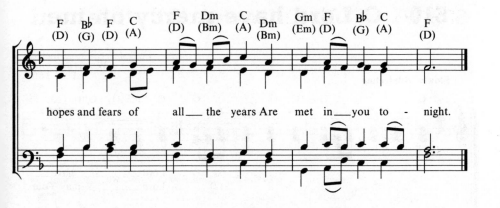

hopes and fears of all___ the years Are met in___you to - night.

1 O little town of Bethlehem,
How still we see you lie!
Above your deep and dreamless sleep
The silent stars go by:
Yet in your dark streets shining
Is everlasting Light;
The hopes and fears of all the years
Are met in you tonight.

2 For Christ is born of Mary;
And, gathered all above
While mortals sleep, the angels keep
Their watch of wondering love.
O morning stars, together
Proclaim the holy birth,
And praises sing to God the King,
And peace to men on earth.

3 How silently, how silently,
The wondrous gift is given!
So God imparts to human hearts
The blessings of His heaven.
No ear may hear His coming;
But in this world of sin,
Where meek souls will receive Him, still
The dear Christ enters in.

4 O holy child of Bethlehem,
Descend to us, we pray;
Cast out our sin, and enter in;
Be born in us today.
We hear the Christmas angels
The great glad tidings tell;
O come to us, abide with us,
Our Lord Immanuel.

Phillips Brooks, 1835–93

510 O Lord have mercy on me

Words and music
Carl Tuttle

Slowly with feeling

1 O Lord_____ have__
(2) Lord_____ may Your

mer - cy on me,
love and Your grace
and
pro -

heal__ me.   O__ Lord_____ have__
tect__ me.   O__ Lord_____ may Your

mer - cy on me,   and free me.
ways and Your truth   dir - ect__me.

Place my feet up-on a ___ rock, Put a new song in my ___

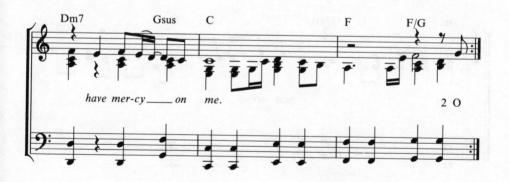

heart, in my heart, _____ O Lord

have mer-cy ___ on me. 2 O

Place my feet up-on a ___ rock, Put a new song in my ___

heart,   in my   heart,_____ O   Lord

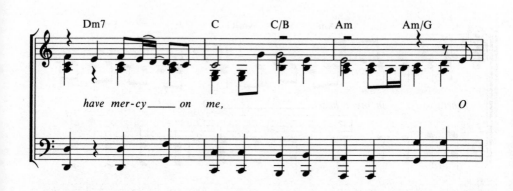

have mer-cy_____ on   me,   O

Lord   have mer-cy_____ on   me,

on__ me.

511　O Lord most Holy God

Worshipfully

Wendy Churchill

O Lord most Ho - ly God, Great are Your pur - po-ses,

Great is Your will for us, Great is Your love.

And we re - joice in You, And we will sing to You,

O Fa - ther have Your way, Your will be done.

1 O Lord most Holy God,
Great are Your purposes,
Great is Your will for us,
Great is Your love.
And we rejoice in You,
And we will sing to You,
O Father have Your way,
Your will be done.

2 For You are building
A temple without hands,
A city without walls
Enclosed by fire.
A place for You to dwell,
Built out of living stones,
Shaped by a Father's hand
And joined in love.

512 O Lord our God

(We will magnify)

Phil Lawson Johnston

O Lord our God,___ how ma-jest - ic is Your___ name,_____ The earth is filled with Your glo - ry.___

O Lord our God,___ You are robed in ma-jes - ty,_____ You've set Your glo-ry a-bove the hea - vens. *We will mag - ni - fy,_____ we will mag - ni - fy___*

The Lord en-throned in Zi - on. We will mag - ni-fy,_____ we will mag - ni-fy_____ The Lord en - throned in Zi - on.

1 O Lord our God, how majestic is Your name,
The earth is filled with Your glory.
O Lord our God, You are robed in majesty,
You've set Your glory above the heavens.

We will magnify, we will magnify
The Lord enthroned in Zion.
We will magnify, we will magnify
The Lord enthroned in Zion.

2 O Lord our God, You have established a throne,
You reign in righteousness and splendour.
O Lord our God, the skies are ringing with Your praise,
Soon those on earth will come to worship.
We will magnify . . .

3 O Lord our God, the world was made at Your command,
In You all things now hold together.
Now to Him who sits on the throne and to the Lamb,
Be praise and glory and power for ever.
We will magnify . . .

513 O Lord, You are my light

Copyright © 1983 Thankyou Music, P.O. Box 75, Eastbourne BN23 6NW
Used by permission

in Your love, You've lift-ed me up, placed my feet on a rock. __

I will shout for joy in the house of God. _____ O

O Lord, You are my light,
O Lord, You are my salvation.
You have delivered me from all my fear,
For You are the defence of my life.

For my life is hidden with Christ in God.
You have concealed me in Your love,
You've lifted me up, placed my feet on a rock.
I will shout for joy in the house of God.

514   O Lord, You're beautiful

Keith Green

do - ing well,___ help me to ne - ver seek a crown,___

___ For my re - ward is giv - ing glo - ry to

D.C. al Fine

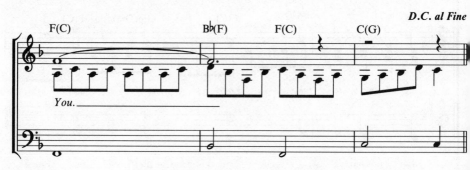

You.___

1 O Lord, You're beautiful,
   Your face is all I seek,
   For When Your eyes are on this child,
   Your grace abounds to me.

2 O Lord, please light the fire
   That once burned bright and clear,
   Replace the lamp of my first love
   That burns with holy fear!

   I want to take Your word and shine it all around,
   But first help me just to live it Lord!
   And when I'm doing well,
   help me to never seek a crown,
   For my reward is giving glory to You.

3 O Lord You're beautiful,
   Your face is all I seek,
   For when Your eyes are on this child,
   Your grace abounds to me.

515   O love of God

MARTHAM L.M.

J.H. Maunder (1858–1920)

1 O love of God, how strong and true!
Eternal and yet ever new;
Uncomprehended and unbought,
Beyond all knowledge and all thought.

2 O heavenly love, how precious still,
In days of weariness and ill,
In nights of pain and helplessness,
To heal, to comfort, and to bless!

3 O wide-embracing, wondrous love,
We see You in the sky above;
We see You in the earth below,
In seas that swell and streams that flow.

4 We see You best in Him who came
To bear for us the cross of shame,
Sent by the Father from on high,
Our life to live, our death to die.

5 We see Your power to bless and save
E'en in the darkness of the grave;
Still more in resurrection-light,
We see the fulness of Your might.

6 O love of God, our shield and stay
Through all the perils of our way;
Eternal love, in You we rest,
For ever safe, for ever blessed!

Horatius Bonar, 1808–89

516 O Lord, You've done great things

Carolyn Govier

I will sing prais - es un - to You and re-mem-ber Your good - ness,_____ My past is for - giv - en_____ and now I have life,_____ You crown me with stead - fast love and ten - der mer - cy,_____ I'll do Your will_____ and bless You, O Lord.

517 O Lord Your tenderness

Graham Kendrick
arr. Phil Burt

O Lord, Your ten-der-ness— Melt-ing all my
bit-ter-ness, O Lord, I re-ceive Your love,_____
— O Lord, Your love-li-ness Chang-ing all my
ug-li-ness, O Lord, I re-ceive Your love,_____

O Lord, Your tenderness
Melting all my bitterness,
O Lord, I receive Your love,
O Lord, Your loveliness
Changing all my ugliness,
O Lord, I receive Your love,
O Lord, I receive Your love,
O Lord, I receive Your love.

518 O my Saviour, lifted

DERBY 6 5. 6 5   Friedrich Filitz (1804–76)

1 O my Saviour, lifted
  From the earth for me,
  Draw me, in Thy mercy,
  Nearer unto Thee.

2 Lift my earth-bound longings,
  Fix them, Lord above;
  Draw me with the magnet
  Of Thy mighty love.

3 And I come, Lord Jesus;
  Dare I turn away?
  No! Thy love hath conquered,
  And I come today.

4 Bringing all my burdens,
  Sorrow, sin, and care;
  At Thy feet I lay them,
  And I leave them there.

William Walsham How, 1823–97

519 O praise ye the Lord!

HOUGHTON 5 5. 5 5. 6 5. 6 5

Henry John Gauntlett (1805–76)

1 O praise ye the Lord!
Praise Him in the height;
Rejoice in His Word,
Ye angels of light;
Ye heavens adore Him
By Whom ye were made,
And worship before Him,
In brightness arrayed.

2 O praise ye the Lord!
Praise Him upon earth,
In tuneful accord,
Ye sons of new birth;
Praise Him Who has brought you
His grace from above,
Praise Him Who has taught you
To sing of His love.

3 O praise ye the Lord!
All things that give sound;
Each jubilant chord,
Re-echo around;
Loud organs, His glory
Forth tell in deep tone,
And sweet harp, the story
Of what He has done.

4 O praise ye the Lord!
Thanksgiving and song
To Him be outpoured
All ages along;
For love in creation,
For heaven restored,
For grace of salvation,
O praise ye the Lord!

Henry Williams Baker, 1821–77

520 O perfect Love

O PERFECT LOVE 11 10. 11 10

Joseph Barnby (1838–96)

O perfect Love, all human thought transcending, Lowly we kneel in
prayer before Your throne, That theirs may be the
love which knows no ending, Whom You for

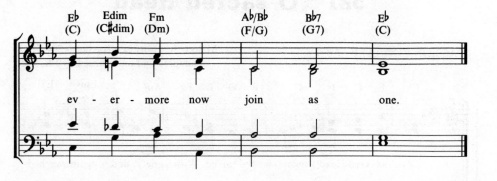

ev - er - more now join as one.

1 O perfect Love, all human thought transcending,
  Lowly we kneel in prayer before Your throne,
  That theirs may be the love which knows no ending,
  Whom You for evermore now join as one.

2 O perfect Life, be now their full assurance
  Of tender charity and steadfast faith,
  Of patient hope, and quiet, brave endurance,
  With child-like trust that fears nor pain nor death.

3 Grant them the joy which brightens earthly sorrow,
  Grant them the peace which calms all earthly strife;
  And to life's day the glorious unknown morrow
  That dawns upon eternal love and life.

Dorothy Frances Gurney, 1858–1932

521 O sacred Head

PASSION CHORALE 7 6. 7 6. D

Melody by Hans Leo Hassler (1564–1612)
adapted and harmonised by J.S. Bach

O sa-cred Head once wound-ed, With grief and pain weighed down, How scorn-ful-ly sur-round-ed With thorns, Thine on-ly crown! How pale art Thou with an-guish, With sore a-buse and scorn! How

does that vis - age lan - guish Which once was bright as morn!

1 O sacred Head once wounded,
   With grief and pain weighed down,
   How scornfully surrounded
   With thorns, Thine only crown!
   How pale art Thou with anguish,
   With sore abuse and scorn!
   How does that visage languish
   Which once was bright as morn!

2 O Lord of Life and Glory,
   What bliss till now was Thine!
   I read the wondrous story,
   I joy to call Thee mine.
   Thy grief and Thy compassion
   Were all for sinners' gain;
   Mine, mine was the transgression,
   But Thine the deadly pain.

3 What language shall I borrow
   To praise Thee, heavenly Friend,
   For this Thy dying sorrow,
   Thy pity without end?
   Lord, make me Thine for ever,
   Nor let me faithless prove;
   O let me never, never
   Abuse such dying love!

4 Be near me, Lord, when dying;
   O show Thyself to me;
   And, for my succour flying,
   Come, Lord, to set me free:
   These eyes, new faith receiving,
   From Jesus shall not move;
   For he who dies believing
   Dies safely through Thy love.

Paulus Gerhardt, 1607–76
from 'Salve caput cruentatum'
attributed to Bernard of Clairvaux, 1091–1153
tr. James Waddell Alexander, 1804–59

522   O teach me what it meaneth

RUTHERFORD 7 6. 7 6. D

Chrétian Urhan (1790–1845)

O teach me what it mean - eth, That cross up - lift - ed high, With One, the Man of Sor - rows, Con - demned to bleed— and— die! O teach me what it cost thee To make a sin - ner whole; And—

teach me, Sav - iour, teach me The va - lue of a soul!

1 O teach me what it meaneth,
   That cross uplifted high,
   With One, the Man of Sorrows,
   Condemned to bleed and die!
   O teach me what it cost thee
   To make a sinner whole;
   And teach me, Saviour, teach me
   The value of a soul!

2 O teach me what it meaneth,
   That sacred crimson tide,
   The blood and water flowing
   From Thine own wounded side.
   Teach me that if none other
   Had sinned, but I alone,
   Yet still Thy blood, Lord Jesus,
   Thine only, must atone.

3 O teach me what it meaneth,
   Thy love beyond compare,
   The love that reacheth deeper
   Than depths of self-despair!
   Yes, teach me, till there gloweth
   In this cold heart of mine
   Some feeble, pale reflection
   Of that pure love of thine.

4 O teach me what it meaneth,
   For I am full of sin;
   And grace alone can reach me,
   And love alone can win.
   O teach me, for I need Thee,
   I have no hope beside,
   The chief of all the sinners
   For whom the Saviour died!

5 O Infinite Redeemer!
   I bring no other plea,
   Because Thou dost invite me
   I cast myself on Thee.
   Because Thou dost accept me
   I love and I adore;
   Because Thy love constraineth,
   I'll praise Thee evermore!

Lucy Ann Bennett, 1850–1927

413

523 O the bitter shame and sorrow

ST. JUDE 8 7. 8 8 7

Charles Vincent (1852–1934)

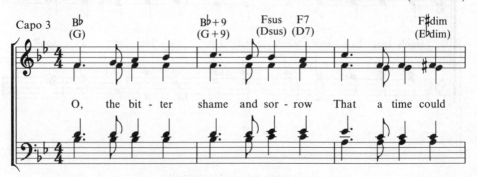

O, the bit - ter shame and sor - row That a time could

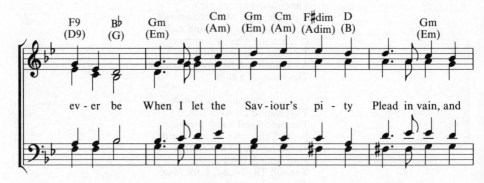

ev - er be When I let the Sav - iour's pi - ty Plead in vain, and

proud - ly ans - wered, 'None of you and all of me.'

1 O, the bitter shame and sorrow
That a time could ever be
When I let the Saviour's pity
Plead in vain, and proudly answered,
'None of you and all of me.'

2 Yet You found me; there I saw You
Dying and in agony,
Heard You pray, 'Forgive them, Father',
And my wistful heart said faintly,
'Some of you and some of me.'

3 Day by day Your tender mercy,
Healing, helping, full and free,
Firm and strong, with endless patience
Brought me lower, while I whispered,
'More of You and less of me.'

4 Higher than the highest heaven,
Deeper than the deepest sea,
Lord, Your love at last has conquered:
Grant me now my spirit's longing,
'All of You and none of me!'

Theodore Monod, 1836–1921
© in this version Jubilate Hymns

524 Oft in danger

UNIVERSITY COLLEGE 77.77

Henry John Gauntlett (1805–76)

Oft in dan - ger, oft in woe,

On - ward, Christ-ians, on - ward go; Bear the toil, main -

tain the strife, Strength-ened with the Bread of life.

1 Oft in danger, oft in woe,
Onward, Christians, onward go;
Bear the toil, maintain the strife,
Strengthened with the Bread of life.

2 Onward, Christians, onward go!
Join the war, and face the foe:
Will ye flee in danger's hour?
Know ye not your Captain's pow'r?

3 Let your drooping hearts be glad;
March in heav'nly armour clad;
Fight, nor think the battle long:
Vict'ry soon shall tune your song.

4 Let not sorrow dim your eye,
Soon shall every tear be dry;
Let not fears your course impede,
Great your strength, if great your need.

5 Onward then in battle move;
More than conquerors ye shall prove;
Though opposed by many a foe,
Christian soldiers, onward go.

Henry Kirke White, 1785–1806 and others

525 O the deep, deep love

EBENEZER (Ton-y-Botel) 8 7. 8 7. D   Thomas John Williams (1869–1944)

416

Is the ___ cur-rent of Thy ___ love; Lead-ing ___ on ward, lead-ing ___ home-ward, To my ___ glo-rious rest ___ a-bove.

1 O the deep, deep love of Jesus!
Vast, unmeasured, boundless, free;
Rolling as a mighty ocean
In its fulness over me.
Underneath me, all around me,
Is the current of Thy love;
Leading onward, leading homeward,
To my glorious rest above.

2 O the deep, deep love of Jesus!
Spread His praise from shore to shore,
How He loveth, ever loveth,
Changeth never, nevermore;
How He watches o'er His loved ones,
Died to call them all His own;
How for them He intercedeth,
Watches over them from the throne.

3 O the deep, deep love of Jesus!
Love of every love the best:
'Tis an ocean vast of blessing,
'Tis a haven sweet of rest.
O the deep, deep love of Jesus!
'Tis a heaven of heavens to me;
And it lifts me up to glory,
For it lifts me up to Thee.

Samuel Trevor Francis, 1834–1925

417

526 O the valleys shall ring

Steadily

Dave Bilbrough

Capo 3

O the val - leys shall ring___ with the sound___ of praise,___ And the li - on shall lie___ with the lamb.___ ___ Of His gov - ern - ment___ there shall be___ no end,___ And His glo - ry shall fill the earth.___

527 Oh! Oh! Oh! how good is the Lord

Anon.
arr. Jeanne Harper

With joyful abandon

Oh! Oh! Oh! how good is the Lord,

Oh! Oh! Oh! how good is the Lord, Oh! Oh! Oh! how

Fine

good is the Lord, I ne-ver will for-get what He has done for me.

He gives me sal-va-tion, how good is the Lord, He

gives me sal-va-tion, how good is the Lord, He gives me sal-va-tion, how good is the Lord, I ne-ver will for-get what He has done for me.

Oh! Oh! Oh! how good is the Lord,
Oh! Oh! Oh! how good is the Lord,
Oh! Oh! Oh! how good is the Lord,
I never will forget what He has done for me.

1 He gives me salvation, how good is the Lord,
　He gives me salvation, how good is the Lord,
　He gives me salvation, how good is the Lord,
　I never will forget what He has done for me.
　　Oh! Oh! Oh! . . .

2 He gives me His blessings . . .
　　Oh! Oh! Oh! . . .

3 He gives me His Spirit . . .
　　Oh! Oh! Oh! . . .

4 He gives me His healing . . .
　　Oh! Oh! Oh! . . .

5 He gives me His glory . . .
　　Oh! Oh! Oh! . . .

OTHER SUITABLE VERSES MAY BE ADDED
He gives us each other . . .
He gives us His body . . .
He gives us His freedom . . . *etc.*

528 On Jordan's bank, the Baptist's cry

WINCHESTER NEW L.M.

From a chorale in the *Musicalisch Hanbuch*,
Hamburg, 1690, arr. W.H. Havergal (1793–1870)

1 On Jordan's bank the Baptist's cry
Announces that the Lord is nigh;
Come then and listen for he brings
Glad tidings from the King of kings.

2 Then cleansed be every heart from sin;
Make straight the way for God within;
Prepare we in our hearts a home,
Where such a mighty guest may come.

3 For You are our salvation, Lord,
Our refuge and our great reward;
Without Your grace we waste away,
Like flowers that wither and decay.

4 To heal the sick stretch out Your hand,
Make wholeness flow at Your command;
Sin's devastation now restore
Earth's own true loveliness once more.

5 To Him who left the throne of heaven
To save mankind, all praise be given;
To God the Father, voices raise,
And Holy Spirit, let us praise.

Charles Coffin, 1676–1749,
tr. John Chandler, 1806–76, altd.,
Altered © 1986 Horrobin/Leavers

529 Our blest Redeemer

ST. CUTHBERT 8 6. 8 4

John Bacchus Dykes (1823–76)

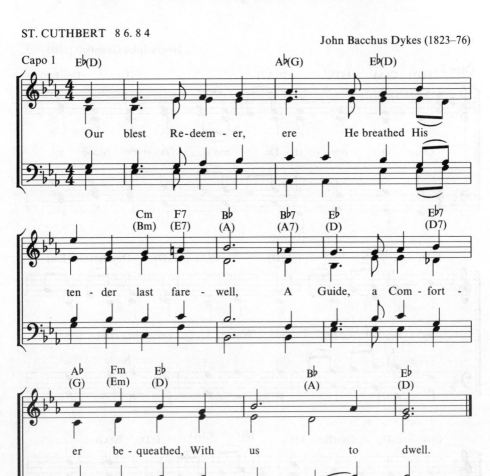

1 Our blest Redeemer, ere He breathed
His tender last farewell,
A Guide, a Comforter bequeathed,
With us to dwell.

2 He came in semblance of a dove,
With shelt'ring wings outspread,
The holy balm of peace and love
On earth to shed.

3 He came in tongues of living flame
To teach, convince, subdue;
All pow'rful as the wind He came
As viewless too.

4 He comes sweet influence to impart,
A gracious, willing Guest,
Where He can find one humble heart
Wherein to rest.

5 And His that gentle voice we hear,
Soft as the breath of even,
That checks each fault, that calms each fear,
And speaks of heaven.

6 For every virtue we possess,
And every victory won,
And every thought of holiness,
Are His alone.

7 Spirit of purity and grace,
Our weakness, pitying, see;
O make our hearts Thy dwelling-place,
And worthier Thee.

Harriet Auber, 1773–1862

423

530   Once in royal David's city

IRBY   8.7.8.7.77

Henry John Gauntlett (1805–76)

Once in roy - al Da - vid's__ ci - ty, Stood a
low - ly cat - tle__ shed, Where a mo - ther laid__ her__
Ba - by, In a man - ger for__ His__ bed. Ma - ry
was that mo-ther mild, Je - sus Christ her lit - tle__ child.

1 Once in royal David's city,
  Stood a lowly cattle shed,
  Where a mother laid her Baby,
  In a manger for His bed.
  Mary was that mother mild,
  Jesus Christ her little child.

2 He came down to earth from heaven,
  Who is God and Lord of all,
  And His shelter was a stable,
  And His cradle was a stall:
  With the poor and mean and lowly
  Lived on earth our Saviour holy.

3 And through all His wondrous childhood
  He would honour and obey,
  Love and watch the lowly mother,
  In whose gentle arms He lay.
  Christian children all should be,
  Kind, obedient, good as He.

4 For He is our childhood's pattern:
  Day by day like us He grew;
  He was little, weak, and helpless;
  Tears and smiles like us He knew:
  And He feels for all our sadness,
  And He shares in all our gladness.

5 And our eyes at last shall see Him
  Through His own redeeming love;
  For that Child, so dear and gentle,
  Is our Lord in heaven above;
  And He leads His children on
  To the place where He is gone.

6 Not in that poor, lowly stable,
  With the oxen standing by,
  We shall see Him, but in heaven,
  Set at God's right hand on high;
  There His children gather round
  Bright like stars, with glory crowned.

Cecil Frances Alexander, 1823–95
Altered © 1986 Horrobin/Leavers

531 One shall tell another

(The wine of the kingdom)

Graham Kendrick

Lightly with increasing pace

One shall tell a - noth - er, And he shall tell his friend,
Hus-bands, wives and child-ren Shall come fol-low-ing on. From
house to house in fam - i - lies Shall more be gath-ered in, And
lights will shine in ev-'ry street, So warm and wel-com - ing.

Come on in and taste the new wine, The wine of the

1 One shall tell another,
  And he shall tell his friend,
  Husbands, wives and children
  Shall come following on.
  From house to house in families
  Shall more be gathered in,
  And lights will shine in ev'ry street,
  So warm and welcoming.

  Come on in and taste the new wine,
  The wine of the kingdom,
  The wine of the kingdom of God.
  Here is healing and forgiveness,
  The wine of the kingdom,
  The wine of the kingdom of God.

2 Compassion of the Father
  Is ready now to flow,
  Through acts of love and mercy
  We must let it show.
  He turns now from His anger
  To show a smiling face
  And longs that men should stand beneath
  The fountain of His grace.
      Come on in . . .

3 He longs to do much more than
  Our faith has yet allowed,
  To thrill us and suprise us
  With His sovereign power.
  Where darkness has been darkest
  The brightest light will shine,
  His invitation comes to us,
  It's yours and it is mine.
      Come on in . . .

427

532 One there is above all others

GOUNOD 8 7. 8 7. 7 7

Charles Gounod (1818–93)

One there is a - bove all oth - ers Well de -
serves the__name of Friend; His is love be - yond__ a__
bro - ther's, Cost - ly, free, and__knows no end: They who
once His__kind - ness prove Find it ev - er - last - ing love.

1 One there is above all others
Well deserves the name of Friend;
His is love beyond a brother's,
Costly, free, and knows no end:
They who once His kindness prove
Find it everlasting love.

2 Which of all our friends, to save us
Could, or would, have shed His blood?
Christ, the Saviour, died to have us
Reconciled in Him to God:
This was boundless love indeed!
Jesus is a Friend in need.

3 When He lived on earth abasèd,
'Friend of sinners' was His name;
Now above all glory raisèd
He rejoices in the same:
Still He calls them brethren, friends,
And to all their wants attends.

4 O for grace our hearts to soften!
Teach us, Lord, at length to love;
We, alas! forget too often
What a Friend we have above;
But when home our souls are brought,
We will love Thee as we ought.

John Newton, 1725–1807

533 Open my eyes that I may see

OPEN MY EYES Irregular

Clara H. Scott (1841–97)
and Fred P. Morris

O - pen my eyes that I may see Glimp-ses of truth Thou hast for me; Place in my hands the won-der-ful key That shall un-clasp and set me free. *Si - lent - ly now I wait for Thee, Read - y, my God, Thy will to see;*

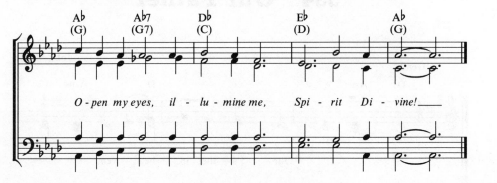

O - pen my eyes, il - lu - mine me, Spi - rit Di - vine!

1 Open my eyes that I may see
  Glimpses of truth Thou hast for me;
  Place in my hands the wonderful key
  That shall unclasp and set me free.

  Silently now I wait for Thee,
  Ready, my God, Thy will to see;
  Open my eyes, illumine me,
  Spirit Divine!

2 Open my ears that may hear
  Voices of truth Thou sendest clear;
  And while the wave-notes fall on my ear,
  Ev'rything false will disappear.
  Silently now . . .

3 Open my mouth and let me bear
  Tidings of mercy ev'rywhere;
  Open my heart and let me prepare
  Love with Thy children thus to share.
  Silently now . . .

4 Open my mind, that I may read
  More of Thy love in word and deed:
  What shall I fear while yet Thou dost lead?
  Only for light from Thee I plead.
  Silently now . . .

Clara H. Scott, 1841–97

534 Our Father

John Marsh

Our eyes have seen the glory

Anon.
arr. Phil Burt

Capo 3

Our eyes have seen the glo - ry Of our Sav-iour, Christ the Lord; He is
seat - ed at His Fa - ther's side In love and full ac-cord; From
there up-on the sons of men His Spi - rit is out-poured, All
hail, as - cend - ed King! Glo - ry, glo - ry hal - le -

lu - jah, Glo - ry, glo - ry hal - le - lu - jah,

Glo - ry, glo - ry hal - le - lu - jah, All hail as - cend - ed King!____

1 Our eyes have seen the glory
   Of our Saviour, Christ the Lord;
   He is seated at His Father's side
   In love and full accord;
   From there upon the sons of men
   His Spirit is out-poured,
   All hail, ascended King!

   Glory, glory hallelujah,
   Glory, glory hallelujah,
   Glory, glory hallelujah,
   All hail ascended King!

2 He came to earth at Christmas
   And was made a man like us;
   He taught, He healed, He suffered –
   And they nailed Him to the cross;
   He rose again on Easter Day –
   Our Lord victorious,
   All hail, ascended King!
     Glory, glory . . .

3 The good news of His kingdom
   Must be preached to every shore,
   The news of peace and pardon,
   And the end of strife and war;
   The secret of His kingdom
   Is to serve Him evermore,
   All hail, ascended King!
     Glory, glory . . .

4 His kingdom is a family
   Of men of every race,
   They live their lives in harmony,
   Enabled by His grace;
   They follow His example
   Till they see Him face to face,
   All hail, ascended King!
     Glory, glory . . .

© *Roland Meredith*

536 Out of my bondage

JESUS, I COME! Irregular

George C. Stebbins (1846–1945)

Out of my bon - dage, sor - row, and night, Je - sus, I come:

Je - sus, I come. In - to Your free - dom, glad - ness, and light,

Je - sus, I come to You.— Out of my sick - ness in - to Your health,

Out of my want and in - to Your wealth, Out of my sin and

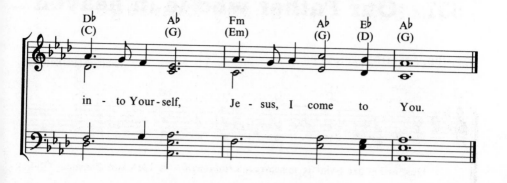

in - to Your-self, Je - sus, I come to You.

1 Out of my bondage, sorrow, and night,
   Jesus, I come: Jesus, I come.
   Into Your freedom, gladness, and light,
   Jesus, I come to You.
   Out of my sickness into Your health,
   Out of my want and into Your wealth,
   Out of my sin and into Yourself,
   Jesus, I come to You.

2 Out of my shameful failure and loss,
   Jesus, I come: Jesus, I come.
   Into the glorious gain of Your cross,
   Jesus, I come to You.
   Out of earth's sorrows into Your balm,
   Out of life's storm and into Your calm,
   Out of distress to jubilant psalm,
   Jesus, I come to You.

3 Out of unrest and arrogant pride,
   Jesus, I come: Jesus, I come.
   Into Your blessèd will to abide,
   Jesus, I come to You.
   Out of myself to dwell in Your love,
   Out of despair into joy from above,
   Upward for ever on wings like a dove,
   Jesus, I come to You.

4 Out of the fear and dread of the tomb,
   Jesus, I come: Jesus, I come.
   Into the joy and light of Your home,
   Jesus, I come to You.
   Out of the depths of ruin untold,
   Into the peace of Your sheltering fold,
   Ever Your glorious face to behold,
   Jesus, I come to You.

W.T. Sleeper, 1840–1920

537 Our Father who is in heaven

CARIBBEAN LORD'S PRAYER   arr. Allen Percival

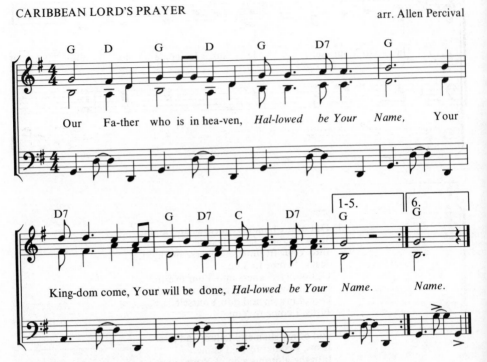

Our Fa-ther who is in hea-ven, *Hal-lowed be Your Name,* Your

King-dom come, Your will be done, *Hal-lowed be Your Name.* Name.

1 Our Father who is in heaven,
   Hallowed be Your Name,
   Your Kingdom come, Your will be done,
   Hallowed be Your Name.

2 On earth as it is in heaven,
   Hallowed be Your Name,
   Give us this day our daily bread,
   Hallowed be Your Name.

3 Forgive us all our trespasses,
   Hallowed be Your Name,
   As we forgive those who trespass against us,
   Hallowed be Your Name.

4 And lead us not into temptation,
   Hallowed be Your Name,
   But deliver us from all that is evil,
   Hallowed be Your Name.

5 For Yours is the Kingdom, the Power and the Glory,
   Hallowed be Your Name,
   For ever and for ever
   Hallowed be Your Name.

6 Amen, Amen, it shall be so,
   Hallowed be Your Name
   Amen, Amen, it shall be so,
   Hallowed be Your Name.

538 Peace I give to you

Graham Kendrick

1 Peace, I give to you, I give to you My peace.
  Peace, I give to you, I give to you My peace.

  Let it flow to one another, let it flow, let it flow.
  Let it flow to one another, let it flow, let it flow.

2 Love I give to you, I give you My love.
  Love I give to you, I give you My love.
  Let it flow . . .

3 Hope I give to you, I give you My hope.
  Hope I give to you, I give you My hope.
  Let it flow . . .

4 Joy I give to you, I give you My joy.
  Joy I give to you, I give you My joy.
  Let it flow . . .

539 Praise Him on the trumpet

John Kennett

With pace and swing

Praise Him on the trum - pet,__ the psalt - ery and harp,__

Praise Him on the tim - brel and the dance,__ Praise Him__

__with stringed in - stru-ments too.__

Praise Him on the loud cym-bals, Praise Him on the loud

cym - bals, _____ Let ev - 'ry - thing that has breath praise the

Lord.   Hal - le - lu - jah, praise the Lord, ___

Hal - le - lu - jah, praise the Lord, _____ Let ev - 'ry - thing that has

1.

breath   praise   the   Lord. _____

2.

breath   praise   the   Lord. _____

540 Praise the Lord

(Praise God in His sanctuary)

David J. Hadden

Brightly with pace

Praise the Lord,___ Praise God in His sanc-tu-a - ry, Praise Him in His migh-ty heavens. Praise Him for His great-ness And praise Him for His power. Praise the Lord, power.

Praise Him with the sound of trum-pets,_____

D

Praise Him with the harp and lyre,_____

Bm　　　　　　　　　　　　　　Em

Praise Him with the tam-bour-ine__ and with danc - ing._____ Let

Am　　　　　　D　　　　　　G　　　　　　*D.C. al Fine*

ev-ery-thing__that has breath　praise　the　Lord.

Praise the Lord,
Praise God in His sanctuary,
Praise Him in His mighty heavens.
Praise Him for His greatness
And praise Him for His power.

1 Praise Him with the sound of trumpets,
　Praise Him with the harp and lyre,
　Praise Him with the tambourine and with dancing.
　Let everything that has breath praise the Lord.
　　Praise the Lord . . .

2 Praise Him with the clash of cymbals,
　Praise Him with the strings and flute,
　Praise Him with the tambourine and with dancing.
　Let everything that has breath praise the Lord.
　　Praise the Lord . . .

541 Praise You, Lord

Praise You, — Lord, for Your love for ——— me.

1 Praise You, Lord, for the wonder of Your healing.
 Praise You, Lord, for Your love so freely given,
 Out-pouring, anointing, flowing in to heal our wounds.
 Praise You, Lord, for Your love for me.

2 Praise You, Lord, for Your gift of liberation.
 Praise You, Lord, You have set the captives free;
 The chains that bind are broken by the sharpness of Your sword,
 Praise You, Lord, You gave Your life for me.

3 Praise You, Lord, You have born the depths of sorrow.
 Praise You, Lord, for Your anguish on the tree;
 The nails that tore Your body and the pain that tore Your soul.
 Praise You, Lord, Your tears, they fell for me.

4 Praise You, Lord, You have turned our thorns to roses.
 Glory, Lord, as they bloom upon Your brow.
 The path of pain is hallowed, for Your love has made it sweet,
 Praise You, Lord, and may I love You now.

542 Reconciled

Words and music
Mike Kerry

With excitment

Capo 3

Re - con-ciled, I'm re - con-ciled, I'm re - con-ciled to God for ev - er, Know He took a - way my sin, I know His love will leave me ne - ver. Re - con-ciled, I am His child, I know it was on me He smiled, I'm re - con-ciled, I'm

re-con-ciled to God, _____Hal-le-lu-jah. I'm ___

1 Reconciled, I'm reconciled,
   I'm reconciled to God for ever,
   Know He took away my sin,
   I know His love will leave me never.
   Reconciled, I am His child,
   I know it was on me He smiled,
   I'm reconciled, I'm reconciled to God,
   Hallelujah.

2 I'm justified, I'm justified,
   It's just as if I'd never sinned,
   And once I knew such guilty fear,
   But now I know His peace with me,
   Justified, I'm justified,
   It's all because my Jesus died,
   I'm justified, I'm justified by God.
   Hallelujah.

3 I'll magnify, I'll magnify,
   I'll magnify His name for ever,
   Wear the robe of righteousness
   And bless the name of Jesus, Saviour,
   Magnify the One who died,
   The One who reigns for me on high.
   I'll magnify, I'll magnify my God.

543 Rejoice!

Graham Kendrick

Triumphantly

Re - joice! Re-joice! Christ is in you, The hope of glo - ry in our hearts. He lives! He lives! His breath is in you, A - rise a migh - ty ar - my, We a - rise.

Now is the time for us To march up - on the land, In-to our

hands He will give the ground we claim.____

He rides in ma-jes-ty___ To lead us in-to vic-to-ry,___

The world shall see that Christ is Lord!_____ Re -

Rejoice! Rejoice! Christ is in you,
The hope of glory in our hearts.
He lives! He lives!
His breath is in you,
Arise a mighty army,
We arise.

1 Now is the time for us
  To march upon the land,
  Into our hands
  He will give the ground we claim.
  He rides in majesty
  To lead us into victory,
  The world shall see that
  Christ is Lord!
      Rejoice! . . .

2 God is at work in us
  His purpose to perform,
  Building a kingdom
  Of power not of words,
  Where things impossible
  By faith shall be made possible;
  Let's give the glory
  To Him now.
      Rejoice! . . .

3 Though we are weak, His grace
  Is everything we need;
  We're made of clay
  But this treasure is within.
  He turns our weakness
  Into His opportunities,
  So that the glory
  Goes to Him.
      Rejoice! . . .

544 Rejoice and be glad

Irregular

J.J. Husband (1760–1825)

Re - joice and be glad! the Re - deem - er has come:

Go,— look on His cra - dle, His cross, and His tomb.

Sound His prai - ses, tell the sto - ry of Him who was slain;

Sound His prai - ses, tell with glad - ness He now lives a - gain.

1 Rejoice and be glad! the Redeemer has come:
Go, look on His cradle, His cross, and His tomb.

Sound His praises, tell the story of Him who was slain;
Sound His praises, tell with gladness He now lives again.

2 Rejoice and be glad! it is sunshine at last;
The clouds have departed, the shadows are past.
Sound His praises . . .

3 Rejoice and be glad! for the blood has been shed;
Redemption is finished, the price has been paid.
Sound His praises . . .

4 Rejoice and be glad! now the pardon is free;
The just for the unjust has died on the tree.
Sound His praises . . .

5 Rejoice and be glad! for the Lamb that was slain,
O'er death is triumphant, and now lives again.
Sound His praises . . .

6 Rejoice and be glad! for our King is on high;
He pleads now for us on His throne in the sky.
Sound His praises . . .

7 Rejoice and be glad! for He's coming again;
He'll come in great glory, the Lamb that was slain.
Sound His praises . . .

Horatius Bonar, 1808–89

545 Rejoice! The Lord is risen!

Words and music
Moira Austin

With strength and joy *Descant (3rd verse only)*

Re - joice!_____

1 Re - joice! The Lord is ris - en!___
2 Re - joice! The Lord is ris - en!___
3 Re - joice! The Lord is ris - en!___

Re - joice!_____ Wis - dom, au -

___ He is the King of glo - ry_____ Migh - ty Re -
___ We are His ho - ly na - tion_____ Ran - somed, for -
___ Bless - ing and hon - our give Him_____ Wis - dom, au -

thor-i-ty, Be - long to His Name:

deem - er, He has made us His own: Re -
giv - en, Washed in His pre - cious Blood: Re -
thor - i - ty, Be - long to His Name: Re -

Re - joice!_____ Re - joice!_____

joice! The Lord is ris - en!_____ O - pened, the
joice! The Lord is ris - en!_____ Worth - y His
joice! The Lord is ris - en!_____ An - gels and

Wor - ship and praise Him, sing - ing

gate of hea - ven_____ Bow down be - fore Him For He
new cre - a - tion,_____ Per - fect and spot - less As the
saints a - dore Him_____ Wor - ship and praise Him, sing - ing

'Je - sus Christ_____ is Lord!'

comes to claim His own!
Lamb up - on the throne.
'Je - sus Christ is Lord!'

Chorus overleaf

453

Chorus: (with increased breadth and fullness)

Glo-ry to the King of Kings!

Glo-ry to the King of Kings! _____ Glo-ry to the

Glo-ry to the Lord of Lords! Je - sus, You are

Lord of Lords! _____ Je-sus, we pro-claim That You are

Lord in ma - jes - ty!

Lord en-throned in ma - jes-ty! _____ Glo-ry to the

546 Reign in me

Chris A. Bowater
arr. G. Baker

Reign in me, so-ve-reign Lord, reign in me,
Reign in me, sove-reign Lord, reign in me,
Cap-ti-vate my heart, let Your king-dom come,
Es-tab-lish there Your throne, let Your will be done.

Reign in me, sovereign Lord, reign in me,
Reign in me, sovereign Lord, reign in me,
Captivate my heart, let Your kingdom come,
Establish there Your throne, let Your will be done.

547 Ride on, ride on in majesty

ST. DROSTANE L.M.

John Bacchus Dykes (1823–76)

1 Ride on, ride on in majesty!
Hark, all the tribes 'Hosanna!' cry!
O Saviour meek, pursue Your road,
With palms and scattered garments strowed.

2 Ride on, ride on in majesty!
In lowly pomp ride on to die:
O Christ, Your triumphs now begin
O'er captive death and conquered sin.

3 Ride on, ride on in majesty!
The angel armies of the sky
Look down with sad and wond'ring eyes
To see th'approaching sacrifice.

4 Ride on, ride on in majesty!
Your last and fiercest strife is nigh:
The Father on His sapphire throne
Awaits His own anointed Son.

5 Ride on, ride on in majesty!
In lowly pomp ride on to die;
Bow Your meek head to mortal pain,
Then take, O God Your power, and reign.

Henry Hart Milman, 1791–1868

548 River wash over me

Unhurried (with strength)

Dougie Brown

Capo 3

1 River wash over me,
Cleanse me and make me new.
Bathe me, refresh me and fill me anew,
River wash over me.

2 Spirit watch over me,
Lead me to Jesus' feet.
Cause me to worship and fill me anew,
Spirit watch over me.

3 Jesus rule over me,
Reign over all my heart.
Teach me to praise You and fill me anew,
Jesus rule over me.

549 Safe in the shadow

CREATOR GOD 8 6 8 6 (CM)

Norman L. Warren (b. 1934)

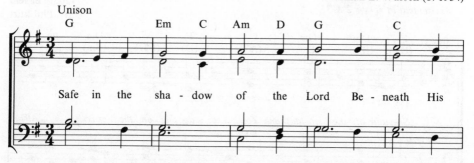

Safe in the sha - dow of the Lord Be - neath His

hand___ and power,_____ I trust in Him,___ I

trust in Him,___ My for - tress and___ my tower.___

1 Safe in the shadow of the Lord
Beneath His hand and power,
I trust in Him,
I trust in Him,
My fortress and my tower.

2 My hope is set on God alone
Though Satan spreads his snare;
I trust in Him,
I trust in Him
To keep me in His care.

3 From fears and phantoms of the night,
From foes about my way,
I trust in Him,
I trust in Him
By darkness as by day.

4 His holy angels keep my feet
Secure from every stone;
I trust in Him,
I trust in Him
And unafraid go on.

5 Strong in the everlasting name,
And in my Father's care,
I trust in Him,
I trust in Him
Who hears and answers prayer.

6 Safe in the shadow of the Lord,
Possessed by love divine,
I trust in Him,
I trust in Him
And meet His love with mine.

© *Timothy Dudley-Smith, b. 1926*

550 Saviour of the world

Begin slowly – with increasing
excitement in verses 2 & 3

Words and music
Greg Leavers
arr. Phil Burt

Sa-viour of the world, thank You for dy-ing on the cross. All
praise to You our ris-en Lord, Hal-le-lu-jah! Je-sus.

In the gar-den of Geth-se-ma-ne Je-sus knelt and prayed,

For He knew the time was near when He would be be-trayed.

last time to Coda

Saviour of the world, thank You for dying on the cross.
All praise to You our risen Lord, Hallelujah! Jesus.

1 In the garden of Gethsemane Jesus knelt and prayed,
   For He knew the time was near when He would be betrayed.
   God gave Him the strength to cope with all that people did to hurt Him;
   Soldiers laughed and forced a crown of thorns upon His head.
       Saviour of the world, . . .

2 On a cross outside the city they nailed Jesus high;
   Innocent, but still He suffered as they watched Him die.
   Nothing that the soldiers did could make Him lose control, for Jesus
   Knew the time to die then 'It is finished', was His cry.
       Saviour of the world, . . .

3 Three days later by God's pow'r He rose up from the dead,
   For the tomb could not hold Jesus it was as He'd said;
   Victor over sin and death He conquered Satan's power; so let us
   Celebrate that Jesus is alive for ever more.
       Saviour of the world, . . .

© *1986 Greg Leavers*

461

551 Saviour! Thy dying love

PHELPS 6 4. 6 4. 6 6. 6 4

Robert Lowry (1826–99)

Sav - iour! Thy dy - ing love Thou gav - est me,

Nor should I aught with-hold, My Lord, from Thee;

In love my soul would bow, My heart ful - fil its vow,

Some of - f'ring bring Thee now, Some - thing for Thee.

1 Saviour! Thy dying love
   Thou gavest me,
   Nor should I aught withhold,
   My Lord, from Thee;
   In love my soul would bow,
   My heart fulfil its vow,
   Some offering bring Thee now,
   Something for Thee.

2 At the blest mercy-seat,
   Pleading for me,
   My feeble faith looks up,
   Jesus, to Thee:
   Help me the cross to bear,
   Thy wondrous love declare,
   Some song to raise, or prayer,
   Something for Thee.

3 Give me a faithful heart,
   Likeness to Thee –
   That each departing day
   Henceforth may see
   Some work of love begun,
   Some deed of kindness done,
   Some wanderer sought and won,
   Something for Thee.

4 All that I am and have –
   Thy gifts so free –
   In joy, in grief, through life,
   O Lord, for Thee!
   And when Thy face I see
   My ransomed soul shall be
   Through all eternity
   Something for Thee.

Sylvanus Dryden Phelps, 1816–95

552 See, amid the winter's snow

HUMILITY (Oxford) 7 7. 7 7 and Refrain

John Goss (1800–80)

See, a-mid the win - ter's snow, Born for us on earth be-low,

See, the Lamb of God ap-pears, Prom-ised from e - ter - nal years.

Hail thou ev - er bless-èd morn! Hail, re-demp-tion's hap - py dawn!

Sing through all Je - ru - sa-lem: Christ is born in Beth - le - hem!

1 See, amid the winter's snow,
Born for us on earth below,
See, the Lamb of God appears,
Promised from eternal years.

Hail thou ever blessèd morn!
Hail, redemption's happy dawn!
Sing through all Jerusalem:
Christ is born in Bethlehem!

2 Lo, within a manger lies
He Who built the starry skies,
He Who, throned in height sublime,
Sits amid the cherubim.
Hail thou . . .

3 Say, ye holy shepherds, say,
What your joyful news today;
Wherefore have ye left your sheep
On the lonely mountain steep?
Hail thou . . .

4 As we watched at dead of night,
Lo, we saw a wondrous light:
Angels, singing peace on earth,
Told us of the Saviour's birth.
Hail thou . . .

5 Sacred Infant, all divine,
What a tender love was Thine,
Thus to come from highest bliss
Down to such a world as this!
Hail thou . . .

6 Teach, O teach us, holy Child,
By Thy face so meek and mild,
Teach us to resemble Thee
In Thy sweet humility.
Hail thou . . .

Edward Caswell, 1814–78

553　See Him lying on a bed of straw

CALYPSO CAROL　Irregular

Michael Perry (b. 1942)
arr. Stephen Coates (b. 1952)

See Him ly - ing on a bed of straw:___ A

draugh-ty sta - ble with an o - pen door; Ma - ry cra - dl-ing the

babe she bore— The Prince of glo - ry is His name.

O now car - ry me to Beth - le - hem___ To

554 See Him on the cross

see the Lord___ ap-pear to men! Just as poor as was the

sta-ble then, The Prince of glo-ry when He came.

1 See Him lying on a bed of straw:
A draughty stable with an open door;
Mary cradling the babe she bore—
The Prince of glory is His name.

O now carry me to Bethlehem
To see the Lord appear to men!
Just as poor as was the stable then,
The Prince of glory when He came.

2 Star of silver, sweep across the skies,
Show where Jesus in the manger lies;
Shepherds swiftly from your stupor rise
To see the Saviour of the world!
O now carry . . .

3 Angels, sing the song that you began,
Bring God's glory to the heart of man;
Sing that Bethl'em's little baby can
Be salvation to the soul.
O now carry . . .

4 Mine are riches, from Your poverty,
From Your innocence, eternity;
Mine forgiveness by Your death for me,
Child of sorrow for my joy.
O now carry . . .

Michael Perry, b. 1942

554 See Him on the cross

Words and music
Ruth Hooke

Verse thoughtfully, chorus triumphantly

1. See Him on the cross of shame Dy - ing for
(2.) laid Him in a gar - den tomb, And sealed it with a

me, Bear - ing all my guilt and pain
stone. Ma - ry wept her tears of grief – Her

Dy - ing for me.
pre - cious Lord had gone,

468

And how I love You
'And how I love You,

Je-sus my Re-deem - er, You gave Your life for
Je-sus my Re-deem - er' Then she looked— the stone was

me, O___ Lord, Now I give my life to__ You.
rolled a - way– He had tri-umphed o - ver__ death.

Chorus overleaf

1 See Him on the cross of shame
  Dying for me,
  Bearing all my guilt and pain
  Dying for me.
  And how I love You
  Jesus my Redeemer,
  You gave Your life for me, O Lord,
  Now I give my life to You.

  Jesus lives, Jesus lives,
  Jesus lives in me.
  I will praise Your name.

2 They laid Him in a garden tomb,
  And sealed it with a stone.
  Mary wept her tears of grief –
  Her precious Lord had gone,
  'And how I love You,
  Jesus my Redeemer'
  Then she looked – the stone was rolled away –
  He had triumphed over death.
      Jesus lives . . .

555 Send forth the gospel

OMBERSLEY L.M.

W.H. Gladstone (1840–91)

1 Send forth the gospel! Let it run
Southward and northward, east and west:
Tell all the earth Christ died and lives,
He offers pardon, life, and rest.

2 Send forth Your gospel, mighty Lord!
Out of the chaos bring to birth
Your own creation's promised hope;
The better days of heaven on earth.

3 Send forth Your gospel, gracious Lord!
Yours was the blood for sinners shed;
Your voice still pleads in human hearts;
To You may all Your sheep be led.

4 Send forth Your gospel, holy Lord!
Kindle in us love's sacred flame;
Love giving all and grudging naught
For Jesus' sake, in Jesus' name.

5 Send forth the gospel! Tell it out!
Go, brothers, at the Master's call;
Prepare His way, who comes to reign
The King of kings and Lord of all.

H.E. Fox, 1841–1926

556 Send me out from here

John Pantry
arr. Christopher Norton

Majestically

Send me out from here, Lord, To serve a world in need, May I know no man by the coat he wears, But the heart that Je - sus sees. And may the light of Your face Shine up - on me Lord, You have filled my heart with the

Verse 2

Go now bearing the light living for oth-er's,

Fear-less-ly walk-ing in-to the night. Take no

thought for your lives, like lambs a-mong wolves, Full of the Spi-rit

D.C. al Coda ⊕ *CODA*

rea-dy to die.

cup is o-ver-

flow-ing with joy.

474

557 Set my spirit free

Author unknown
arr. Phil Burt

Set my spi-rit free that I might wor - ship You,

Set my spi-rit free that I might praise Your name.

Let all bond-age go and let de - liv - erance flow,

Set my spi-rit free to wor-ship You.____

558 Silent night

STILL NACHT

F. Gruber (1787–1863)

Si - lent night, ho - ly night! Sleeps the world; hid from sight, Ma - ry and Jo - seph in sta - ble bare Watched o'er the Child—be - lov - ed and fair Sleep-ing in hea - ven-ly rest,_____ Sleep - ing in hea - ven - ly rest._____

2 Silent night, holy night!
  Shepherds first saw the light;
  Heard resounding clear and long,
  Far and near, the angel song:
  'Christ the Redeemer is here,
  Christ the Redeemer is here.'

3 Silent night, holy night!
  Son of God, O how bright
  Love is smiling from Your face!
  Strikes for us now the hour of grace,
  Saviour, since You are born,
  Saviour, since You are born.

J. Mohr, d. 1848
tr. S.A. Brooke, d. 1916

559 Souls of men, why will ye scatter

CROSS OF JESUS 8 7. 8 7

John Stainer (1840–1901)
from *The Crucifixion*

1 Souls of men, why will ye scatter
Like a crowd of frightened sheep?
Foolish hearts, why will ye wander
From a love so true and deep?

2 Was there ever kindest shepherd
Half so gentle, half so sweet,
As the Saviour Who would have us
Come and gather round His feet?

3 There's a wideness in God's mercy
Like the wideness of the sea;
There's a kindness in His justice,
Which is more than liberty.

4 There is plentiful redemption
In the blood that has been shed;
There is joy for all the members
In the sorrows of the Head.

5 For the love of God is broader
Than the measures of man's mind;
And the heart of the Eternal
Is most wonderfully kind.

6 If our love were but more simple,
We should take Him at His word,
And our lives would be all sunshine
In the sweetness of our Lord.

Frederick William Faber, 1814–63

477

560 Sing to God

ODE TO JOY 8 7 8 7 D

L. van Beethoven (1770–1827)

Sing to God new songs of wor-ship— All His deeds are mar-vel-lous;

He has brought sal - va-tion to us With His hand and ho - ly arm:

He has shown to all the—na-tions Right-eous-ness and sa-ving power;

He re-called His truth and mer - cy To His peo-ple Is - ra-el.

1 Sing to God new songs of worship—
All His deeds are marvellous;
He has brought salvation to us
With His hand and holy arm:
He has shown to all the nations
Righteousness and saving power;
He recalled His truth and mercy
To His people Israel.

2 Sing to God new songs of worship—
Earth has seen His victory;
Let the lands of earth be joyful
Praising Him with thankfulness:
Sound upon the harp His praises,
Play to Him with melody;
Let the trumpets sound His triumph,
Show your joy to God the king!

3 Sing to God new songs of worship—
Let the sea now make a noise;
All on earth and in the waters
Sound your praises to the Lord:
Let the hills be joyful together,
Let the rivers clap their hands,
For with righteousness and justice
He will come to judge the earth.

from Psalm 98
© *Michael Baughen, b. 1930*

561   So freely

With a sense of mystery

Dave Bilbrough

Capo 2

So free - ly,____ Flows the end-less love_ You give____ to me;_ So free - ly,__ ____ Not de - pen-dent on__ my part.__ As I am reach-ing out_Re-veal the love with-in Your heart,_____

As I am reach-ing out— Re-veal the love with-in Your—

heart._____ 2. Com - ___

1 So freely,
  Flows the endless love You give to me;
  So freely,
  Not dependent on my part.
  As I am reaching out
  Reveal the love within Your heart,
  As I am reaching out
  Reveal the love within Your heart.

2 Completely,
  That's the way You give Your love to me,
  Completely,
  Not dependent on my part.
  As I am reaching out
  Reveal the love within Your heart,
  As I am reaching out
  Reveal the love within Your heart.

3 So easy,
  I receive the love You give to me.
  So easy,
  Not dependent on my part.
  Flowing out to me
  The love within Your heart,
  Flowing out to me
  The love within Your heart.

562 Speak, Lord, in the stillness

QUIETUDE 6 5. 6 5

Harold Green (1871–1931)

Speak, Lord, in the still - ness, While I wait on Thee;

Hushed my heart to lis - ten In ex-pec - tan - cy.

1 Speak, Lord, in the stillness,
While I wait on Thee;
Hushed my heart to listen
In expectancy.

2 Speak, O blessèd Master,
In this quiet hour;
Let me see Thy face, Lord,
Feel Thy touch of power.

3 For the words Thou speakest,
'They are life' indeed;
Living Bread from heaven,
Now my spirit feed!

4 All to Thee is yielded,
I am not my own;
Blissful, glad surrender—
I am Thine alone.

5 Speak, Thy servant heareth!
Be not silent, Lord;
Waits my soul upon Thee
For the quickening word!

6 Fill me with the knowledge
Of Thy glorious will;
All Thine own good pleasure
In Thy child fulfil.

E. May Grimes, 1868–1927

563 Spirit Divine

EMMAUS C.M.

Source unknown

1 Spirit Divine, attend our prayers
  And make this house Thy home;
  Descend with all Thy gracious powers,
  O come, great Spirit, come!

2 Come as the Light: to us reveal
  Our emptiness and woe;
  And lead us in those paths of life
  Where all the righteous go.

3 Come as the Fire, and purge our hearts
  Like sacrificial flame;
  Let our whole soul an offering be
  To our Redeemer's name.

4 Come as the Dove, and spread Thy wings,
  The wings of perfect love;
  And let Thy church on earth become
  Blest as the church above.

5 Spirit Divine, attend our prayers;
  Make a lost world Thy home;
  Descend with all Thy gracious powers,
  O come, great Spirit, come!

Andrew Reed, 1787–1862

564 Spirit of God Divine

Colin Preston
arr. Chris Mitchell

Spi - rit of God Di - vine____

Fill this heart of____ mine____ With ho - ly

flame To praise the name Of Je - sus my

Lord.____ *Fill me a - gain,____*

Fill me a - gain,_____ Fill me a -

gain_____ O Spi - rit of the Lord._____

1 Spirit of God Divine
  Fill this heart of mine
  With holy flame
  To praise the name
  Of Jesus my Lord.

> *Fill me again,*
> *Fill me again,*
> *Fill me again*
> *O Spirit of the Lord.*

2 Spirit of God Divine,
  Fill this mouth of mine
  With holy praise
  To set the earth ablaze
  And glorify Your name.
      Fill me again . . .

3 Spirit of God Divine,
  Take this heart of mine
  To Your throne this day,
  Help me I pray
  My offering to give.
      Fill me again . . .

565 Spirit of holiness

BLOW THE WIND SOUTHERLY
12 10 12 10 12 11 12 11

Traditional melody
arr. John Barnard (b. 1948)

Spi - rit of ho - li - ness, wis - dom and faith - ful - ness, Wind of the

Lord, blow - ing strong - ly and free: Strength of our ser - ving and

joy of our wor - ship - ping – Spi - rit of God, bring Your ful - ness to me!

You came to in - ter - pret and teach us ef - fec - tive - ly All that the

Sav-iour has spo-ken and done; To glo-ri-fy Je-sus is
all Your ac - ti - vi - ty – Pro-mise and gift of the Fa-ther and Son:

Spirit of holiness, wisdom and faithfulness,
Wind of the Lord, blowing strongly and free:
Strength of our serving and joy of our worshipping –
Spirit of God, bring Your fulness to me!

1 You came to interpret and teach us effectively
   All that the Saviour has spoken and done;
   To glorify Jesus is all Your activity –
   Promise and gift of the Father and Son:
      Spirit of holiness . . .

2 You came with Your gifts to supply all our poverty,
   Pouring Your love on the church in her need;
   You came with Your fruit for our growth to maturity,
   Richly refreshing the souls that You feed:
      Spirit of holiness . . .

© *Christopher Idle, b. 1938*

566 Stand up and bless the Lord

Andy Silver

Stand up and bless the Lord___ your God, Stand up___ and

bless the Lord. His name is ex-al-ted___ a-bove all names, Stand up___

___ and bless the Lord. For our God is good to us,___

___ Al-ways rea-dy to for-give,

Stand up and bless the Lord your God,
Stand up and bless the Lord.
His name is exalted above all names,
Stand up and bless the Lord.

For our God is good to us,
Always ready to forgive,
He is gracious and merciful,
Slow to anger and very kind.

So, stand up and bless the Lord your God,
Stand up and bless the Lord.
Stand up and bless the Lord your God,
Stand up.

567 Sun of my soul

ABENDS L.M.

Herbert Stanley Oakley (1830–1903)

Sun of my soul, My Sav - iour dear,

It is not night if You are near;

O may no earth - born cloud a - rise

To hide You from Your ser - vant's eyes.

1 Sun of my soul, My Saviour dear,
  It is not night if You are near;
  O may no earth-born cloud arise
  To hide You from Your servant's eyes.

2 When the soft dews of kindly sleep
  My wearied eyelids gently steep,
  Be my last thought, how sweet to rest
  For ever on my Saviour's breast!

3 Abide with me from morn till eve,
  For without You I cannot live;
  Abide with me when night is nigh,
  For without You I dare not die.

4 If some poor wandering child of Yours
  Have spurned today Your holy voice,
  Now, Lord, the gracious work begin;
  Let them no more be ruled by sin.

5 Watch by the sick; enrich the poor
  With blessings from Your boundless store;
  Be every mourner's sleep tonight
  Like infant's slumbers, pure and light.

UNISON
6 Come near and bless us when we wake,
  Ere through the world our way we take;
  Till in the ocean of Your love
  We lose ourselves in heaven above.

John Keble, 1792–1866

568 Sweet is the work

DEEP HARMONY L.M.

Handel Parker (1857–1929)

1 Sweet is the work, my God, my King,
  To praise Thy name, give thanks and sing;
  To show Thy love by morning light,
  And talk of all Thy truth at night.

2 Sweet is the day of sacred rest,
  No mortal cares disturb my breast;
  O may my heart in tune be found,
  Like David's harp of solemn sound.

3 My heart shall triumph in the Lord,
  And bless His works, and bless His word;
  Thy works of grace, how bright they shine,
  How deep Thy counsels, how divine!

4 And I shall share a glorious part,
  When grace has well refined my heart,
  And fresh supplies of joy are shed,
  Like holy oil, to cheer my head.

5 Then shall I see, and hear, and know
  All I desired or wished below;
  And every power find sweet employ
  In that eternal world of joy.

Isaac Watts, 1674–1748

569 Teach me Thy way

THE PATH DIVINE 6 4. 6 4. 6 6. 6 4

B. Mansell Ramsey, 1849–1923

Teach me Thy way, O Lord, Teach me Thy way!

Thy gra-cious aid af-ford, Teach me Thy way!_____

Help me to walk a-right, More by faith, less by sight;

Lead me with heav'n - ly light: Teach me Thy way!

2 When doubts and fears arise,
Teach me Thy way!
When storms o'erspread the skies,
Teach me Thy way!
Shine through the cloud and rain,
Through sorrow, toil, and pain;
Make Thou my pathway plain:
Teach me Thy way!

3 Long as my life shall last,
Teach me Thy way!
Where'er my lot be cast,
Teach me Thy way!
Until the race is run,
Until the journey's done,
Until the crown is won,
Teach me Thy way!

B. Mansell Ramsey, 1849–1923

570 Take, eat, this is My body

Paul Simmons

Slowly

Take, eat, this is My bo - dy, Bro - ken for you, For I am come that you might have life; Eat of My flesh and live,___

last time **to Coda**

Eat of My flesh and live.

1. My blood was shed for ma-ny, Tak-ing a-
2. Though your sins be as scar-let They shall be
3. For God so loved the world He gave His

way your sin, And if I shall
white as snow, Though___ they be
on - ly Son, That___ who - so - ev - er be -

make you free then___ You shall be free in -
red like crim - son They___ shall be as
lie - veth on Him Might have ev - er - last - ing

deed,___ You shall be free in - deed.
wool,___ They___ shall be as wool.
life,___ Might have ev - er - last - ing life.

D.C. al Coda

live.___

495

Take, eat, this is My body,
Broken for you,
For I am come that you might have life;
Eat of My flesh and live,
Eat of My flesh and live.

1 My blood was shed for many,
   Taking away your sin,
   And if I shall make you free then
   You shall be free indeed,
   You shall be free indeed.
     Take, eat, . . .

2 Though your sins be as scarlet
   They shall be white as snow,
   Though they be red like crimson
   They shall be as wool,
   They shall be as wool.
     Take, eat, . . .

3 For God so loved the world
   He gave His only Son,
   That whosoever believeth on Him
   Might have everlasting life,
   Might have everlasting life.
     Take, eat, . . .

571 Thank You God for sending Jesus

Composer unknown
arr. Phil Burt

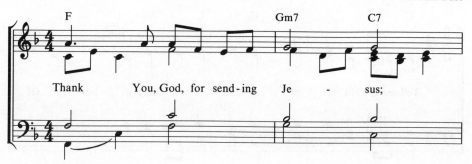

Thank You, God, for send-ing Je - sus;

Thank You, Je-sus, that You came; Ho - ly Spi-rit, won't You

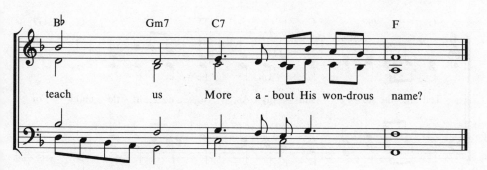

teach us More a - bout His won-drous name?

Thank You, God, for sending Jesus;
Thank You, Jesus, that You came;
Holy Spirit, won't You teach us
More about His wondrous name?

Copyright control

572 Tell me the old, old story

7 6. 7 6. D with chorus

W.H. Doane (1832–1915)

Tell me the old, old sto - ry Of un-seen things a - bove, Of Je - sus and His glo - ry, Of Je - sus and His love.

Tell me the sto - ry sim - ply, As to a lit - tle child, For I am weak and wea - ry, And help - less and de - filed.

Tell me the old, old sto - ry, Tell me the old, old sto - ry,

Tell me the old, old sto - ry, Of Je - sus and His love.

1 Tell me the old, old story
Of unseen things above,
Of Jesus and His glory,
Of Jesus and His love.
Tell me the story simply,
As to a little child,
For I am weak and weary,
And helpless and defiled.

> *Tell me the old, old story,*
> *Tell me the old, old story,*
> *Tell me the old, old story,*
> *Of Jesus and His love.*

2 Tell me the story slowly,
That I may take it in—
That wonderful redemption,
God's remedy for sin.
Tell me the story often,
For I forget so soon:
The early dew of morning
Has passed away at noon.
Tell me the old, . . .

3 Tell me the story softly,
With earnest tones and grave;
Remember! I'm the sinner
Whom Jesus came to save.
Tell me the story always,
If you would really be,
In any time of trouble,
A comforter to me.
Tell me the old, . . .

4 Tell me the same old story,
When you have cause to fear
That this world's empty glory
Is costing me too dear.
Yes, and when that world's glory
Is dawning on my soul,
Tell me the old, old story;
'Christ Jesus makes you whole.'
Tell me the old, . . .

Arabella C. Hankey, 1834–1911, altd.

499

573 Tell me the stories of Jesus

STORIES OF JESUS 84.84.54.54

F.A. Challinor (1866–1952)

Tell me the sto-ries of Je-sus I love to hear;

Things I would ask Him to tell me If He were here;

Scenes by the way-side, Tales of the sea,

Sto-ries of Je-sus, Tell them to me.

1 Tell me the stories of Jesus
  I love to hear;
  Things I would ask Him to tell me
  If He were here;
  Scenes by the wayside,
  Tales of the sea,
  Stories of Jesus,
  Tell them to me.

2 First let me hear how the children
  Stood round His knee;
  That I may know of His blessing
  Resting on me;
  Words full of kindness,
  Deeds full of grace,
  Signs of the love found
  In Jesus' face.

3 Tell me in words full of wonder,
  How rolled the sea,
  Tossing the boat in a tempest
  On Galilee.
  Jesus then doing
  His Father's will,
  Ended the storm say'ng
  'Peace, peace be still.'

4 Into the city I'd follow
  The children's band,
  Waving a branch of the palm-tree
  High in my hand;
  Worshipping Jesus,
  Yes, I would sing
  Loudest Hosannas,
  For He is King.

5 Show me that scene in the garden,
  Of bitter pain;
  And of the cross where my Saviour
  For me was slain;
  And, through the sadness,
  Help me to see
  How Jesus suffered
  For love of me.

6 Gladly I'd hear of His rising
  Out of the grave,
  Living and strong and triumphant,
  Mighty to save;
  And how He sends us
  All men to bring
  Stories of Jesus,
  Jesus, their King.

W.H. Parker, 1845–1929, altd.
v.6 by Hugh Martin, 1890–
Altered © 1986 Horrobin/Leavers

574 Tell my people

Leonard Bartlotti
verses and descant by Jan Harrington

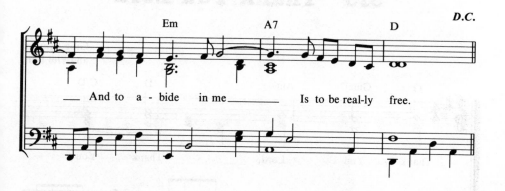

And to a - bide in me_____ Is to be real-ly free.

Optional descant for refrain

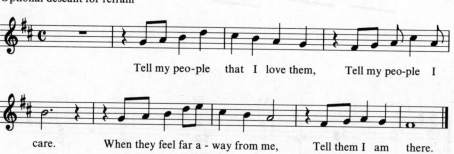

Tell my peo-ple that I love them, Tell my peo-ple I care. When they feel far a - way from me, Tell them I am there.

Tell my people I love them,
Tell my people I care.
When they feel far away from me,
Tell my people I am there.

1 Tell my people I came and died
To give them liberty,
And to abide in me
Is to be really free.
    Tell my people . . .

2 Tell my people where'er they go
My comfort they can know.
My peace and joy and love
I freely will bestow.
    Tell my people . . .

575 Thank You Lord

Greg Leavers
and Phil Burt

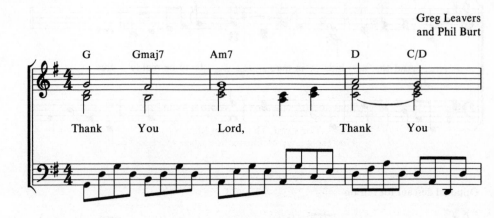

Thank You Lord, Thank You

Lord That no - thing can sep - ar - ate us

from Your love.

Copyright © 1987 Greg Leavers / Phil Burt

504

316 Thank you, Lord, for Your presence here

SELECT VERSES AS APPROPRIATE

1 Thank You Lord, Thank You Lord
   That nothing can separate us from Your love.

2 Thank You Lord, Thank You Lord
   That there is no condemnation when we're in You.

CONFESSION VERSES
3 Search my heart, Search my heart
   And show me the sin I need to confess to You.

4 Sorry Lord, Sorry Lord,
   I humbly now ask forgiveness for my sin.

5 Cleanse me Lord, Cleanse me Lord
   Through Your precious blood make my heart clean before You.

6 Thank You Lord, Thank You Lord
   That You've now removed the guilt of all my sin.

COMMUNION
7 Take this bread, Take this bread,
   For this is Christ's body which was broken for you.

8 Thank You Lord, Thank You Lord
   For dying on Calv'ry so that I can know You.

9 Take this cup, Take this cup
   And drink it rememb'ring Jesus Christ died for you.

10 Thank You Lord, Thank You Lord,
   That through Your shed blood we are made one with God.

PRAISE AND WORSHIP
11 Fill me Lord, Fill me Lord,
   So that I might learn to live through Your power alone.

12 We love You, We love You,
   We open our hearts in adoration to You.

13 Holy Lord, Holy Lord,
   Your Name is far higher than any other name.

14 Worthy Lord, Worthy Lord,
   We offer our sacrifice of worship to You.

15 Reigning King, Reigning King,
   You're glorious in Majesty, almighty in power.

© *1987 Greg Leavers*

576 Thank you, Lord, for Your presence here

Guitar: Tune 6th string to D

Roland Fudge

thank You, we bless You, Christ Je - sus our

Lord, We thank You, Lord._____

Thank You, Lord._____ Thank You, Lord._____

1 Thank You, Lord, for Your presence here,
  Thank You Lord, thank You Lord.
  Thank You Lord, You remove all fear,
  Thank You Lord, thank You Lord.

2 For the love that You showed
  As You poured out Your life,
  We thank You, we bless You,
  Christ Jesus our Lord,
  We thank You, Lord.
  Thank You, Lord.

577 Thanks be to God

Words and music by
Robert Stoodley

Thanks be to God___ Who gives us the vic - to - ry,___ Gives us the vic - to - ry,___ Through our Lord Je-sus Christ.___ our Lord Je-sus Christ. He is ab - le to keep us from fall - ing And to

set us free from sin.___ So let us each live

up to our call - ing And com - mit our way___ to Him.___

Thanks be to God
Who gives us the victory,
Gives us the victory,
Through our Lord Jesus Christ.

1 He is able to keep us from falling
   And to set us free from sin.
   So let us each live up to our calling
   And commit our way to Him.
   Thanks be to God . . .

2 Jesus knows all about our temptations,
   He has had to bear them too;
   He will show us how to escape them
   If we trust Him He will lead us through:
   Thanks be to God . . .

3 He has led us from the power of darkness
   To the kingdom of His blessed Son;
   So let us join in praise together
   And rejoice in what the Lord has done.
   Thanks be to God . . .

4 Praise the Lord for sending Jesus
   To the cross of Calvary:
   Now He's risen, reigns in power
   And death is swallowed up in victory.
   Thanks be to God . . .

578 Thank You, Jesus, for Your love to me

Alison Huntley

Happily

Thank You, Je - sus,_____ for Your love to me._____

_____ Thank You, Je - sus,_____ for Your grace so free._____

_____ I'll lift my voice to praise Your name, Praise You a-gain and a-

gain. You are ev - ery - thing,_____ You are my Lord._____

579 The battle belongs to the Lord

Jamie Owens-Collins
arr. Christopher Norton

us will stand,—
of His blood, *mp* The bat-tle be-longs— to the Lord.—
tion is near,—

We sing glo - ry, hon - our,

f

pow-er and strength to the Lord!— We sing glo - ry,

hon - our, pow-er and strength to the Lord!—

4th time
to Coda ⊕

512

513

580 The first nowell

THE FIRST NOWELL Irregular

English traditional carol
arr. David Willcocks (b. 1919)

The __ first _____ no - well the __ an - gel did

say Was to Beth - le - hem's shep-herds in fields as they

lay; In __ fields _____ where they lay __ keep - ing their

sheep On a cold win - ter's night __ that was __ so

deep: *No - well,_____ no - well, no - well, no -*

well, Born is the king___ of Is - ra - el!

1 The first nowell the angel did say
   Was to Bethlehem's shepherds in fields as they lay;
   In fields where they lay keeping their sheep
   On a cold winter's night that was so deep:

     Nowell, nowell, nowell, nowell,
     Born is the king of Israel!

2 Then wise men from a country far
   Looked up and saw a guiding star;
   They travelled on by night and day
   To reach the place where Jesus lay:
     Nowell, nowell . . .

3 At Bethlehem they entered in,
   On bended knee they worshipped Him;
   They offered there in His presence
   Their gold and myrrh and frankincense:
     Nowell, nowell . . .

4 Then let us all with one accord
   Sing praises to our heavenly Lord;
   For Christ has our salvation wrought
   And with His blood mankind has bought:
     Nowell, nowell . . .

Author unknown (c. 17th cent.)
© *in this version Jubilate Hymns*

581 The God of Abraham praise

LEONI 66.84.D

Adapted from a Hebrew Melody
by Thomas Olivers (1725–99)

The God of Abra-ham praise, Who reigns en-throned a-

bove, An - cient of ev - er - last - ing days, And

God of love. Je - ho - vah, great I

AM! By___ earth___ and___heaven con - fessed; We

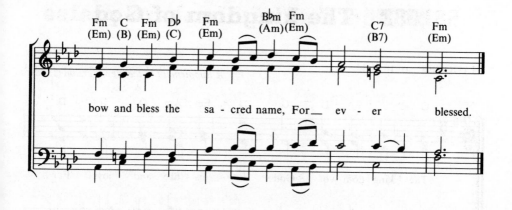

bow and bless the sa - cred name, For__ ev - er blessed.

1 The God of Abraham praise,
Who reigns enthroned above,
Ancient of everlasting days,
And God of love.
Jehovah, great I AM!
By earth and heaven confessed;
We bow and bless the sacred name,
For ever blessed.

2 The God of Abraham praise,
At whose supreme command
From earth we rise, and seek the joys
At His right hand;
We all on earth forsake,
Its wisdom, fame, and power;
And Him our only portion make,
Our shield and tower.

3 The God of Abraham praise,
Whose all-sufficient grace
Shall guide us all our happy days,
In all our ways:
He is our faithful friend;
He is our gracious God;
And He will save us to the end,
Through Jesus' blood.

4 He by Himself has sworn—
We on His oath depend—
We shall, on eagles' wings upborne,
To heaven ascend:
We shall behold His face,
We shall His power adore,
And sing the wonders of His grace
For evermore.

5 The whole triumphant host
Give thanks to God on high:
'Hail, Father, Son, and Holy Ghost!'
They ever cry.
Hail, Abraham's God and ours!
We join the heavenly lays;
And celebrate with all our powers
His endless praise.

Thomas Olivers, 1725–99, altd.

582 The kingdom of God

HANOVER   10 10 11 11

A Supplement to the New Version (1708)

The king-dom of God is jus-tice and joy; For Je - sus re - stores what sin would de - stroy. God's pow - er and glo - ry in Je - sus we know; And here and here - af - ter the king - dom shall grow.

1 The kingdom of God is justice and joy;
  For Jesus restores what sin would destroy.
  God's power and glory in Jesus we know;
  And here and hereafter the kingdom shall grow.

2 The kingdom of God is mercy and grace;
  The captives are freed, the sinners find place,
  The outcast are welcomed God's banquet to share;
  And hope is awakened in place of despair.

3 The kingdom of God is challenge and choice:
  Believe the good news, repent and rejoice!
  His love for us sinners brought Christ to His cross:
  Our crisis of judgement for gain or for loss.

4 God's kingdom is come, the gift and the goal;
  In Jesus begun, in heaven made whole.
  The heirs of the kingdom shall answer His call;
  And all things cry 'Glory!' to God all in all.

Bryn Rees, 1911–1983
© *M.E. Rees*

583 The Lord has given

Author unknown
arr. Phil Burt

The Lord has gi - ven____ a land of good things, I will press on____ and make them mine.____ I'll know His pow - er____ I'll know His glo - ry,____ And in His king - dom I will shine. *With the* *high* *prai-ses* *of God in* *our mouth And a* *two-edged sword in our*

hand, We'll march right on to the vic-to-ry side,___

Right in - to Ca - naan's land.___

1 The Lord has given a land of good things,
   I will press on and make them mine.
   I'll know His power I'll know His glory,
   And in His kingdom I will shine.

   With the high praises of God in our mouth
   And a two-edged sword in our hand,
   We'll march right on to the victory side,
   Right into Canaan's land.

2 Gird up your armour, ye sons of Zion,
   Gird up your armour, let's go to war.
   We'll win the battle with great rejoicing
   And so we'll praise Him more and more.
   With the high praises . . .

3 We'll bind their kings in chains and fetters,
   We'll bind their nobles tight in iron,
   To execute God's written judgement.
   March on to glory, sons of Zion!
   With the high praises . . .

Anon

584 The Lord reigns

Angela Pack

Steadily

The Lord reigns,_____ the Lord reigns,_____ He is robed_____ in ma-jes-ty,_____ The Lord is robed_____ in ma-jes-ty,_____

The Lord reigns, the Lord reigns,
He is robed in majesty,
The Lord is robed in majesty,
And He is girded with strength.

1 The Lord has established the world,
It shall never be moved,
Thy throne is established of old,
Thou art from everlasting.
The Lord reigns, . . .

2 The floods have lifted up, O Lord,
Lifted up their voice,
Mightier than the thunder of the waves,
The Lord on high is mighty.
The Lord reigns, . . .

585 The strife is o'er

VICTORY 8 8 8. 4

First three lines adapted from a 'Gloria Patri'
by G.P. da Palestrina (1525–94)
Hallelujah by William Henry Monk (1823–89)

The strife is o'er, the bat - tle done; The vic - to -
ry of life____ is won; The song of tri - umph
has____ be - gun: Hal - le - lu - jah!

2 The powers of death have done their worst,
But Christ their legions has dispersed;
Let shouts of holy joy outburst:
Hallelujah!

3 The three sad days have quickly sped;
He rises glorious from the dead;
All glory to our risen Head:
Hallelujah!

4 He broke the bonds of death and hell;
The bars from heaven's high portals fell;
Let hymns of praise His triumphs tell:
Hallelujah!

5 Lord, by the stripes which wounded Thee,
From death's dread sting Thy servants free,
That we may live, and sing to Thee;
Hallelujah!

tr. from the Latin by Francis Pott, 1832–1909

525

586 The Lord's Prayer

Joseph Lees

Our Fa-ther which art in heaven, Hal-low-ed

be Thy name, Thy king-dom come, Thy will be done, In

earth, as it is in heaven. Give us this day our dai-ly

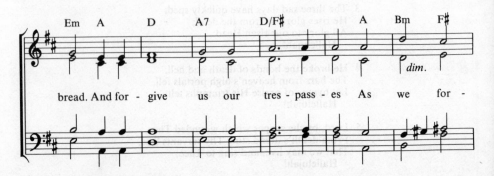

bread. And for-give us our tres-pass-es As we for-

587 The price is paid

Graham Kendrick

Triumphantly

The price is paid, Come let us en-ter in To all that Je-sus died To make our own. For ev-'ry sin More than e-nough He gave, And bought our free-dom From each guil-ty stain. *The price is paid, Al-le-lu - ia, A-maz-ing grace, So strong and*

sure. And so with all my heart, My life in ev-'ry part,__ I live to

thank You For the price You paid.__

The price is

paid.

1 The price is paid,
   Come let us enter in
   To all that Jesus died
   To make our own.
   For ev'ry sin
   More than enough He gave,
   And bought our freedom
   From each guilty stain.

The price is paid,
Alleluia,
Amazing grace,
So strong and sure.
And so with all my heart,
My life in ev'ry part,
I live to thank You
For the price You paid.

2 The price is paid,
  See Satan flee away;
  For Jesus crucified
  Destroys his power.
  No more to pay,
  Let accusation cease,
  In Christ there is
  No condemnation now.
  The price is paid, . . .

3 The price is paid,
  And by that scourging cruel
  He took our sickness
  As if His own.
  And by His wounds
  His body broken there,
  His healing touch may now
  By faith be known.
  The price is paid, . . .

4 The price is paid,
  'Worthy the Lamb' we cry,
  Eternity shall never
  Cease His praise.
  The Church of Christ
  Shall rule upon the earth,
  In Jesus' name we have
  Authority.
  The price is paid, . . .

588 The Spirit lives

WALK IN THE LIGHT

Andy Silver

1 The Spirit lives to set us free,
  Walk, walk in the light.
  He binds us all in unity,
  Walk, walk in the light.

    Walk in the light,
    Walk in the light,
    Walk in the light,
    Walk in the light of the Lord.

2 Jesus promised life to all,
  Walk, walk in the light.
  The dead were wakened by His call,
  Walk, walk in the light.
    Walk in the light . . .

3 He died in pain on Calvary,
  Walk, walk in the light.
  To save the lost like you and me,
  Walk, walk in the light.
    Walk in the light . . .

4 We know His death was not the end,
  Walk, walk in the light.
  He gave His Spirit to be our friend,
  Walk, walk in the light.
    Walk in the light . . .

5 By Jesus' love our wounds are healed,
  Walk, walk in the light.
  The Father's kindness is revealed,
  Walk, walk in the light.
    Walk in the light . . .

6 The Spirit lives in you and me,
  Walk, walk in the light.
  His light will shine for all to see,
  Walk, walk in the light.
    Walk in the light . . .

Damian Lundy

589 Then I saw a new heaven and earth

Norman Warren

Then I saw a new heaven and earth For the first had passed a -
way, And the ho - ly ci - ty, come down from God, Like a
bride on her wed - ding day. And I know how He loves His
own For I heard His great voice tell They would be His peo - ple, and

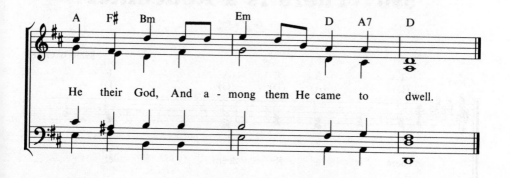

He their God, And a-mong them He came to dwell.

1 Then I saw a new heaven and earth
For the first had passed away,
And the holy city, come down from God,
Like a bride on her wedding day.
And I know how He loves His own
For I heard His great voice tell
They would be His people, and He their God,
And among them He came to dwell.

2 He will wipe away every tear,
Even death shall die at last;
There'll be no more crying, or grief, or pain,
They belong to the world that's past.
And the One on the throne said 'Look!
I am making all things new';
He is A and Z, He is first and last,
And His words are exact and true.

3 So the thirsty can drink their fill
At the fountain giving life;
But the gates are shut on all evil things,
On deceit and decay and strife.
With foundations and walls and towers
Like a jewel the city shines,
With its streets of gold and its gates of pearl
In a glory where each combines.

4 As they measured its length and breadth
I could see no temple there,
For its only temple is God the Lord
And the Lamb in that city fair.
And it needs neither sun nor moon
In a place which knows no night,
For the city's lamp is the Lamb Himself
And the glory of God its light.

5 And I saw by the sacred throne
Flowing water, crystal clear,
And the tree of life with its healing leaves
And its fruit growing all the year.
So the worshippers of the Lamb
Bear His Name, and see His face;
And they reign and serve and for ever live
To the praise of His glorious grace.

© *Chris Idle, b. 1938*

590 There is a Redeemer

Melody Green

534

Son,_____ And leav - ing Your Spi - rit Till the

work on earth is done. done.

1 There is a Redeemer,
  Jesus, God's own Son,
  Precious Lamb of God,
  Messiah, Holy One.

  Thank You, O my Father,
  For giving us Your Son,
  And leaving Your Spirit
  Till the work on earth is done.

2 Jesus my Redeemer,
  Name above all names,
  Precious Lamb of God, Messiah,
  O for sinners slain.
  Thank You . . .

3 When I stand in glory
  I will see His face.
  And there I'll serve my King for ever,
  In that Holy Place.
  Thank You . . .

591 There is no love like the love of Jesus

THE LOVE OF JESUS 10. 6. 10. 6 with chorus

T.E. Perkins (1831–1912)

There is no love like the love of Je - sus,

Ne - ver to fade or fall, Till in - to the fold of the

peace of God He has ga - thered us all.

Je - sus' love, pre-cious love, Bound-less and pure and free! O

turn to that love, wea-ry wand-ering soul, Je-sus plea - deth with thee.

1 There is no love like the love of Jesus,
  Never to fade or fall,
  Till into the fold of the peace of God
  He has gathered us all.

  Jesus' love, precious love,
  Boundless and pure and free!
  O turn to that love, weary wandering soul,
  Jesus pleadeth with thee.

2 There is no heart like the heart of Jesus,
  Filled with a tender love,
  No throb nor throe that our hearts can know
  But He feels it above.
      Jesus' love, . . .

3 O let us hark to the voice of Jesus!
  O may we never roam,
  Till safe we rest on His loving breast
  In the dear heavenly home.
      Jesus' love, . . .

W.E. Littlewood, 1831–86

592　There's a light upon the mountains

15 15. 15 15.

M.L. Wostenholm (1887–1959)

There's a light u-pon the moun-tains, and the day is at the spring, When our eyes shall see the beau-ty and the glo-ry of the King; Wea-ry was our heart with wait-ing, and the night-watch seemed so long; But His tri-umph day is

break-ing, and we hail it with a song.

1 There's a light upon the mountains, and the day is at the spring,
  When our eyes shall see the beauty and the glory of the King;
  Weary was our heart with waiting, and the night-watch seemed so long;
  But His triumph-day is breaking, and we hail it with a song.

2 In the fading of the starlight we can see the coming morn;
  And the lights of men are paling in the splendours of the dawn:
  For the eastern skies are glowing as with light of hidden fire,
  And the hearts of men are stirring with the throbs of deep desire.

3 There's a hush of expectation, and a quiet in the air;
  And the breath of God is moving in the fervent breath of prayer:
  For the suffering, dying Jesus is the Christ upon the throne,
  And the travail of our spirit is the travail of His own.

4 He is breaking down the barriers, He is casting up the way;
  He is calling for His angels to build up the gates of day:
  But His angels here are human, not the shining hosts above;
  For the drum-beats of His army are the heart-beats of our love.

5 Hark! we hear a distant music, and it comes with fuller swell;
  'Tis the triumph-song of Jesus, of our King, Immanuel:
  Zion, go ye forth to meet Him; and, my soul, be swift to bring
  All thy sweetness and thy dearest for the triumph of our King!

Henry Burton, 1840–1930

593   Therefore the redeemed

Ruth Lake

With pace and swing

Capo 3

There-fore the re-deemed of the Lord shall re - turn And come with sing-ing___ un - to Zi - on,___ And ev - er - last - ing___ joy shall be up - on their head. There-fore the re- head. They shall ob - tain

594 There is no condemnation

Joan Parsons

With feeling

There is no con-dem-na-tion for those who are in Christ,

For the Spi-rit of life in Christ has set me free.

O He's a-live, He's a-live, He's a-live, O He's a-

live, He's a-live, He's a-live, Praise the Lord.

1 There is no condemnation for those who are in Christ,
For the Spirit of life in Christ has set me free.

O He's alive, He's alive, He's alive,
O He's alive, He's alive, He's alive,
Praise the Lord.

2 If the Spirit of Him who raised Christ from the dead
Be born in you, then He will give you life.
O He's alive, . . .

3 If God be for us, who can be against us?
For He who sent His Son will freely give us all things.
O He's alive, . . .

595 These are the facts

YVONNE 10 10 11 10

Norman L. Warren (b. 1934)

These are the facts as we have re-ceived them,
These are the truths that the Christ-ian be-lieves, This is the ba-sis of
all of our preach-ing: Christ died for sin-ners and rose from the tomb.

2 These are the facts as we have received them:
Christ has fulfilled what the scriptures foretold,
Adam's whole family in death had been sleeping,
Christ through His rising restores us to life.

3 These are the facts as we have received them:
We, with our Saviour, have died on the cross;
Now, having risen, our Jesus lives in us,
Gives us His Spirit and makes us His home.

4 These are the facts as we have received them:
We shall be changed in the blink of an eye,
Trumpets shall sound as we face life immortal,
This is the victory through Jesus our Lord.

5 These are the facts as we have received them,
These are the truths that the Christian believes,
This is the basis of all of our preaching:
Christ died for sinners and rose from the tomb.

© *Michael Saward, b. 1932*

596 They that wait upon the Lord

Andy Silver

They that wait up-on___ the Lord Shall re-new their
strength and mount on ea - gles wings.___
They that wait up-on___ the Lord Shall re - new their
strength and mount on ea - gles wings.

They that wait upon the Lord
Shall renew their strength and mount on eagles wings.
They that wait upon the Lord
Shall renew their strength and mount on eagles wings.
They will run and not grow weary,
They will walk and not be faint.
Those whose hope is in the Lord
Shall renew their strength.

545

597 This is what our Saviour said

Music by Greg Leavers
and Phil Burt

This is what our Sav-iour said, He will re-turn to the
Com-ing on the clouds from heaven All earth shall see Him and

earth in pow-er, He is the Al-pha and O-me-ga,
bow be-fore Him.

Who is and who was and who is to come;— Once He was dead and be-

hold He now is Liv-ing for ev-er-more. -men!

2 With a shout and trumpet sound
He'll fetch His bride for the marriage feast,
And then we'll see Him face to face,
Joining all heaven in praise and worship.

Blessing and glory and thanksgiving
Be to the Lamb reigning now and forever,
Honour and power belong to Jesus,
Come quickly Lord, Amen!

598 The heavens declare

Andy Silver

The heavens declare the glory of God,
And the heavens proclaim the work of His hands,
And day after day they pour forth speech,
And night after night they display what He knows.

599   Thou art the everlasting word

PALMYRA   8 6. 8 6. 8 8

Joseph Summers (1843–1916)

Thou art the ev - er - last - ing Word, The
Fa - ther's on - ly Son; God ma - ni - fest - ly
seen and heard, And Heav'n's be - lov - èd One: *Wor - thy, O Lamb of*
God,   art   Thou   That   ev - 'ry knee   to   Thee   should   bow.

1 Thou art the everlasting Word,
The Father's only Son;
God manifestly seen and heard,
And Heaven's belovèd One:

Worthy, O Lamb of God, art Thou
That every knee to Thee should bow.

2 In Thee most perfectly expressed
The Father's glories shine;
Of the full Deity possessed,
Eternally Divine:
Worthy, O Lamb . . .

3 True image of the Infinite,
Whose essence is concealed;
Brightness of uncreated light,
The heart of God revealed:
Worthy, O Lamb . . .

4 But the high mysteries of Thy name
An angel's grasp transcend;
The Father only – glorious claim! –
The Son can comprehend:
Worthy, O Lamb . . .

5 Throughout the universe of bliss,
The centre Thou, and sun;
The eternal theme of praise is this,
To Heaven's belovèd One:
Worthy, O Lamb . . .

Josiah Conder, 1789–1855

600 Through our God

(Victory song)

Resolutely with steady pace

Dale Garratt

Capo 3

Through our God we shall do val-iant-ly,__ It is
He__ who will tread down our e-ne-mies. We'll
sing__ and shout His vic-to-ry,__ Christ is King! For God__ has won the

Cm(Am) · G7(E7) · Cm(Am) · G7(E7) · Cm(Am) · Bb(G)

3rd time to Coda ⊕

vic - to - ry___ And set___ His peo - ple
free, His word___ has slain the e - ne - my,___ The
earth shall stand and see that through our

⊕ CODA

Christ is King! Christ is
King! Christ is King!

601 Through the love of our God

SOUTHGATE 8 4. 8 4. 8 8 8 4

Thomas B. Southgate (1814–68)

Through the love of God our Sav-iour, All will be

well; Free and change-less is His fa-vour, All, all is

well: Pre-cious is the blood that heals us,

Per-fect is the grace that seals us,

Strong the hand stretched out to shield us, All must be well.

1 Through the love of God our Saviour,
  All will be well;
  Free and changeless is His favour,
  All, all is well:
  Precious is the blood that heals us,
  Perfect is the grace that seals us,
  Strong the hand stretched out to shield us,
  All must be well.

2 Though we pass through tribulation,
  All will be well;
  Ours is such a full salvation,
  All, all is well:
  Happy, still in God confiding,
  Fruitful, if in Christ abiding,
  Holy, through the Spirit's guiding,
  All must be well.

3 We expect a bright tomorrow,
  All will be well;
  Faith can sing, through days of sorrow,
  All, all is well:
  On our Father's love relying,
  Jesus every need supplying,
  Or in living or in dying,
  All must be well.

Mary Peters, 1813–56

602 To Him we come

LIVING LORD

Patrick Appleford

To Him we come — Je - sus Christ our Lord,
God's own liv - ing Word, His dear Son.
In Him there is no east and west, In Him all na - tions shall be blessed;
To all He of - fers peace and rest — Lov - ing Lord!

1 To Him we come –
Jesus Christ our Lord,
God's own living Word,
His dear Son.
In Him there is no east and west,
In Him all nations shall be blessed;
To all He offers peace and rest –
Loving Lord!

2 In Him we live –
Christ our strength and stay,
Life and truth and way,
Friend divine:
His power can break the chains of sin,
Still all life's storms without, within,
Help us the daily fight to win –
Living Lord!

3 For Him we go –
Soldiers of the cross,
Counting all things loss
Him to know;
Going to every land and race,
Preaching to all redeeming grace,
Building His church in every place –
Conquering Lord!

4 With Him we serve –
His the work we share
With saints everywhere,
Near and far;
One in the task which faith requires,
One in the zeal which never tires,
One in the hope His love inspires –
Coming Lord!

5 Onward we go –
Faithful, bold, and true,
Called His will to do
Day by day
Till, at the last, with joy we'll see
Jesus, in glorious majesty;
Live with Him through eternity –
Reigning Lord!

James E. Seddon, 1915–83
© Mavis Seddon / Jubilate Hymns

603 To Him who is able to keep us

Andy Silver

In Hebrew style

To Him who is a - ble to keep us, To
keep us from fall - ing a - way, Who'll
bring us spot - less and joy - ful In - to God's
pre - sence one day. To the on - ly God

our Sav - iour, Through Je - sus Christ___ our

Lord Be glo - ry, ma - jes - ty, might and

pow - er, Now, al-ways___ A - men.

To Him who is able to keep us,
To keep us from falling away,
Who'll bring us spotless and joyful
Into God's presence one day.
To the only God our Saviour,
Through Jesus Christ our Lord
Be glory, majesty, might and power,
Now, always – Amen.

604 True-hearted, whole-hearted

TRUE-HEARTED 11 10. 11 10

Josiah Booth (1852–1930)

True - heart - ed, whole - heart - ed! faith - ful and loy - al,
King of our lives, by Your grace we'll stay true! Un - der Your stand - ard, ex -
alt - ed and roy - al, Strong in Your strength we will bat - tle for You!
Peal out the watch - word, and si - lence it ne - ver,

Song of our spirits, rejoicing and free: 'True-hearted, whole-hearted,
now and for ev-er, King of our lives, by Your grace we will be.'

1 True-hearted, whole-hearted! faithful and loyal,
King of our lives, by Your grace we'll stay true!
Under Your standard, exalted and royal,
Strong in Your strength we will battle for You!

Peal out the watchword, and silence it never,
Song of our spirits, rejoicing and free:
'True-hearted, whole-hearted, now and for ever,
King of our lives, by Your grace we will be.'

2 True-hearted, whole-hearted! Fullest allegiance
Yielding each day to our glorious King!
Valiant endeavour and loving obedience,
Freely and joyously now would we bring.
Peal out the . . .

3 True-hearted, Saviour, You know all our story,
Weak are the hearts that we lay at Your feet;
Sinful and treacherous! Yet, for Your glory,
Heal them and cleanse them from sin and deceit.
Peal out the . . .

4 True-hearted, whole-hearted! Saviour, all-glorious,
Take Your great power and You reign alone,
Over our wills and affections victorious –
Freely surrendered and wholly Your own.
Peal out the . . .

Frances Ridley Havergal, 1836–79
Altered © 1987 Horrobin/Leavers

605 Thou art the Way

ST. JAMES C.M.

Raphael Courteville (d. c. 1772)

Thou art the Way, to Thee a - lone From

sin and death we flee: And he who would the

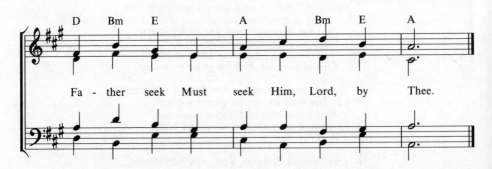

Fa - ther seek Must seek Him, Lord, by Thee.

1 Thou art the Way, to Thee alone
From sin and death we flee:
And he who would the Father seek
Must seek Him, Lord, by Thee.

2 Thou art the Truth, Thy word alone
True wisdom can impart;
Thou only canst inform the mind,
And purify the heart.

3 Thou art the Life, the rending tomb
Proclaims Thy conquering arm:
And those who put their trust in Thee
Nor death nor hell shall harm.

4 Thou art the Way, the Truth, the Life;
Grant us that Way to know,
That Truth to keep, that Life to win
Whose joys eternal flow.

George Washington Doane, 1799–1859

560

606 Unto us a Boy is born

PUER NOBIS

German carol melody
harm. Geoffrey Shaw (1879–1943)

Un - to us a Boy is born! King of all cre - a - tion, Came He to a world for - lorn The Lord of ev - ery na - tion, The Lord of ev - ery na - tion.

1 Unto us a Boy is born!
  King of all creation,
  Came He to a world forlorn
  The Lord of every nation,
  The Lord of every nation.

2 Cradled in a stall was He
  With sleepy cows and asses;
  But the very beasts could see
  That He all men surpasses,
  That He all men surpasses.

3 Herod then with fear was filled:
  'A Prince,' he said, 'in Jewry!'
  All the little boys he killed
  At Bethlehem in his fury,
  At Bethlehem in his fury.

4 Now may Mary's Son, who came
  So long ago to love us,
  Lead us all with hearts aflame
  Unto the joys above us,
  Unto the joys above us.

5 Alpha and Omega He!
  Let the organ thunder,
  While the choir with peals of glee
  Doth rend the air asunder!
  Doth rend the air asunder!

*German (15th cent.)
tr. Percy Dearmer, 1867–1936*

607 We are a chosen people

David J. Hadden

Triumphantly

We are a cho - sen peo - ple, A roy - al priest - hood, A ho - ly na - tion be - long - ing to God. We are a God. You have called us out of dark - ness

To de-clare_____ Your praise._

We ex-alt_____ You_____ and en-throne___ You.___

D.C. al Fine

Glo-ri-fy_____ Your name.___

We are a chosen people,
A royal priesthood,
A holy nation belonging to God

1 You have called us out of darkness
   To declare Your praise.
   We exalt You and enthrone You.
   Glorify Your name.
      We are a chosen . . .

2 You have placed us into Zion
   In the new Jerusalem.
   Thousand thousand are their voices,
   Singing to the Lamb.
      We are a chosen . . .

608   We are here to praise You

We are here to praise You,
Lift our hearts and sing.
We are here to give You
The best that we can bring.
And it is our

1 We are here to praise You,
  Lift our hearts and sing.
  We are here to give You
  The best that we can bring.

2 And it is our love rising from our hearts,
  Ev'rything within us cries:
  'Abba Father.'
  Help us now to give You pleasure and delight,
  Heart and mind and will that say:
  'I love You Lord.'

609 We are marching

(O give thanks)

Graham Kendrick

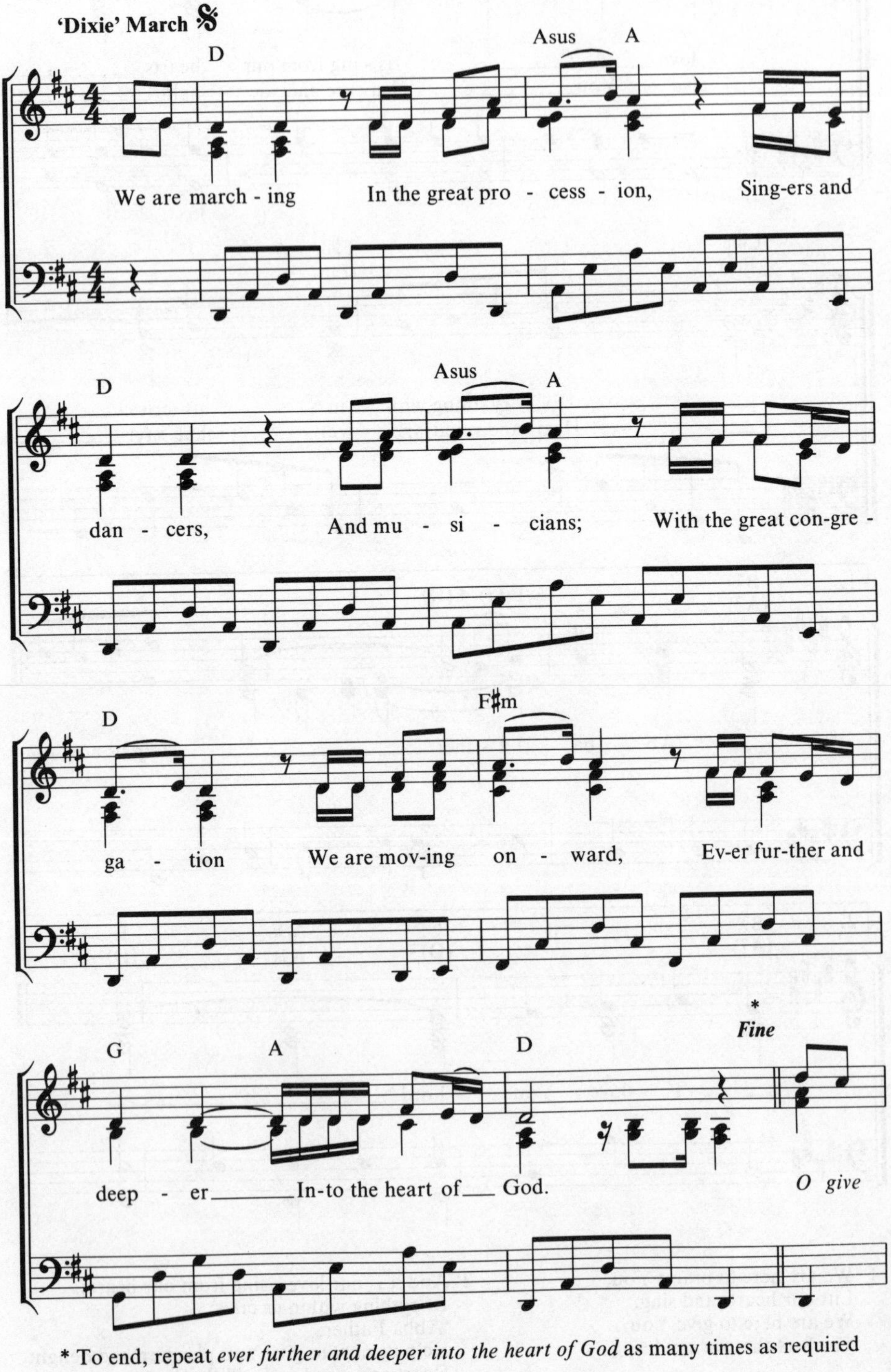

'Dixie' March
D
Asus A
We are march - ing In the great pro - cess - ion, Sing-ers and
D
Asus A
dan - cers, And mu - si - cians; With the great con-gre -
D
F♯m
ga - tion We are mov-ing on - ward, Ev-er fur-ther and
G A D
*
Fine
deep - er In-to the heart of God. O give

* To end, repeat *ever further and deeper into the heart of God* as many times as required

D.S. al Fine

thanks ... to the Lord ... For His love will ne - ver end. 2. It's a march of___

1 We are marching
In the great procession,
Singers and dancers,
And musicians;
With the great congregation
We are moving onward,
Ever further and deeper
Into the heart of God.

*O give thanks to the Lord
For His love will never end.*

2 It's a march of victory,
It's a march of triumph,
Lifting Jesus higher
On a throne of praise.
With the banner of love
Flying over us
Ever further and deeper
Into the heart of God.
O give thanks . . .

3 We will go to the nations
Spreading wide the fragrance
Of the knowledge of Jesus
Into every place.
Hear the great cloud of witnesses
Cheer us onward
Ever further and deeper
Into the heart of God.
O give thanks . . .

4 And the whole creation
Waits in expectation
Of the full revelation
Of the sons of God;
As we march through history
To our blood-bought destiny
Ever further and deeper
Into the heart of God.

Ever further and deeper
Into the heart of God.

610　We are moving on

Grace it seems is all He has, And one big op-en heart; And it's

so good___ Be-ing loved by You, my Lord.___

1 We are moving on into
A deep appreciation
Of the love which flows from Father out
To ev'ry child of God,
Of the grace with which He handles
Ev'ry minute situation,
How He wants the best for ev'ryone
Who gives to Him his all.

Grace it seems is all He has,
And one big open heart;
And it's so good
Being loved by You, my Lord.

2 We will know and understand
His purposes more clearly,
O, the mystery of the things He does
In making us more whole.
With His love He woos us,
By His grace He sets us free;
We can only trust Him
And just hold on to His hand.
Grace it seems . . .

611 We believe

Graham Kendrick

We be-lieve in God the Fa-ther, Ma-ker of the u-ni-verse, And in Christ His Son our sa-viour, Come to us by vir-gin birth. We be-lieve He died to save us, Bore our sins was cru-ci-fied. Then from death He rose vic-tor-ious, A-scen-ded to the Fa-ther's side.

Je - sus, Lord of all, Lord of all,___ Je -

sus, Lord of all, Lord of all,___ Je - sus, Lord of

all, Lord of all,___ Je - sus, Lord of all,

Lord of all.___ Name a-bove all names, Name a-bove

second chorus only

all names.___ Name a-bove all names.___

2 We believe He sends His Spirit,
   On His church with gifts of power.
   God His word of truth affirming,
   Sends us to the nations now.

He will come again in glory,
Judge the living and the dead.
Every knee shall bow before Him,
Then must every tongue confess.
   Jesus, Lord of all, . . .

571

612   We bring the sacrifice of praise

fi - ces of thanks-giv-ing, And we of - fer up to You___ The sac-ri - fi - ces of joy.

We bring the sacrifice of praise
Into the house of the Lord,
We bring the sacrifice of praise
Into the house of the Lord.
And we offer up to You
The sacrifices of thanksgiving,
And we offer up to You
The sacrifices of joy.

613 We come as guests invited

Melody by Hans Hassler (1564–1612)
adapted and harmonised by
J.S. Bach (1685–1750)

PASSION CHORALE 7 6 7 6 D

We come as guests in - vi - ted When Je - sus bids us

dine, His friends on earth u - ni - ted To

share the bread and wine; The bread of life is

bro - ken, The wine is free - ly poured, For

1 We come as guests invited
When Jesus bids us dine,
His friends on earth united
To share the bread and wine;
The bread of life is broken,
The wine is freely poured,
For us, in solemn token
Of Christ our dying Lord.

2 We eat and drink, receiving
From Christ the grace we need,
And in our hearts believing
On Him by faith we feed;
With wonder and thanksgiving
For love that knows no end,
We find in Jesus living
Our ever-present Friend.

3 One Bread is ours for sharing,
One single fruitful Vine,
Our fellowship declaring
Renewed in bread and wine –
Renewed, sustained and given
By token, sign and word,
The pledge and seal of heaven,
The love of Christ our Lord.

Timothy Dudley-Smith, b. 1926

614 We come unto our father's God

THE GOLDEN CHAIN 8 7. 8 7. 8 8. 7

Joseph Barnby (1838–96)

We come un-to our fa-ther's God: Their
Rock is our sal-va-tion: Th'e-ter-nal arms, their
dear a-bode, We make our ha-bi-ta-tion: We
bring Thee, Lord, the praise they brought; We seek Thee as Thy

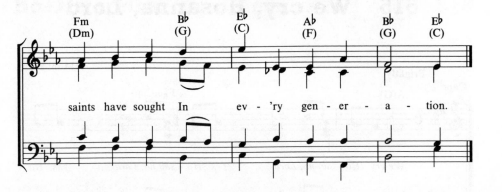

saints have sought In ev - 'ry gen - er - a - tion.

1 We come unto our father's God:
   Their Rock is our salvation:
   The eternal arms, their dear abode,
   We make our habitation:
   We bring Thee, Lord, the praise they brought;
   We seek Thee as Thy saints have sought
   In ev'ry generation.

2 The fire divine, their steps that led,
   Still goeth bright before us;
   The heav'nly shield, around them spread,
   Is still high holden o'er us:
   The grace those sinners that subdued,
   The strength those weaklings that renewed,
   Doth vanquish, doth restore us.

3 The cleaving sins that brought them low
   Are still our souls oppressing;
   The tears that from their eyes did flow
   Fall fast, our shame confessing;
   As with Thee, Lord, prevailed their cry,
   So now our prayer ascends on high,
   And bringeth down Thy blessing.

4 Their joy unto their Lord we bring;
   Their song to us descendeth:
   The Spirit Who in them did sing
   To us His music lendeth.
   His song in them, in us, is one;
   We raise it high, we send it on—
   The song that never endeth!

5 Ye saints to come, take up the strain,
   The same sweet theme endeavour!
   Unbroken be the golden chain,
   Keep on the song for ever!
   Safe in the same dear dwelling-place,
   Rich with the same eternal grace,
   Bless the same boundless Giver!

Thomas Hornblower Gill, 1819–1906

615 We cry, Hosanna, Lord

God.   He of - fers____ Him - self and He
by.   Should we for - get to praise our____
ty.   His vic - t'ry o - ver death is th'e -

D.C. al Fine

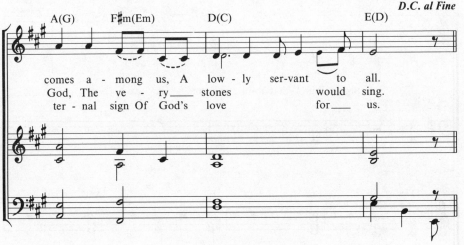

comes a - mong us, A low - ly ser-vant to all.
God, The ve - ry____ stones   would sing.
ter - nal sign Of God's love for____ us.

We cry, 'Hosanna, Lord,'
Yes, 'Hosanna, Lord,'
Yes, 'Hosanna, Lord,' to You.
We cry, 'Hosanna, Lord,'
Yes, 'Hosanna, Lord,'
Yes, 'Hosanna, Lord,' to You.

1 Behold, our Saviour comes.
  Behold the Son of our God.
  He offers Himself and He comes among us,
  A lowly servant to all.
    We cry, 'Hosanna, Lord,' . . .

2 Children wave their palms as the
  King of all kings rides by.
  Should we forget to praise our God,
  The very stones would sing.
    We cry, 'Hosanna, Lord,' . . .

3 He comes to set us free.
  He gives us liberty.
  His victory over death is th'eternal sign
  Of God's love for us.
    We cry, 'Hosanna, Lord,' . . .

616 We declare Your majesty

Malcolm du Plessis

Majestically

We de - clare Your ma - jes - ty,___ ___ We pro - claim that Your name__ is ex - alt - ed;___ For You reign mag - ni - fi - cent - ly, rule vic - to - ri - ous - ly, And Your power is shown through - out the

earth. And we ex - claim_____ our God is migh - ty,_____

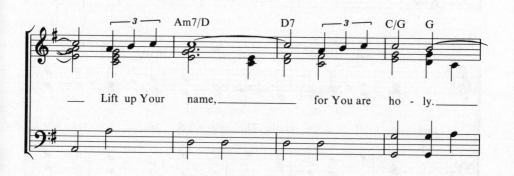

_____ Lift up Your name,_____ for You are ho - ly._____

_____ Sing it a - gain,_____ all hon-our and glo - ry,_____

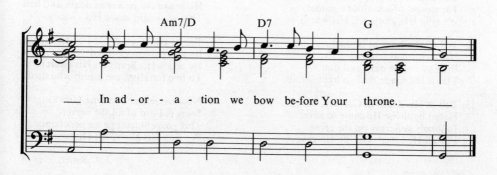

_____ In ad - or - a - tion we bow be-fore Your throne._____

617 We have a gospel to proclaim

FULDA 8 8 8 8 (LM)   W. Gardiner's *Sacred Melodies* (1815)

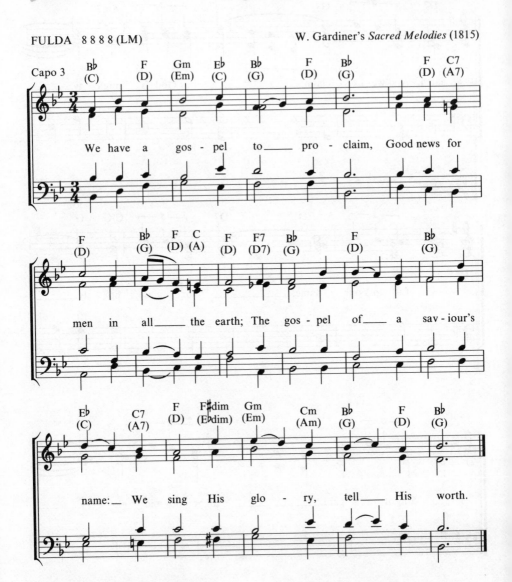

1 We have a gospel to proclaim,
  Good news for men in all the earth;
  The gospel of a saviour's name:
  We sing His glory, tell His worth.

2 Tell of His birth at Bethlehem,
  Not in a royal house or hall
  But in a stable dark and dim:
  The Word made flesh, a light for all.

3 Tell of His death at Calvary,
  Hated by those He came to save;
  In lonely suffering on the cross
  For all He loved, His life He gave.

4 Tell of that glorious Easter morn:
  Empty the tomb, for He was free;
  He broke the power of death and hell
  That we might share His victory.

5 Tell of His reign at God's right hand,
  By all creation glorified;
  He sends His Spirit on His church
  To live for Him, the Lamb who died.

6 Now we rejoice to name Him king:
  Jesus is Lord of all the earth;
  This gospel-message we proclaim:
  We sing His glory, tell His worth.

© *E.J. Burns, b. 1938*

582

618 We love the place O God

QUAM DILECTA 6 6. 6 6

Henry Lascelles Jenner (1820–98)

1 We love the place, O God,
   Where in Thine honour dwells;
   The joy of Thine abode
   All earthly joy excels.

1 We love the place, O God,
  Wherein Thine honour dwells;
  The joy of Thine abode
  All earthly joy excels.

2 It is the house of prayer,
  Wherein Thy servants meet;
  And Thou, O Lord, art there,
  Thy chosen flock to greet.

3 We love the word of life,
  The word that tells of peace,
  Of comfort in the strife,
  And joys that never cease.

4 We love to sing below
  Of mercies freely given;
  But O we long to know
  The triumph song of heaven!

5 Lord Jesus, give us grace,
  On earth to love Thee more,
  In heaven to see Thy face,
  And with Thy saints adore.

William Bullock, 1798–1874

619 We plough the fields

WIR PFLÜGEN 76.76.D with Refrain

J.A.P. Schulz (1747–1800)

We plough the fields and scat - ter The good seed on the land, But
it is fed and wa - tered By God's al - migh - ty hand; He
sends the snow in win - ter, The warmth to swell the grain, The
breez - es and the sun - shine And soft re-fresh - ing rain.

All good gifts a - round us Are sent from heaven a - bove, Then

thank the Lord, O thank the Lord, For all____ His love.

1 We plough the fields and scatter
The good seed on the land,
But it is fed and watered
By God's almighty hand;
He sends the snow in winter,
The warmth to swell the grain,
The breezes and the sunshine
And soft refreshing rain.

   *All good gifts around us
   Are sent from heaven above,
   Then thank the Lord, O thank the Lord,
   For all His love.*

2 He only is the Maker
Of all things near and far;
He paints the wayside flower,
He lights the evening star;
The wind and waves obey Him,
By Him the birds are fed;
Much more to us, His children,
He gives our daily bread.
   All good gifts . . .

3 We thank You then, O Father,
For all things bright and good,
The seed-time and the harvest,
Our life, our health, our food.
Accept the gifts we offer
For all Your love imparts,
We come now Lord to give You
Our humble, thankful hearts.
   All good gifts . . .

Matthias Claudius, 1740–1815
tr. Jane Montgomery Campbell, 1817–78
Altered © 1986 Horrobin/Leavers

620 We praise You, we bless You

ST. LUKE 11 11. 11 11

Anonymous

We praise You, we bless You, our Sav-iour Di-vine, All
pow'r and do-min-ion are Yours for all time! We
sing of Your mer-cy with joy-ful ac-claim, For
You have re-deemed us: all praise to Your name!

1 We praise You, we bless You, our Saviour Divine,
   All power and dominion are yours for all time!
   We sing of Your mercy with joyful acclaim,
   For You have redeemed us: all praise to Your name!

2 All honour and praise to Your excellent name,
   Your love is unchanging – for ever the same!
   We bless and adore You, O Saviour and King;
   With joy and thanksgiving Your praises we sing!

3 The strength of the hills and the depths of the sea,
   The earth and its fulness, Yours always shall be,
   And yet to the lowly You listen with care,
   So ready their humble petitions to hear.

4 Your infinite goodness our tongues shall employ;
   You give to us richly all things to enjoy;
   We'll follow Your footsteps, we'll rest in Your love,
   And soon we shall praise You in mansions above!

Fanny J. Crosby, 1823–1915
Altered © 1987 Horrobin/Leavers

621 We rest on Thee

FINLANDIA 11 10 11 10 11 10

Jean Sibelius (1865–1957)

'We rest on Thee,' our Shield and our De-fend-er!

We go not forth a-lone a-gainst the foe;

Strong in Thy strength, safe in Thy keep-ing ten-der,

'We rest on Thee, and in Thy name we go.'

1 'We rest on Thee,' our Shield and our Defender!
    We go not forth alone against the foe;
    Strong in Thy strength, safe in Thy keeping tender,
    'We rest on Thee, and in Thy name we go.'
    Strong in Thy strength, safe in Thy keeping tender.
    'We rest on Thee, and in Thy name we go.'

2 Yes, 'in Thy name,' O captain of salvation!
    In Thy dear Name, all other names above;
    Jesus our Righteousness, our sure Foundation,
    Our Prince of glory and our King of love.
    Jesus our Righteousness, our sure Foundation.
    Our Prince of glory and our King of love.

3 We go in faith, our own great weakness feeling,
    And needing more each day Thy grace to know:
    Yet from our hearts a song of triumph pealing;
    'We rest on Thee, and in Thy name we go.'
    Yet from our hearts a song of triumph pealing.
    'We rest on Thee, and in Thy name we go.'

4 'We rest on Thee,' our Shield and our Defender!
    Thine is the battle, Thine shall be the praise;
    When passing through the gates of pearly splendour,
    Victors – we rest with Thee, through endless days.
    When passing through the gates of pearly splendour,
    Victors – we rest with Thee, through endless days.

Edith Gilling Cherry, 1872–97

622 We three kings of Orient are

Words and music
J.H. Hopkins Jnr. (d. 1891)

We three kings of Or - i - ent are; Bear - ing

gifts we tra - vel a - far, Field and foun - tain,

moor and moun - tain, Fol - low - ing yon - der star:

O_____ star of won - der, star of night, Star with

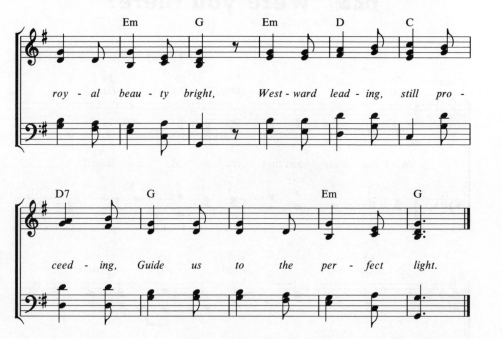

royal beauty bright, Westward leading, still proceeding, Guide us to the perfect light.

1 We three kings of Orient are;
  Bearing gifts we travel afar,
  Field and fountain, moor and mountain,
  Following yonder star:

  O star of wonder, star of night,
  Star with royal beauty bright,
  Westward leading, still proceeding,
  Guide us to the perfect light.

2 Born a King on Bethlehem plain,
  Gold I bring, to crown Him again –
  King for ever, ceasing never,
  Over us all to reign:
  O star of wonder . . .

3 Frankincense for Jesus have I,
  God on earth yet Priest on high;
  Prayer and praising all men raising
  Worship is earth's reply.
  O star of wonder . . .

4 Myrrh is mine; its bitter perfume
  Tells of His death and Calvary's gloom;
  Sorrowing, sighing, bleeding, dying,
  Sealed in a stone-cold tomb:
  O star of wonder . . .

5 Glorious now, behold Him arise,
  King, and God, and sacrifice:
  Heaven sings out 'Alleluia',
  'Amen' the earth replies:
  O star of wonder . . .

J.H. Hopkins Jnr., d. 1891
Altered © 1986 Horrobin/Leavers

623 Were you there?

arr. Francis B. Westbrook (1903–1975)

Were you there when they cru-ci-fied my Lord?____ Were you there when they cru-ci-fied my Lord?____ Oh!____ Some-times it cau-ses me to trem-ble, trem-ble,

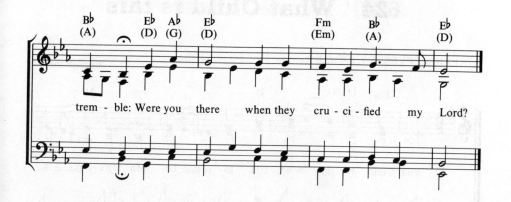

trem - ble: Were you there when they cru - ci - fied my Lord?

1 Were you there when they crucified my Lord?
Were you there when they crucified my Lord?
Oh! Sometimes it causes me to tremble, tremble, tremble:
Were you there when they crucified my Lord?

2 Were you there when they nailed Him to the tree?
Were you there when they nailed Him to the tree?
Oh! Sometimes it causes me to tremble, tremble, tremble:
Were you there when they nailed Him to the tree?

3 Were you there when they laid Him in the tomb?
Were you there when they laid Him in the tomb?
Oh! Sometimes it causes me to tremble, tremble, tremble:
Were you there when they laid Him in the tomb?

4 Were you there when God raised Him from the dead?
Were you there when God raised Him from the dead?
Oh! Sometimes it causes me to tremble, tremble, tremble:
Were you there when God raised Him from the dead?

624 What Child is this

GREENSLEEVES 87.87 with Refrain

English melody

What Child is this, Who, laid to rest,—On Ma-ry's lap—is

sleep - ing? Whom an - gels greet—with an - thems sweet, While

shep - herds watch—are keep - ing? *This,* *this—is*

Christ *the* *King,—Whom* *shep - herds guard—and* *an - gels sing:*

Haste, haste to bring Him praise, The Babe, the Son of Ma - ry.

1 What Child is this, Who, laid to rest,
On Mary's lap is sleeping?
Whom angels greet with anthems sweet,
While shepherds watch are keeping?

> *This, this is Christ the King,*
> *Whom shepherds guard and angels sing:*
> *Haste, haste to bring Him praise,*
> *The Babe, the Son of Mary.*

2 Why lies He in such mean estate
Where ox and ass are feeding?
Good Christian fear: for sinners here
The silent Word is pleading.
> *This, this is Christ . . .*

3 So bring Him incense, gold, and myrrh,
Come, peasant, king, to own Him.
The King of kings salvation brings,
Let loving hearts enthrone Him.
> *This, this is Christ . . .*

William Chatterton Dix, 1837–98

625 When He comes

Sue Read

Gently

1. When He comes we'll see just a child, No war-rior Lord but a ba-by so mild. The Lord says: 'Beth - le - hem though you are but small, In____ you shall be born the King.' When He comes, when He comes.____

tears   For the Lord will wipe them all   a-way.____ And on that

day, men shall be bro-thers, Re-con - ciled to God and each oth-er, The world shall

D.S.

see   the King in His glo - ry,   When He   comes.____

Verse 3 – use verse 2 accompaniment

3. When He   comes   He'll be of Da - vid's   line,

The migh-ty   God   and ru - ler di - vine.   They'll call Him

Won - der - ful____ and Coun-sell-or,   And His king-dom shall ne - ver cease___

Back to the Chorus

____ When He   comes,   when___ He   comes.

598

1 When He comes we'll see just a child,
No warrior Lord but a baby so mild.
The Lord says: 'Bethlehem though you are but small,
In you shall be born the King.'
When He comes, when He comes.

2 When He comes His reign shall bring peace,
When He comes all fighting shall cease.
Men shall hammer their spears into pruning hooks
And prepare for battle no more.
When He comes, when He comes.

And on that day there will be laughter,
On that day joy ever after, no more tears
For the Lord will wipe them all away.
And on that day, men shall be brothers,
Reconciled to God and each other,
The world shall see the King in His glory,
When He comes.

3 When He comes He'll be of David's line,
The mighty God and ruler divine.
They'll call Him Wonderful and Counsellor,
And His kingdom shall never cease
When He comes, when He comes.
And on that day . . .

626 When I look into Your holiness

Anon.
arr. Phil Burt

When I look in-to Your ho - li - ness,___ When I

gaze in-to Your love - li - ness, When all

things that sur-round Be-come sha-dows in the light of You.___

___ When I've found the joy___ of reach-ing Your

heart,_____ When my will be-comes en-throned in Your

love, When all things that sur - round Be - come

sha - dows in the light of You._____ I wor-ship

You,_____ I wor-ship You._____ The

rea-son I live_____ is to wor-ship You._____ I wor-ship

You,_____ I wor-ship You._____ The

rea-son I live_____ is to wor-ship You._____

When I look into Your holiness,
When I gaze into Your loveliness,
When all things that surround
Become shadows in the light of You.

When I've found the joy of reaching Your heart,
When my will becomes enthroned in Your love,
When all things that surround
Become shadows in the light of You.

I worship You, I worship You.
The reason I live is to worship You.
I worship You, I worship You.
The reason I live is to worship You.

Copyright control

627 When to our world the Saviour came

James W. Elliott (1833–1915)

When to our world the Sav-iour came The____
sick and__help-less heard His name, And in their weak-ness
longed to see The heal-ing Christ of Ga - li - lee.

2 That good physician! night and day
The people thronged about His way;
And wonder ran from soul to soul –
'The touch of Christ has made us whole!'

3 His praises then were heard and sung
By opened ears and loosened tongue,
While lightened eyes could see and know
The healing Christ of long ago.

4 Of long ago – yet living still.
Who died for us on Calvary's hill;
Who triumphed over cross and grave,
His healing hands stretched forth to save.

5 Those wounded hands are still the same,
And all who serve that saving Name
May share today in Jesus' plan –
The healing Christ of everyman.

6 Then, grant us, Lord, in this our day,
To hear the prayers the helpless pray;
Give to us hearts their pain to share,
Make of us hands to tend and care.

7 Make us your hands! For Christ to live,
In prayer and service, swift to give;
Till all the world rejoice to find
The healing Christ of all mankind.

628 When the Lord in glory comes

GLORIOUS COMING 77 77 77 D

Michael Baughen (b. 1930)
and D.G. Wilson (b. 1940)

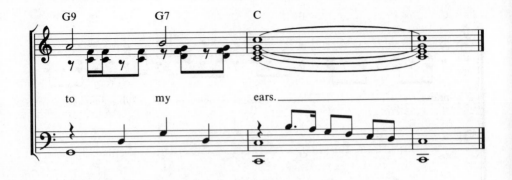

to my ears.

1 When the Lord in glory comes
Not the trumpets, not the drums,
Not the anthem, not the psalm,
Not the thunder, not the calm,
Not the shout the heavens raise,
Not the chorus, not the praise,
Not the silences sublime,
Not the sounds of space and time,
But His voice when He appears
Shall be music to my ears—
But His voice when He appears
Shall be music to my ears.

2 When the Lord is seen again
Not the glories of His reign,
Not the lightnings through the storm,
Not the radiance of His form,
Not His pomp and power alone,
Not the splendours of His throne,
Not His robe and diadems,
Not the gold and not the gems,
But His face upon my sight
Shall be darkness into light—
But His face upon my sight
Shall be darkness into light.

3 When the Lord to human eyes
Shall bestride our narrow skies,
Not the child of humble birth,
Not the carpenter of earth,
Not the man by all denied,
Not the victim crucified,
But the God who died to save,
But the victor of the grave,
He it is to whom I fall,
Jesus Christ, my All in all—
He it is to whom I fall,
Jesus Christ, my All in all.

© *Timothy Dudley-Smith, b. 1926*

629 While shepherds watched

WINCHESTER OLD C.M.

First appeared in *Este's Psalter*, (1592)

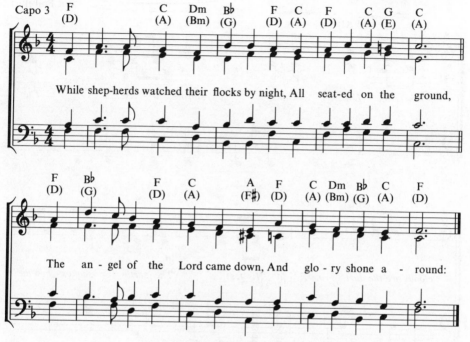

1 While shepherds watched their flocks by night,
All seated on the ground,
The angel of the Lord came down,
And glory shone around:

2 'Fear not!' said he (for mighty dread
Had seized their troubled mind)
'Glad tidings of great joy I bring
To you and all mankind.

3 'To you in David's town, this day
Is born, of David's line,
A Saviour, who is Christ the Lord;
And this shall be the sign:

4 'The heavenly babe you there shall find
To human view displayed.
All meanly wrapped in swaddling bands,
And in a manger laid.'

5 Thus spake the angel; and forthwith
Appeared a shining throng
Of angels, praising God, who thus
Addressed their joyful song:

6 'All glory be to God on high,
And to the earth be peace;
Goodwill henceforth from heaven to men
Begin and never cease.'

Nahum Tate, 1652–1715

630 Where the Lord walks

NAHUM

Words and music
Anne Horrobin and Sue Cartwright
arr. Phil Burt

Where the Lord walks, storms a - rise, ___ The
clouds are the dust raised by His feet, ___ The earth shakes when the
Lord ap - pears, The world and its peo - ple trem - ble.
You, Ni - ne - veh, are a wick - ed ci - ty, Your

*Where the Lord walks, storms arise,
The clouds are the dust raised by His feet,
The earth shakes when the Lord appears,
The world and its people tremble.*

1 You, Nineveh, are a wicked city,
Your people plot against me,
You've made my people Israel suffer,
But now I'm going to set them free.
    Where the Lord walks . . .

2 The Lord will always protect His people,
He'll care for those who trust Him,
But turn against Him, oppose the Lord,
And His judgement then is death.
    Where the Lord walks . . .

3 I say to my people Israel,
A messenger is bringing good news,
Stand in the victory I've given you,
For your enemy has been destroyed.
    Where the Lord walks . . .

631 Wind, wind blow on me

WIND, WIND

Jane and Betsy Clowe
arr. David Peacock

Wind, Wind blow on me;___ Wind, Wind set me free!___

Wind, Wind my Fa-ther sent The bless-èd Ho-ly Spi-rit.___

Je-sus told us all a-bout You, How we could not live with-out___You,

With His blood the pow-er bought To help us live the life He taught.

Wind, Wind blow on me;
Wind, Wind set me free!
Wind, Wind my Father sent
The blessèd Holy Spirit.

1 Jesus told us all about You,
  How we could not live without You,
  With His blood the power bought
  To help us live the life He taught.
  Wind, Wind . . .

2 When we're weary You console us,
  When we're lonely You enfold us,
  When in danger You uphold us,
  Blessèd Holy Spirit.
  Wind, Wind . . .

3 When into the church You came,
  It was not in Your own but Jesus' name:
  Jesus Christ is still the same—
  He sends the Holy Spirit.
  Wind, Wind . . .

4 Set us free to love our brothers,
  Set us free to live for others,
  That the world the Son might see
  And Jesus' name exalted be.
  Wind, Wind . . .

632 With harps and viols

THE NEW SONG   11 12 with chorus

Philip Bliss (1838–76)

Capo 1

With__ harps and with__ vi - ols there__ stand a great throng In the pre - sence of Je - sus, and sing this new song: *Un - to Him Who has__ loved us and washed us from sin, Un - to*

Him be the glo - ry for ev - er! A - men.

1 With harps and with viols there stand a great throng
   In the presence of Jesus, and sing this new song:

   Unto Him Who has loved us and washed us from sin,
   Unto Him be the glory for ever! Amen.

2 All these once were sinners, defiled in His sight,
   Now arrayed in pure garments in praise they unite:
   Unto Him Who has . . .

3 He's made of the rebel a priest and a king,
   He has bought us, and taught us this new song to sing:
   Unto Him Who has . . .

4 How helpless and hopeless we sinners had been,
   If He never had loved us till cleansed from our sin!
   Unto Him Who has . . .

5 Aloud in His praises our voices shall ring,
   So that others, believing, this new song shall sing:
   Unto Him Who has . . .

                    Arthur Tappan Pierson, 1837–1911

633　Wonderful Counsellor

614

1 Wonderful Counsellor,
The Mighty God,
The Everlasting Father,
The Prince of Peace,
The Prince of Peace,
The Everlasting Father,
The Mighty God.

2 Wonderful Counsellor,
Wonderful Counsellor,
Wonderful is the name of Jesus,
Wonderful Counsellor,
Wonderful Counsellor,
Wonderful is the name of Jesus.

634   With my heart I worship You

Words and music
Norman Warren

Gently

With my heart I wor-ship You Je - sus,
Je - sus; With my heart I wor-ship You Je - sus,
Je - sus: You gave all in love for me, Saved me for e-
ter - ni - ty; With my heart I wor - ship You.

ALTERNATIVE VERSES:

With my lips I praise You . . .

With my life I serve You . . .

635 Worthy is the Lamb seated on the throne

David J. Hadden

Worthy is the Lamb seated on the throne, Worthy is the Lamb who was slain, To receive power and riches, And wisdom and strength, Honour and glory, Glory and praise, For ever and ever more.

636 Worthy, O worthy are You Lord

Words and music
Mark S. Kinzer

Wor-thy, O wor-thy are You Lord, Wor-thy to be thank'd and prais'd And wor - shipp'd and a - dor'd. Wor - thy, O wor - thy are You Lord, Wor-thy to be thank'd and prais'd And wor - shipp'd and a - dor'd.

Sing-ing Hal - le-lu - jah, Lamb up-on the throne,

We wor-ship and a - dore You,

Make Your glo - ry known. Hal - le-lu - jah,

Glo-ry to the King: You're more than a con - quer-or, You're

Lord of ev - 'ry - thing.

637 Ye holy angels bright

DARWELL'S 148th   6 6. 6 6. 4 4. 4 4

John Darwell (1731–89)

1 Ye holy angels bright,
   Who wait at God's right hand,
   Or through the realms of light
   Fly at your Lord's command,
   Assist our song,
   Or else the theme
   Too high doth seem
   For mortal tongue.

2 Ye blessèd souls at rest,
   Who see your Saviour's face,
   Whose glory, e'en the least
   Is far above our grace,
   God's praises sound,
   As in His sight
   With sweet delight
   Ye do abound.

3 Ye saints, who toil below,
   Adore your heavenly King,
   And onward as ye go,
   Some joyful anthem sing;
   Take what He gives,
   And praise Him still
   Through good and ill,
   Who ever lives.

4 My soul, bear thou thy part,
   Triumph in God above,
   And with a well-tuned heart
   Sing thou the songs of love.
   Let all the days
   Till life shall end,
   Whate'er He send,
   Be filled with praise.

Richard Baxter, 1615–91
alt. John Hampden Gurney, 1802–62
and Richard Robert Chopf, 1830–1928

638 Yes, power belongs to You O Lord

Words and music
Colin Preston
arr. Chris Mitchell

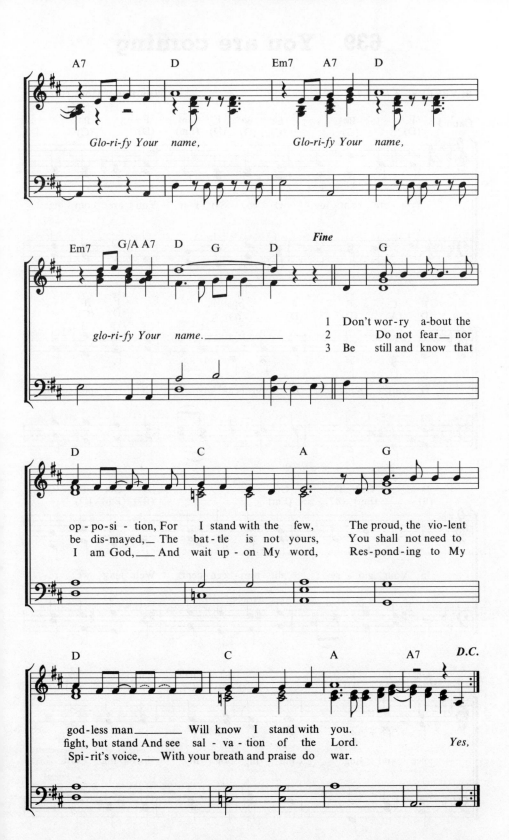

Glo-ri-fy Your name,   Glo-ri-fy Your name,

glo-ri-fy Your name.

1 Don't wor-ry a-bout the
2   Do not fear nor
3 Be   still and know that

op - po-si - tion, For   I stand with the few,   The proud, the vio-lent
be dis-mayed, The   bat - tle   is not yours,   You shall not need to
I am God, And   wait up - on My word,   Res-pond-ing to My

god-less man Will know I stand with you.
fight, but stand And See sal - va - tion of the Lord.
Spi - rit's voice, With your breath and praise do war.   Yes,

623

639 You are coming

BEVERLEY 8 7. 8 8 7. 7 7. 7 7   William Henry Monk (1823–89)

You are com-ing, O my Sav-iour, You are com-ing,

O my King; In Your beau-ty all re-splen-dent,

In Your glo-ry all tran-scen-dent; Well may we re-

joice and sing. Com-ing soon my liv-ing Lord,

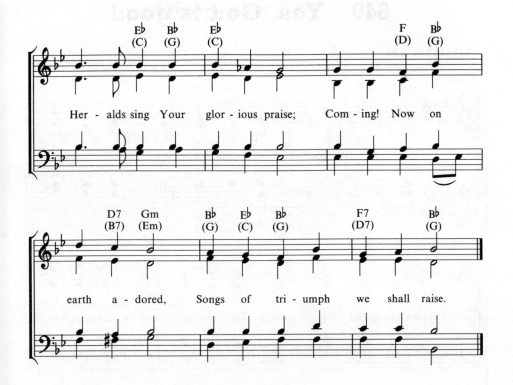

Her - alds sing Your glor - ious praise; Com - ing! Now on earth a - dored, Songs of tri - umph we shall raise.

1 You are coming, O my Saviour,
You are coming, O my King;
In Your beauty all resplendent,
In Your glory all transcendent;
Well may we rejoice and sing.
Coming soon my living Lord,
Heralds sing Your glorious praise;
Coming! Now on earth adored,
Songs of triumph we shall raise.

2 You are coming, You are coming;
We shall meet You on Your way,
We shall see You, we shall see You,
We shall bless You, we shall show You
All our hearts could never say.
What an anthem that will be,
Ringing out eternally,
Earth's and heaven's praises meet,
At Your own all glorious feet!

3 O the joy to see You reigning,
You, my own beloved Lord!
Every tongue Your name confessing,
Worship, honour, glory blessing
Brought to You with glad accord –
You, my Master and my Friend,
Vindicated and enthroned,
Unto earth's remotest end
Glorified, adored, and owned!

Frances Ridley Havergal, 1836–79
Altered © 1986 Horrobin/Leavers

640　Yes, God is good

WILLIAMS LM

From *Templi Carmina* (1829)

1　Yes, God is good—in earth and sky,
　From ocean depths and spreading wood,
　Ten thousand voices seem to cry:
　God made us all, and God is good.

2　The sun that keeps His trackless way,
　And downward pours His golden flood,
　Night's sparkling hosts, all seem to say
　In accents clear, that God is good.

3　The joyful birds prolong the strain,
　Their song with every spring renewed;
　The air we breathe, and falling rain,
　Each softly whispers: God is good.

4　I hear it in the rushing breeze;
　The hills that have for ages stood,
　The echoing sky and roaring seas,
　All swell the chorus: God is good.

5　Yes, God is good, all nature says,
　By God's own hand with speech endued;
　And man, in louder notes of praise,
　Should sing for joy that God is good.

6　For all Your gifts we bless You Lord,
　But chiefly for our heavenly food;
　Your pardoning grace, Your quickening word,
　These prompt our song, that God is good.

John Hampden Gurney, 1802–1862

641　You are my hiding place

Round

Slowly with feeling

Michael Ledner

You are my hid-ing place,_____ You al-ways fill my heart With

songs of de-liv-er-ance When-ev-er I am a-fraid. I will trust in

You,_____ I will trust in You,_____ Let the weak say

I am strong in the strength of my God.

642 You are the Mighty King

Eddie Espinosa

Stately

You are the Might - y King,
The liv - ing Word;
Mas - ter of ev - 'ry-thing,
You are the Lord.

1 You are the Mighty King,
  The living Word;
  Master of ev'rything,
  You are the Lord.

  And I praise Your name,
  And I praise Your name.

2 You are Almighty God,
  Saviour and Lord;
  Wonderful Counsellor,
  You are the Lord.

  And I praise Your name,
  And I praise Your name.

3 You are the Prince of Peace,
  Emmanuel;
  Everlasting Father,
  You are the Lord.

  And I love Your name,
  And I love Your name.

4 You are the Mighty King,
  The living Word;
  Master of ev'rything,
  You are the Lord.

643   You are the Vine

644 You laid aside Your majesty

(I really want to worship You, my Lord)

Noel Richards

Majestically

You laid a - side Your ma - jes - ty, Gave up ev - 'ry-thing for me, Suf-fer'd at the hands Of those You had cre - a - ted.

You took all my guilt and shame, When You died___ and rose a-gain;___ Now to-day___You reign, In heav'n and earth ex - alt - ed.

I real-ly want to wor-ship You, my Lord, You have won my heart and I am Yours For ev-er and ev-er; I will love You. You are the on-ly one who died for me, Gave Your life to set me free, So I lift my voice to You in ad-or-a-tion.

645   Your love is to me

Richard Taylor
arr. Phil Burt

Your＿ love is to me like an ev - er - flow - ing stream, Your love is to me like an ev - er - flow - ing stream Reach-ing out Lord.＿ ＿ Lord we need Your love, Yes, we need Your

Your love is to me like an everflowing stream,
Your love is to me like an everflowing stream,
Your love is to me like an everflowing stream
Reaching out Lord.
Lord we need Your love,
Yes, we need Your love,
We need Your love to make it through;
Lord we need Your love,
Yes, we need Your love,
We need Your love to make it through.

646   You are worthy

John Daniel Lawtum

With breadth

You are wor-thy,_____ Lord, You are wor-thy,_____

__ so I lift my heart, I lift my voice and cry 'Ho-ly'.__

__ You have sav'd__ me,_____ and I__ love__ You,__

__ Je-sus ev-er-more I live to praise Your name._____

647   Yours, Lord, is the greatness

Helen Thomas

Yours, Lord, is the greatness,
The power, the glory.
Yours, Lord, is the greatness,
The victory, the majesty.

1 For everything in heaven and earth is Yours,
  You are the King, supreme over all.
   Yours, Lord . . .

2 All riches and honour come from You;
  You are our God, You make us strong.
   Yours, Lord . . .

3 And now, our God, we give You thanks,
  We praise Your glorious name.
   Yours, Lord . . .

Notes for Guitarists

One of the most important considerations for both *Mission Praise 1* and *Mission Praise 2* was the addition of guitar chords for all the hymns and songs. For in a growing number of church and fellowship situations the guitar is the primary instrument for leading worship. But this growth appears to have been accompanied by a certain amount of complacency amongst some guitarists who try to get by with as few chords as possible!

We do appreciate, however, that the experience and ability of guitarists varies considerably and we have, therefore, attempted to make the arrangements as simple as possible without destroying the richness of the music. We suggest that if your chord knowledge is currently very limited that it would be well worthwhile learning a few more chords (e.g. F#m, C#m, Bm, Gm, Bb and diminished chords), for you would then be able to play nearly all the hymns and songs we have included. There follows an easy-to-use chord chart which will enable you to learn all the chords you will need.

To enable relatively simple chords to be regularly used we have often included two sets of chords, so that with the use of a capo, as directed at the top of the music, the guitarist can follow the set of easier bracketed chords e.g. Eb(D). Where a chord is written, e.g. A/C# the letter before the slash is the chord, and the letter after is the bass note. If you know how to play the chord with the appropriate bass note, do so, if not, just play the chord (the first letter). Bass guitarists should follow the chords, or bass note where it is given beneath the chord.

We want guitarists to enjoy their playing, but we also want to encourage those with limited ability to learn new chords and techniques. Here are a few practical tips:

1. Practice strumming so that you learn what types of rhythm suit particular sorts of hymn. If you have a steel strung guitar, get used to using a plectrum.
2. Be confident when you lead. Practice does make an enormous difference!! You will find that people will sing confidently if you play confidently.
3. Learn the chords well so that you don't have to stop half way through a song to look one up in the chord chart.
4. Make sure your guitar is in tune, (i) with itself, and (ii) with any other instrument you're playing with.
5. Make sure you and any other instrument player know what key you are going to play a particular song in.
6. Lastly, but most importantly, pray about your music. Don't just treat it as a hobby but see it as a ministry through which the Lord can draw people's attention to Himself.

Greg Leavers

Using the Chord Chart

This chart contains all the chords you will need to play all the hymns and songs in this book. Even if a chord looks more difficult than those you are used to playing, DO TRY. Always seek to improve your knowledge and playing ability. It may seem to you that you have a very large number of chords to learn, bu don't panic! For example, look at Fm, F#m, Gm and G#m, and you will see that they all have the same finger formation, but are on different frets for each chord. So, if you learn the ONE finger formation, you can immediately play *four new chords*!

If you want to play chords in a different key to the one set (because, for example, of a limited chord knowledge) you can very simply use this chart to discover the chords you need. Here's how you do it:

1. Locate the key chord that is set in the original. Find it on the chart in the SECOND COLUMN for *major* keys and the THIRD COLUMN for *minor* keys.
2. Locate on the chart the new key that you wish to play the music in (also in the second column for *major* keys and the third column for *minor* keys).
3. Work out the rest of the chords that need to be changed by noting their position around the original key chord and finding the chord that is *exactly the same position* around the new key chord.

Example:
When changing from key chord F to key chord E, find F and E in the second column of the chart. On the left of F you will find C7. The equivalent chord in key E is therefore the one on the left of E, B7. Similarly Dm would become C#m, and B♭ would become A.

Chord Chart

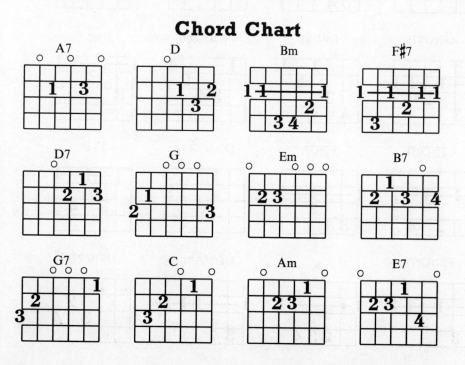

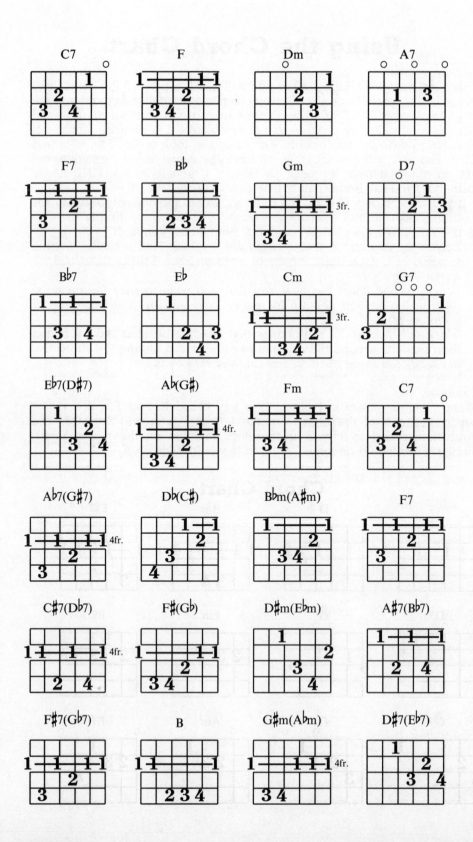

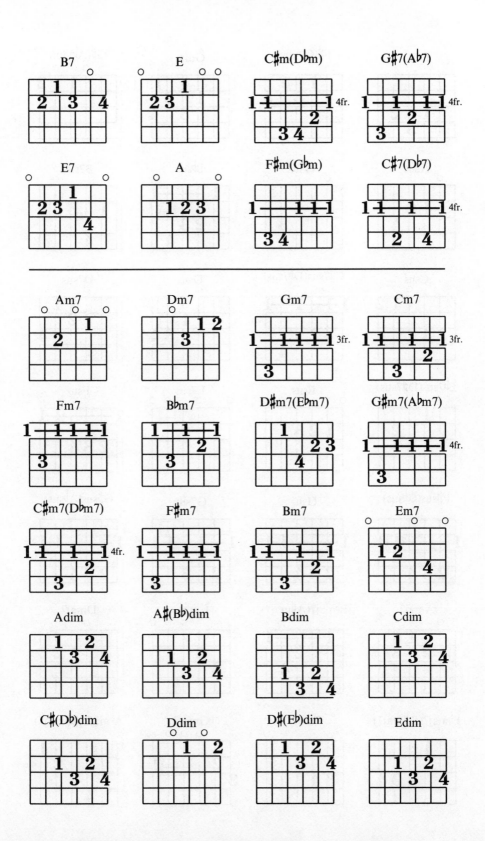

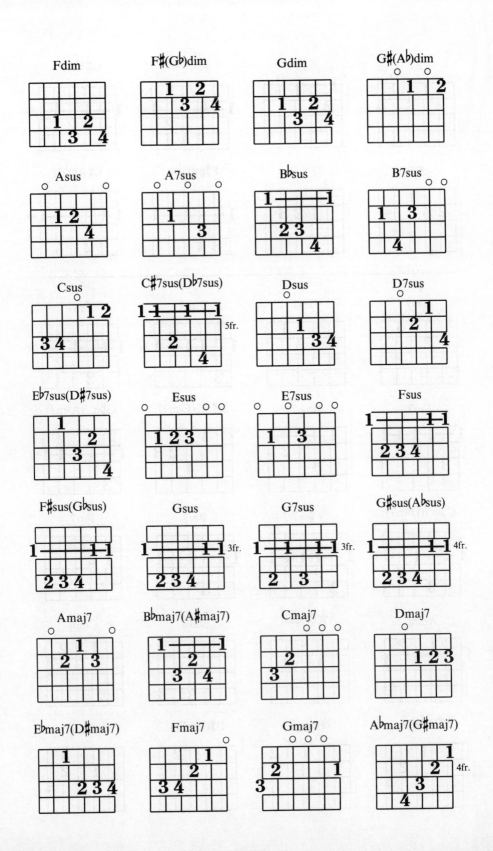

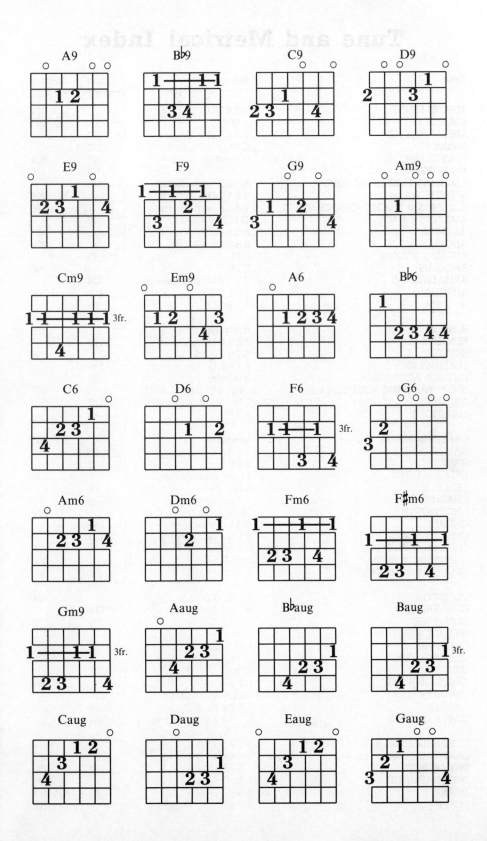

Tune and Metrical Index

Tune	Metre	Mission Praise 1	Mission Praise 2
ABBOTS LEIGH	8.7.8.7.D.		371
ABENDS	L.M.		567
ABERYSTWYTH	7 7.7 7.D.	120	
ABRIDGE	C.M.	167(i)	
ADELES FIDELES	Irregular	165	504
ALLELUIA No.1		9	
ALL THAT THRILLS MY SOUL	8.7.8.7. with chorus	270	
ALL THE WAY	8.7.8.7.D.		296
ALL THINGS BRIGHT AND BEAUTIFUL	7.6.7.6. with chorus		298
AMAZING GRACE	C.M.	10	
ANCHOR	8 8.8 8.8 8.		501
ANGEL VOICES	8.5.8.5.8.4.3.		304
ANGEL'S SONG	L.M.	55	
ANGELUS	L.M.		306
ARMAGEDDON	6.5.6.5.D. with chorus	274	
AURELIA	7.6.7.6.D.	217	346
AUSTRIA	8.7.8.7.D.	59	
BENSON	Irregular		373
BENTLEY	7.6.7.6.D.	177	
BEVERLY	8 7.8 8 7.7 7.7 7.		639
BLAENWERN	8.7.8.7.D.	149	
BLESSED ASSURANCE	Irregular	22	
BLOW THE WIND SOUTHERLY	12.10.12.10.12.11.12.11.		565
BODMIN	L.M.	110	
BULLINGER	8.5.8.3.	81	
CALYPSO CAROL	Irregular		553
CAMBERWELL	6.5.6.5.D.	15(i)	
CASWELL	6.5.6.5.	125	
CELEBRATIONS	11.14. with chorus		326
CELESTE	L.M.	77	
CHARITY	7 7 7.5.		377
CHEDWORTH	10.11.11.11.		479
CHESHIRE	C.M.	166(i)	
CHRIST AROSE	6.5.6.4. with chorus	150	
CHRIST'S OWN PEACE	Irregular		478
CHRISTMAS CAROL	D.C.M.		509
CHURCH TRIUMPHANT	L.M.	86(i) 226(i)	627
CLOISTERS	11.11.11.5.		484
CONSTANCE	8.7.8.7.D. Iambic	113	
CONVERSE	8.7.8.7.D.	262	
CRADLE SONG			310
CRANHAM	Irregular		437
CREATOR GOD	C.M.		549
CRIMOND	C.M.	227	
CROSS OF JESUS	8.7.8.7.		559
CRUCIFER	10.10. with chorus	139	
CRUGER	7.6.7.6.D.	64	
CWN RHONDDA	8.7.8.7.4.7. extended	63	
DAMBUSTERS MARCH	7 7.7 5.7 7.11.		372
DARWELL'S 148th	6.6.6.6.4.4 4.4.		637
DAY OF REST	7.6.7.6.D.	172	
DEEP HARMONY	L.M.		568
DENNIS	S.M.		311
DERBY	6.5.6.5.		518

Index of First Lines

Titles which differ from first lines are shown in italics

Song No.

'Praise' Books Published by Marshall Pickering

Mission Praise I

WORDS AND MUSIC EDITIONS

Combining traditional hymns with modern songs and choruses, and with an outstanding sales record behind it (over two million copies of the words edition sold to date), *Mission Praise 1* has established itself as a world-wide phenomenon and as **the** worship songbook of the 80s for all denominations. In its emphasis on evangelistic hymns and songs expressing the central truths of Christianity, it provides the foundation companion volume for *Mission Praise 2*.

Junior Praise

WORDS AND MUSIC EDITIONS

The perfect songbook for school assemblies, Sunday schools, and special festivals and national days. Drawing on a wide selection of sources and including easy-to-read melody lines for recorders, flutes, xylophones etc., it aims to make children's worship both fun and varied.

PRAYERS AND READINGS

A compilation of Bible readings and prayers closely linked to the songs and hymns included in the words / music editions, which outlines children's worship throughout the year.

Carol Praise

Only the best of songs, hymns and carols are included in this seasonal selection for Advent, Christmas and Epiphany. What better way to tell the significance of the new-born Saviour to a larger-than-usual congregation than through this sparkling array of Christian music, which includes the most up-to-date with the old favourites.

MAKE WAY!
Graham Kendrick

LP SFR134, CASSETTE SFC134, SONGBOOK & INSTRUCTION MANUAL

MAKE WAY is the creative new album from singer-songwriter and worship leader Graham Kendrick.

It explores the possibilities of taking our worship to the streets, shopping centres and public places of our towns and cities and includes songs of reflection and preparation as well as declaration.

The songs declare Christian truth in a clear, jargon-free fashion and were carefully written with public witness in mind.

Also available is the *MAKE WAY Songbook and Instruction Manual,* a step-by-step guide to the principles and practicalities of praise processions. All the songs are included with melody line and guitar chords.

Available from your local Christian Bookshop, or in case of difficulty direct from:
The Rainbow Company, PO Box 77, Hailsham, E. Sussex BN27 3EF.